THE USA BASKETBALL COACHING GUIDE FOR ALL LEVELS

THE USA BASKETBALL COACHING GUIDE FOR ALL LEVELS

Coaching Philosophy & Player Development Curriculum
from the National Governing Body of Basketball

USA BASKETBALL

BOOKLOGIX®
Alpharetta, Georgia

The information in this book is meant to supplement and guide, not replace, proper basketball training. Like any sport involving speed, equipment, balance, and physical contact, basketball poses some inherent risk, including the risk of injury and even death. USA Basketball advises readers to take full responsibility for their safety and to know their limits. Do not take risks beyond your level of experience, aptitude, training, and comfort level. USA Basketball does not assume and hereby disclaims, and the readers of this book hereby release USA Basketball from, any and all liability to any party for any loss, damage, or disruption caused by your use of this book, including errors or omissions, whether such errors or omissions result from negligence, accident, or any other cause.

Copyright © 2025 by USA Basketball

All rights reserved. No part of this book may be reproduced or transmitted in any form or by any means, electronic or mechanical, including photocopying, recording, or any information storage and retrieval system, without permission in writing from the publisher.

ISBN: 978-1-6653-0196-1 – Paperback
eISBN: 978-1-6653-0197-8 – ePub
eISBN: 978-1-6653-0198-5 – mobi

These ISBNs are the property of BookLogix for the express purpose of sales and distribution of this title. The content of this book is the property of the copyright holder only. BookLogix does not hold any ownership of the content of this book and is not liable in any way for the materials contained within. The views and opinions expressed in this book are the property of the Author/Copyright holder, and do not necessarily reflect those of BookLogix.

Library of Congress Control Number: 2024927227

⊚This paper meets the requirements of ANSI/NISO Z39.48-1992 (Permanence of Paper)

011625

ACKNOWLEDGMENTS

USA BASKETBALL WOULD LIKE TO ACKNOWLEDGE THE FOLLOWING CONTRIBUTORS:

Jamie Carey — Former USA Basketball Assistant Director, Women's National Team

Jason Demings — USA Basketball 3x3 National Teams Director and Former Youth & Sport Development Director

Christopher Keller, Ed. D — Professional Educator, Barrington Public Schools, Rhode Island

Dr. Kristin Neff — Associate Professor, Human Development and Culture, University of Texas at Austin

Don Showalter — USA Basketball Coach Development Director and Former Men's Junior National Team Head Coach

Andrea Travelstead — USA Basketball Youth & Sport Development Director

CONTENTS

FOREWORD *by Retired General Martin E. Dempsey, USA Basketball Board of Directors Chairperson* — ix

CURRICULUM INTRODUCTION & FRAMEWORK — 1
IMPARTING LIFE SKILLS — 7
TEACHING TECHNIQUES — 15
BUILDING YOUR TEAM: CULTURE & COACHING PHILOSOPHY — 21
USA BASKETBALL PLAYER DEVELOPMENT CURRICULUM — 31
- Introductory Level — 41
- Foundational Level — 71
- Advanced Level — 145
- Performance Level — 219

PRACTICE PLANNING & GUIDELINES — 273
- Introductory Level Practice Plans — 285
- Foundational Level Practice Plans — 295
- Advanced Level Practice Plans — 305
- Performance Level Practice Plans — 317

As the national governing body for basketball, USA Basketball provides this resource to serve those who uphold our values and positively impact the game. By sharing our history, legacy, and knowledge with the dedicated coaches, administrators, players, parents, officials, and fans of this game, we hope to help you pursue your gold medal goals at any level.

—Jim Tooley
USA Basketball Chief Executive Officer

FOREWORD *by Retired General Martin E. Dempsey, USA Basketball Board of Directors Chairperson*

As the National Governing Body (NGB) of basketball in the United States, USA Basketball is committed to developing players to represent our country in international competition. We take this responsibility seriously and work tirelessly to provide young men and women with the skills and attributes that will contribute to their success, both on and off the court.

The men and women who travel the globe proudly wearing USA on their jerseys have been remarkably successful at every level – junior and senior, 5-on-5 and 3x3 – including the Olympic Games, World Cup, AmeriCup, Pan American Games, and much more.

Since becoming the national governing body for basketball in the United States in 1974 and assigned the mission of forming teams for international competition, USA Basketball has amassed an extraordinary twenty-one Olympic gold medals and seventeen World Cup gold medals and qualified four teams for Olympic basketball competition – men's and women's 5-on-5 and men's and women's 3x3 – for the first time ever for the Olympic Games Paris 2024.

USA Basketball firmly believes there are both athletic and life lessons to be learned through the game of basketball. Well beyond preparing elite athletes for competition, we seek to expand the game by promoting grassroots youth programs, establishing ability level-specific standards of play, conducting coaching clinics and women's conferences, certifying and screening coaches and administrators, and by sharing guidelines and resources on player health, participation segmentation, playing rules, and leadership development.

We make all of this content available in person, online, and now, for the first time, in this book.

USA Basketball has a hard-earned and internationally recognized reputation for excellence. Our athletes and coaches are among the very best in the world, and our culture is purpose-built to last from team to team and from year to year. In fact, it is our culture that is actually the "special sauce" of USA Basketball.

One important aspect of our culture and curriculum is that we believe excellence in competition must be built on a foundation of fundamentals. USA Basketball's most prominent players through the years, from Kobe Bryant to Jayson Tatum and from Dawn Staley to Breanna Stewart, have also been our hardest workers in practice. In this book, we deliver practical strategies to help coaches prepare developmentally appropriate, skill-focused, and productive practices.

Throughout the chapters, some of the most knowledgeable basketball personalities in the game share their insights and wisdom about building strong and agile individuals and cohesive and resilient teams.

Before I became Chairperson of USA Basketball, I spent forty-one years learning how to build high performing teams in our military. The military is populated with hundreds of thousands of young men and women from across the country who come together and learn to work as a unit toward a common goal. Crucial to their success, they must learn to trust each other. This takes dedicated and determined leaders who are committed to continuing to learn how to become even better leaders.

Though the stakes are lower, the challenges in building sports teams—in our case basketball—are ultimately the same. We believe that coaches should see themselves not just as coaches of the game, but as leaders of a group, with all of the responsibilities that implies.

Consider that when we succeed as coaches and leaders, when we build cohesive, disciplined teams, teams that trust each other, that treat each other with dignity and respect, and that perform at a high level, we are fulfilling a responsibility not just to a single group, or a single institution, but to the game of basketball. It's that important.

Anyone who wants to be the best possible player, coach, leader, or support system in basketball will benefit tremendously from reading this book and applying these on- and off-court life lessons and curriculum practices.

CURRICULUM INTRODUCTION & FRAMEWORK

USA BASKETBALL YOUTH DEVELOPMENT GUIDEBOOK

USA Basketball, which celebrated its 50th anniversary in 2024, is the national governing body for the sport of basketball in the United States. As the recognized governing body by the International Basketball Federation (FIBA) and the United States Olympic and Paralympic Committee (USOPC), USA Basketball is responsible for the selection and training of USA teams that compete in FIBA-sponsored basketball competitions and select national events and for the development of youth basketball initiatives that address player development, coach education, and safety.

USA Basketball was organized in 1974, then known as the Amateur Basketball Association of the United States of America (ABAUSA). In 1978, Congress passed the Amateur Sports Act which created the US Olympic Committee, which exists today as the US Olympic and Paralympic Committee, and also established governing bodies for individual sports. The ABAUSA was selected as the national governing body of basketball. The name change to USA Basketball occurred October 12, 1989, shortly after FIBA modified its rules to allow professional basketball players to participate in international competitions. USA Basketball then admitted the NBA as an active member.

USA Basketball's Youth & Sport Development Division was formed in 2013 to promote, grow, and elevate the game of basketball throughout the United States. As part of the initiative, the USA Basketball Development Model was created to help guide players, coaches, parents, and administrators through the sport. The model includes many initiatives, tools, resources, and offerings, all of which focus on the health and well-being of young people to enhance enjoyment, participation, and development in the game.

USA Basketball is excited to present this book as a resource for players, coaches, parents, and administrators. Inside is the **USA Basketball Player Development Curriculum**, a robust and progressive teaching and playing standard for all levels of the game. Whether you are a basketball novice or a veteran of the game, we hope that you will utilize this curriculum while guiding young people.

Continue your development in the game by visiting us at USAB.com to take advantage of all the resources and initiatives that USA Basketball has to offer.

THE USA BASKETBALL DEVELOPMENT PATHWAY

The USA Basketball Development Pathway describes the road that players take while experiencing the game. The experiences that make up the pathway should be designed to promote "Basketball for Life," which encourages everyone to continue on in the sport. Positive basketball experiences ensure those who enjoy the game will continue to take part as players and also will stay involved in the sport as coaches, trainers, administrators, fans, officials, and referees.

START. Everyone starts the game in a different fashion. Some of us are first introduced to basketball in school, while some of us start as toddlers with a toy hoop in our home. In either case, this introduction sparks our interest in the sport.

EXPLORE. With initial interest comes exploration. Often, we are entered into our local basketball league or registered for instructional lessons as children. Also, we begin to play the sport with friends in our neighborhood or in pickup games at school. Exploring opportunities to play basketball is vital to our continued interest.

LEARN. During the exploration phase and beyond, we learn a basic understanding of how to play. Basketball often is learned from parents or guardians, local coaches, and from those we play with and against. Many players develop skills by emulating their peers or the athletes they watch at higher levels of play.

PARTICIPATE. The next stage is participation, where players take part in the sport at all levels. This includes continued structured play on local recreation teams, travel teams, club programs, and school teams. Participation also includes nonstructured play without coaching, such as pickup games, playing in the driveway, or perhaps at an outdoor court.

ADVANCE & PERFORM. Some of us will find that we will advance into higher levels of basketball. Through hard work, dedication, and natural talent, we may perform basketball well enough to become very good high school players or college athletes at both the scholarship and nonscholarship levels.

ADVANCE & EXCEL. There are a small number of players who possess the attributes of talent, physical and mental ability, and extreme dedication who will go on to excel in the sport. These players move from the perform stage into the excel stage to play basketball professionally. An even smaller number of those players will be selected to play for their country's national team.

BASKETBALL FOR LIFE. It is important to understand and accept that while some will advance to play basketball at higher levels, and some will simply continue to participate in the game, everyone eventually will enter the "Basketball for Life" stage. This stage includes those who continue to play the game, but also includes those who continue to take part as coaches, trainers, administrators, fans, officials, and referees.

The USA Basketball Development Pathway is a road map to enjoying the sport forever. Great experiences along the pathway will ensure growth of the individual, growth of the game, and the future of the sport.

PLAYER DEVELOPMENT PATHWAY

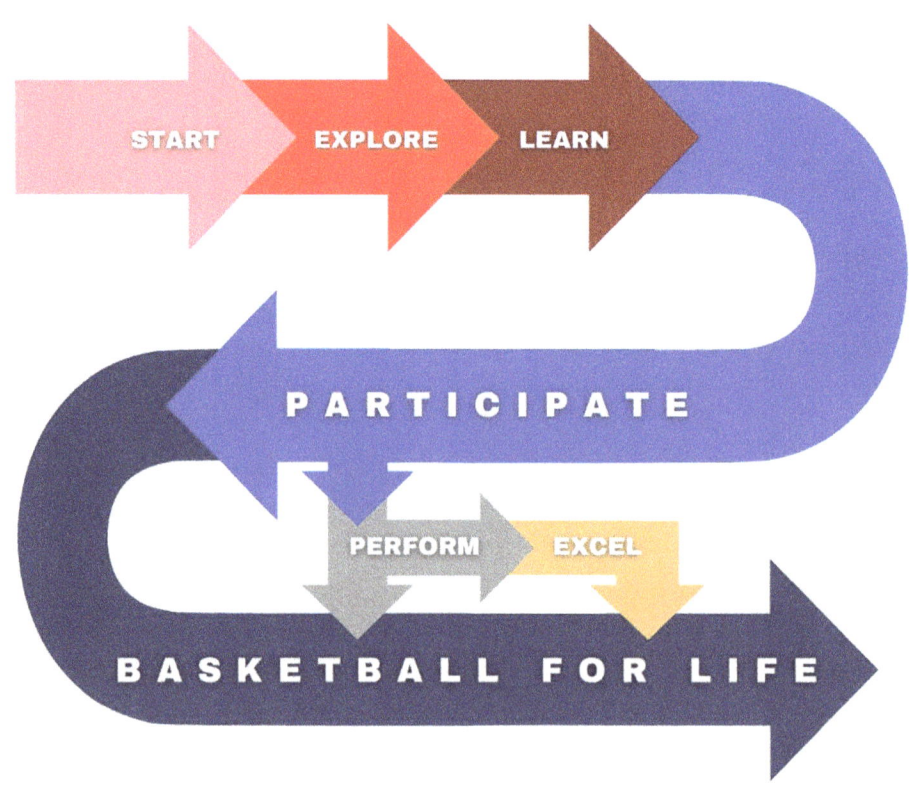

COACHING THE GAME

There are many reasons why an individual has decided to become a basketball coach. Some of us are former players who are looking to give back or stay involved in the game. Some of us have children who play, and we volunteer to coach their team. Others are asked to coach within their community to fill a need. There also are coaches, often referred to as trainers, who work out players in the off-season but don't coach them in games. Whatever your reason, coaching young players requires a high level of responsibility and maturity.

Coaching young players should be thrilling, exciting, rewarding, and fun. To prepare yourself, take into consideration the following characteristics that make for a successful youth coach.

PATIENCE. Remember that you are coaching kids. Young people need teaching, but they also need the opportunity and freedom to make mistakes. Your role as coach is to teach and to help your players learn from their mistakes. Rather than expecting your players to play flawlessly, allow them to demonstrate mistakes. This approach requires a substantial amount of patience but will maximize long-term player and team development.

EMOTIONAL MATURITY. Even at foundational levels of play, basketball games can become heated. It is your duty to act like a responsible adult under any circumstance. This means keeping your temper under control, even when you know that you are right in a particular situation. Your dealings with players, officials, parents, scorekeepers, and others are under a microscope as a leader, and it will require you to demonstrate restraint in all situations.

BASKETBALL KNOWLEDGE. As the coach of a team, group, or individual, you will need to develop an understanding of fundamentals, rules, and various strategies based on the level you are coaching. Introductory levels of play will require only basic education, but also will require a deeper sense of your impact on a beginner's continued involvement in the sport. Advanced levels will require deeper basketball education, as well as a more philosophical approach to coaching. This book and our online resources at USAB.com will serve as valuable tools as you develop as a coach.

TIME COMMITMENT. Games certainly are important, but being a good coach involves more than simply showing up for the game. To be effective you will need to organize and execute practices, provide fundamental skill instruction, decide on playing time, communicate frequently with players and parents, and much more. Coaching is a commitment of your time to the development of players both on and off the court. Make the full commitment to coaching. It will maximize the benefit to your players and make the experience more rewarding for you.

PRIORITIZE. Winning can be a healthy goal, but striving to win is where lessons are learned regardless of the final score. A truly effective coach will evaluate a team's level of play, set attainable goals, and assess outcomes based on development rather than on wins or losses. Identify your players' values and establish your values as a coach, then use those values as guiding principles in prioritizing team and player goals. Perhaps you are coaching a recreation team, and a goal is for everyone to play equal time. Or maybe you are coaching at the high school level, and a goal is to win a state title. In either case, make the journey to achieve the goal a priority.

IMPARTING LIFE SKILLS

COACHABILITY

"Coachability describes someone who wants to be coached. This manifests itself as someone who likes being challenged, loves learning, strives for more and more, and then works tirelessly at what they've been taught."

—Coach Geno Auriemma

Being coachable and being teachable go hand in hand. Above all things, coaches are teachers, players are students, and basketball is the subject matter. Coaches want to feel that players care about what they say. During training, practice, and games, a coachable player will give the coach their undivided attention. Also, a player who is coachable will act on what the coach teaches.

There are four main traits that a player needs to possess to be considered coachable. When selecting a team or deciding to coach a group of young people, you should look for these characteristics among each prospective player.

HUMILITY. A player who has humility accepts and admits that there are things they do not know and cannot do within the sport of basketball. Further, the player is willing to concede when they cannot accomplish a certain task alone, and they are willing to allow the coach to help.

SENSE OF PURPOSE. A player who is willing to state their goals and demonstrate their motivation typically will be easier to reach through coaching.

SURRENDERING CONTROL. A player who can give up control to another, in this case a coach, initially is doing so without seeing results. For a player to make true change to improve their game, a journey into uncertainty is necessary along the way. Once you have been verified as a credible and qualified teacher, a coachable player will be fully invested in the journey.

FAITH. Improvement or nonimprovement as a player can only be determined after the player has been through experiences with you as the coach. A player who puts faith in you is forgoing the benefit of hindsight, understanding that sometimes things need to get worse before they get better.

At the same time that you are seeking or imparting these characteristics to your players, you should also encourage players and their parents to seek the same in a prospective coach.

CONFIDENCE

"Confidence is about more than just thinking the shot will go in. A confident player competes with poise, determination, and a willing attitude that is infectious. The best thing I can do as a coach is help my players find that internal confidence."

—Coach Cheryl Reeve

Confidence is the players' belief in their ability to perform. Some players derive this confidence from possessing natural talent, and some acquire it from training and mastering skills. As a coach, it is imperative that you provide your players with enough confidence to drive their passion to advance in the sport.

Here are five ways to promote and instill confidence in the players you coach.

HELP PLAYERS COPE WITH FEAR OF FAILURE. Fear of failure is a natural trait that derives from a player's desire to succeed. The fear is based on the player's need for social acceptance and approval. Talk openly with players about their personal fears. Coach them to identify and openly discuss what scares them the most.

ASSIST IN SETTING EXPECTATIONS. It's great to have expectations, but when players set their own expectations too high, they will lose confidence and, perhaps, interest in basketball. Assist your players in identifying reasonable expectations so they don't sabotage their experiences.

AID IN NAVIGATING DISTRACTIONS. The ability for a player to concentrate can become blocked by distractions. For that reason, help your players to focus on processes rather than outcomes. Emphasize the importance of living in each moment so as to minimize the distraction of outside forces. For example, teach your players to keep focus on a particular play instead of emphasizing how that play may win or lose the game.

SERVE AS YOUR PLAYERS' BIGGEST FAN. As a coach, you should teach and support your players throughout the confidence-building process. Help players erase doubts and beliefs that undermine their confidence. Demonstrate loudly to your players that you are behind them by using positive reinforcement during both favorable and unfavorable situations.

HELP PLAYERS DEAL WITH SETBACKS. Mistakes, errors, and poor judgment on the part of young people is inevitable, especially in sports. Helping your players cope with those setbacks instills composure in them. Teach your players to learn from and then let go of the past. Keep your players moving forward at all times.

HARD WORK & DISCIPLINE

"Our job is really to help them become the best players they can be. So, helping them to understand the work ethic and habits that it takes to really be a good professional. That is what our job is."

—*Coach Steve Kerr*

Hard work and discipline complement each other in basketball. A hardworking player often will demonstrate a sense of self-discipline. Likewise, a disciplined player typically will appreciate the value of hard work in achieving goals. As a coach, you must set this tone by putting in extra effort and training yourself to uphold the same expectations you have for your players.

It is important to recognize that the definition of hard work for one player may not be the same as it is for another. For example, players with high stamina may perform the same sprinting drill as their teammates but may find the drill unchallenging. Encourage players to discipline themselves to do more when they are able. Conversely, it is equally as valuable for players who struggle with a drill to acknowledge that struggle and work with you to learn how they can improve. Train your players to accept situations that require hard work, and also train them to demonstrate discipline while performing that work.

LEADERSHIP

"If you can learn to lead from your position, you will always have an important role on a team. Leadership comes in many forms. You can lead through your actions on the court or in the locker room, and regardless your impact will be felt."

—*Coach Nell Fortner*

Leadership plays an important role in basketball, especially in team situations. A team can be made up of different levels of leaders on and off the court. Ultimately, the coach will lead the group; however, the coach will need to rely on others to lead at various points. Teaching your players and assistant coaches how to lead allows your coaching philosophy to spread consistently throughout the group.

There are multiple ways to select leaders, although as coaches you should recognize that leaders aren't always your best players. Players learn to lead from the experience of leading and following. There is value in your players learning by emulating the best player, but there is equal value in players learning from those who have had the experience as followers. As a coach, make it a point to identify, train, and appoint both types of leaders within your team or group. This will help to build trust in you as a coach amongst your players, parents, and administrators.

As a leader yourself, it's important to gain the trust of those who follow you. Those who are unfamiliar with you as a person will be apprehensive to trust you as a leader, especially at first. Demonstrate to your players that, as their coach, you embrace initial skepticism and encourage them to do the same. Inform players from the start that you are under the microscope as their coach and let them know that tomorrow it could be them under that same microscope. Finally, impart to your entire group that being under scrutiny doesn't have to be viewed as bad. We should encourage constructive feedback to better ourselves as coaches, players, and as people.

RESPONSIBILITY

"I think a player's choices and more so their accountability to those choices exposes their character better than any other action they could ever take or words they could ever speak."

—*Coach Monty Williams*

Coaching basketball provides a great opportunity to teach young players the value of responsibility. Responsibility involves making choices and then accepting the results of the choices that were made. Often, young people allow circumstances to dictate poor choices. Players often will minimize or ignore their power to choose so they can satisfy short-term wants and needs.

For example, a player may miss a practice or training session when a perceived better opportunity presents itself in the moment, such as playing video games with friends. This doesn't necessarily mean the player doesn't want to improve, but in that moment the player casts aside their long-term goals in basketball to fulfill a short-term desire. As a coach, it is your duty to consider a player's long-term growth and impart true responsibility in your players in order to produce long-term results.

To teach responsibility in your players, take these steps:

- Develop and adhere to consistent consequences for every player you coach. Apply grace to situations that warrant it, but do so equally for all players.
- Reward positive behavior as often as you correct negative actions. If you only recognize negative behavior, a player will respond negatively, and you will impede the long-term growth of the player and the team.
- Model responsible behavior by acknowledging your own choices and how they may impact the player or group.

A responsible player has more of an ability to decide between right and wrong than an irresponsible player. Insist that all players you coach own their responsibilities so they can make informed decisions when faced with choices.

SPORTSMANSHIP & FAIR PLAY

"I want our players to always respect our opponents and respect the game of basketball. We only know one way to play and that's to play hard, play as one, and play the game the way it's supposed to be played."

—*Coach Dawn Staley*

Young players should treat teammates, coaches, opponents, and officials the same way they would like to be treated—fairly and with respect. Coping with winning and losing is a major part of sportsmanship in basketball. Ideally, young people first learn about how to deal with challenges from behavior modeled by their parents or guardians. As a coach, however, it's up to you to reinforce the appropriate behavior for winning and losing, as well as during individual situations.

Rarely does a player enter a game or contest exhibiting poor sportsmanship. Typically, an unfavorable situation arises within an activity that prompts the player to act unruly. Prepare your players for these moments ahead of time by simulating challenging situations in training or practice sessions. For example, have an assistant coach purposely make a wrong out-of-bounds call while officiating a scrimmage. Then, explain to the complaining players that calls like that will happen frequently over the course of basketball. Emphasize to all that acting unruly and complaining about a call is a backward action, and that it takes important focus away from the next play.

Do not tolerate regressive thinking by your players, and do not exhibit regressive thinking in your coaching style. Players will mirror the behavior of their coach as their leader. Set the example for your team by controlling your own emotions toward officials, parents, your own players, and your opponents. Don't allow unfavorable situations to permit you, your assistant coaches, or your players to discredit your team.

TEAMWORK

"To me, teamwork is the beauty of our sport, where you have five acting as one and you become selfless."

—*Coach Mike Krzyzewski*

Teamwork is an essential part of basketball success. Every player and coach has a specific role to play in accomplishing team goals. Although it may seem as if one player scored the basket, that basket was made possible by planning, coordinating, and cooperating to get that player the ball. As a coach, you develop people to work well with others, but you also need to ensure that every player understands their particular role in that process. When everyone focuses on performing within their role, then everyone achieves more.

Teaching the value of teamwork and becoming an effective member of a team is an important first step to developing leadership skills. For impressionable youth, the development of these skills is critical. Young people who lack a team experience have limited exposure to positive and proactive support systems through basketball. Affording young people experiences from which they learn to rely on themselves and on others is an important factor in the development of a productive mentality.

As a coach, encourage each of the following habits in all players:

- Cooperation
- Contributing ideas, suggestions, and effort.
- Communication (giving and receiving.)
- A sense of responsibility.
- Respect and tolerance for different opinions, customs, and individual preferences.

Teach your players that "we over me" is what most often leads to "us over them" in team sport competitions. Encourage your players to be selfless and supportive teammates in both losing and winning efforts.

TEACHING TECHNIQUES

BEHAVIOR MANAGEMENT

Behavior management is the focus on maintaining order and behavior among a group or with an individual. As a basketball coach or administrator, you will find an infinite amount of personalities, behaviors, and mentalities on your team, in your camp or clinic, and throughout your organization. Without effective behavior management techniques, it is impossible to keep athletes focused on training, practices, games, or other team activities. By keeping athletes engaged, you will find that group activities can be effective and efficient.

The key to effective behavior management is to develop clear and concise expectations for each and every member of the group. Try to include your athletes and parents in this development process as much as possible, while still maintaining your authority as the leader. It is very important that everyone in the program is involved in upholding the set expectations. Also, the group should discuss and agree upon the repercussions for not maintaining expectations. Any player, coach, parent, or staff member who fails to behave accordingly should be held accountable for their actions. The decided course of action must be performed by the coach as the leader in order for the message to resonate throughout the program.

By establishing clear and concise expectations in your organization, and by following up with appropriate action when those expectations aren't met, you will instill a sense of personal responsibility in others for their behavior. This will set a consistent tone and help alleviate challenges that arise within your program.

BUILDING SELF-COMPASSION

Having compassion for oneself is no different than having compassion for others. Just like recognizing and acknowledging when someone else is going through a difficult circumstance, self-compassion is the ability to recognize and accept your own difficult circumstances. As defined by researcher Kristin Neff, self-compassion is made up of three main components: mindfulness of your own thoughts, a sense of common humanity, and treating yourself kindly.

Things will not always go the way your players would like them to go. Use these five techniques to instill self-compassion in your players, so they can understand how to deal with the good and bad moments in basketball, as well as in life:

1. Take time to teach players the truth that, no matter what they try to control, life always will be made up of highs and lows. Getting them to accept this reality sets the foundation for dealing with issues that arise.
2. Listen to your players empathetically to help them label what they are feeling. For example: "It sounds like you are feeling aggravated." Or: "Did the situation make you angry?" Young people need to trust that you are hearing them.
3. Honestly critique the player's behavior within a situation, but don't criticize the player's overall character. For example, it is far more effective to say, "That situation caused us to lose possession of the ball. You can do better than that." Than to say something like, "You never listen."
4. Speak to a player's past behavior but shape the future of the behavior with action. An example would be discussing the ramifications of a past turnover, and then next practice working extensively on technique to prevent future mistakes.
5. Model self-compassion by showing your own composure to your players when faced with unfavorable situations. Coaches with self-compassion are better liked, have higher standards, and present a greater work ethic to those who follow them.

CRITIQUE VS. CRITICISM

It is important that all coaches understand the differences between critique and criticism. A critique is an evaluation or an assessment of a particular skill. An example of a critique would be assessing how effectively a player can use their strong and weak hand during a layup drill. Criticism is expressing disapproval of someone based on a mistake they have made. An example of criticism would be simply telling a right-handed player they are awful at left-handed layups. Knowing the difference in these terms is crucial in teaching and evaluating players in youth basketball.

While coaching young people, it is essential to consider the psyche of the players that you are coaching. It has been proven at all levels that players are more likely to build long-term confidence in their game after receiving positive feedback as opposed to negative feedback. For the sake of the lesson, let's say that Michael just completed a basic layup drill session. During the drill, Michael makes fifteen right-handed layups and only two left-handed layups.

An example of critiquing would be communicating to Michael that you have noticed he did extremely well on his right-handed layups and that, with consistent practice, he will perform just as well with his left hand. The comment would confidently motivate Michael into training for the long term on his left-handed layups. An example of criticism would be telling Michael that his left-handed layups are useless, and that he's wasting his time in trying them. This comment can only produce poor results for Michael, his progress as a player, and for you as his coach.

It is important that coaches strive to critique athletes instead of criticizing them. This method used to provide feedback to players will instill long-term confidence to excel on and off the court and stay active in the game.

ESTABLISHING POSITIVE BEHAVIOR

One of the largest challenges coaches face is establishing positive behavior within the team. Whether it is personality conflicts, playing time, parental concerns, or win/loss records, it is difficult for coaches to maintain a positive culture in the program. In order to establish a culture that promotes positive behavior, you must establish clear and concise expectations on behavior from day one. All coaches, players, and personnel must be involved in the process of establishing guidelines for the team and developing the repercussions if said rules were violated. It is important you maintain a positive attitude with the team, and players should be recognized for demonstrating positive behavior. By having clear and concise expectations, involving the players in the process, and commending positive behavior, you will produce a positive atmosphere for your team.

GOAL SETTING

As a coach, it is important to require that each player set personal goals for themselves. The team or group also establishes a set of goals to accomplish throughout their time together. Goal setting is choosing the skills and concepts that a player or a team wishes to accomplish throughout a set period of time. By setting attainable goals, the team will have its focus and motivation on the areas in which they need to improve upon. This provides everyone with a series of finish lines to cross. Once the individual or team has achieved the goal, they can build upon these skills to set more rigorous goals.

In order to implement goals, coaches must facilitate discussion with the team or group and the individual. There are three steps that should go into goal setting:

1. While it may seem obvious, insist that players discuss why they chose the established goal(s). For example, while watching film, a team realized they do not rebound well. The team decides to focus on rebounding to improve on a deficiency. Remind players of the reasoning while working toward the goal.

2. The player or the team must identify the actions they will take to achieve this goal. For example, the team decides it will make a concentrated effort to box out an opponent on every shot attempt.
3. Focus players on what they would like to achieve in a specified amount of time. For example, during drill work, set a requirement that the team must secure three rebounds in a row before moving to the next drill.

By following each of the steps, players will grow, teams will grow together, and growth will take place in areas other than wins and losses. As coaches, we must continue to encourage all players and teams to set realistic goals and make constant plans to achieve those goals.

BUILDING YOUR TEAM: CULTURE & COACHING PHILOSOPHY

CULTURE

WHAT IS CULTURE?

Culture is how you do things. It defines your program's values and sets the tone of team practices, games, and interactions. Culture penetrates all who are involved in a program, from coaches to players to parents and administrators.

The best cultures consistently uphold and reinforce four Cs: **communication**, **competition**, getting outside your **comfort zone** and making the right **choices**. These four Cs are discussed in more detail below, as well as practical strategies to impart these principles to your teams.

HOW DO YOU CREATE CULTURE?

Creating a culture takes discipline and is an everyday effort. Culture must be clearly defined and communicated to your team. Coaches should outline their expectations and standards in a meeting at the beginning of the season and continue to revisit the topics throughout the season. Establish a positive culture by being transparent about the vision. Talking about culture with your team will spread the culture.

Remember, stating what your culture is and holding your team accountable to those standards are two different things. If you don't hold players, parents, and staff accountable to your standards, your culture will suffer and lose credibility.

For example, if your culture values a commitment to being on time and players consistently show up late to practices, as a coach you need to address the issue. By letting things slide you are communicating the message that timeliness really isn't important to you. This makes it harder to enforce with credibility down the road.

THE USA BASKETBALL CULTURE

USA Basketball uses the term **Gold Standards** when describing its culture. Treating everyone with the gold standard means valuing every person in the highest regard and recognizing the important role each person plays. The term is a reminder of the overall goal for USA Basketball national teams in international competition and how that mindset can permeate all other areas of USA Basketball operations.

A gold-standard culture is what we should all strive to achieve. Create specific standards to describe this culture so players understand the expectations they will be held to. Use the term **standards** instead of rules when outlining these expectations. Rules has a negative connotation that a player "must" follow them and "can" break them. Standards has a positive connotation as something a player wants to "uphold" and "strive" to meet.

At the start of the season, sit your team down to have an honest discussion about what the team wants to be known for and what standards matter to them. Formulate a list of your team's Gold Standards with input from everyone. Asking for players to contribute to the list makes them feel involved and more apt to follow through personally, as well as to hold each other accountable.

USA Basketball has identified fifteen Gold Standards used for national teams. Not all of these will apply to your program, but they can be a model to set the direction of conversation when your team collaborates on its standards.

USA BASKETBALL GOLD STANDARDS

NO EXCUSES. With the top talent assembled on national teams, we have what it takes to win. We won't make excuses for our performance, and we will recognize everyone's abilities.

GREAT DEFENSE. While all aspects of the game are important, we believe the key to winning a gold medal is our defensive performance. We will do the hard work in practice and games to always improve in this area.

COMMUNICATION. When we communicate with each other, we will look each other in the eye and have good body language. We will tell the truth even if it's uncomfortable so we can build on an honest foundation.

TRUST. We will believe in each other. Our team is our family.

COLLECTIVE RESPONSIBILITY. We are committed to each other on and off the floor. We win together, and we lose together.

CARE. We will have each other's back in every situation. We will be there for each other in competition as well as emotionally and mentally. We give aid to a teammate however appropriate.

RESPECT. We respect each other, our opponents, and the officials. We will always be on time. We will always be prepared.

INTELLIGENCE. We take good shots that are within our wheelhouse. We will be aware of team and individual fouls. We will know the scouting report for opponents.

POISE. We will show no weaknesses. We appreciate that every minute of a practice or game is important and outcomes aren't decided until the final horn sounds.

FLEXIBILITY. We can handle any situation, because we have the support of our teammates and coaches. We will not complain. We will see obstacles as challenges.

UNSELFISHNESS. We are connected as a team. We will make the extra pass to find the best shot, not just a shot. Our value is not measured in playing time but overall team success.

AGGRESSIVENESS. We will play hard every possession.

ENTHUSIASM. We will never lose sight that basketball is fun.

PERFORMANCE. We are ready to push ourselves to be our best every day. We will not have a bad practice.

PRIDE. We believe it is an honor to represent our country.

THE FOUR Cs OF CULTURE

USA Basketball developed the four Cs of culture as a way to help players remember the important actions that establish a great team culture. The four Cs—Communication, Competition, Comfort Zone, and Choices—represent the pillars upon which to build strong programs.

As defined earlier in this chapter, culture is how you do things. Therefore, the four Cs describe how those things are done within a basketball program. Communication is an action between players and coaches that builds relationships. A competition mindset pushes players to be their best. Getting outside of one's comfort zone raises their level of play. And, making proper choices on and off the court impacts one's game and character.

COMMUNICATION

It has been proven that the vast majority of all communication is nonverbal. Your actions as a coach speak much louder than your words. Through posture, facial expressions, body language, gestures and tone, players and coaches send each other unspoken cues.

It's important that you coach your players to say what they mean and mean what they say. This is extremely valuable as your players communicate amongst themselves and others.

Interactive communication is needed to effectively send and receive messages. There are many obstacles in the way of clear communication, and pushing through those obstacles is a challenge you must overcome as a coach. Obstacles, such as nonlisteners, misinformation, and interpretation, are barriers to interacting with your players and having them interact with each other. A major barrier in communication is sarcasm. It is your responsibility as a coach to remove sarcasm from all communication in order to keep messages clear and effective.

Sarcasm, mocking jokes, or exaggerated negative reactions all are forms of demeaning behavior. Learn to control yourself and be aware of how players can internalize your words. Good coaches can be demanding without being demeaning. Find the appropriate tone and balance to drive your players forward in a supportive manner.

Here are six communication principles to impart to your players:

CARE. Communicators must have a genuine concern for other people, their development, and their needs.

CANDID. Great communicators remain transparent, fair, and competent. Their actions dictate how they are perceived and valued.

CONSTRUCTIVE. Communicators are consistently positive, full of energy, and only see challenges as temporary obstacles.

CONSISTENT. Use every opportunity to communicate at the appropriate level, with simple and direct language to keep and hold someone's attention.

CONFIRM. Check back with the other person or group to ensure messages are understood.

CONCENTRATE. Give opportunity for others to respond, and listen intently to responses and feedback.

COMPETITION

Competition is an integral part of the game, but it must be introduced appropriately. For many, competition and wins are not the driving factor to play the game. Particularly at younger ages and with newer players, introduce competition in a way that does not discourage learning or having fun.

As coaches, we must teach players to embrace competition in a way that encourages them to strive to do their best. Healthy competition makes everyone better and prepares players for competition in life. In a team setting, there will be varying levels of ability, and coaches should look to incorporate unique opportunities for every player's strength to shine through. Maybe you have a player who is struggling with their shooting form but has mastered dribbling. End practice with a dribbling relay race to engage and allow them to demonstrate success.

Competition is critical for players who demonstrate advanced-level skills to teach them how to use their skills in game scenarios. Coaches can put a time limit or scoring goal on just about any drill to teach players how to compete. Competition teaches adversity and how to overcome challenges. If your team has become familiar with a certain drill, then require them to perform the drill successfully in a certain time limit. Set goals for how many baskets the team must make in the drill, or another measure to track successful repetitions.

Whether the competition is individual, in groups, or as a whole team, these metrics help players set goals, work to accomplish their goals, and take their skills to the next level.

COMFORT ZONE

Everyone has a place, whether a physical location or a mindset, where they feel most comfortable. A comfort zone could be your family, your home court, your favorite meal, or your group of longtime friends. Comfort zones make us feel safe and known. While the comfort zone serves a lot of purposes, it is not a place for personal growth. The comfort zone doesn't challenge you, doesn't make you try something new, and doesn't allow you to discover.

As players work to improve their skills and achieve new levels of success, they must be comfortable being uncomfortable. The skill-development process requires players to work hard at something until they can do it well. It is not expected that new skills will be learned the first time they are attempted. When coaches can devise drills that take players outside of their comfort zone, they are more likely to master that skill.

As a coach, you want to put your players in vulnerable, yet healthy, situations to grow as individuals and as a team. In addition to trying new drills, another way you can do this is by setting up disadvantage situations in practice. Modify 3-on-3 half court to limit the offense to only dribble with their weak hand, or not allow any dribbling at all as they try to score. In a defensive transition drill, make one player on defense touch the far baseline before joining their team, so the defense is down a player for the first few seconds of the possession and needs to scramble to cover the offense.

When players experience repetition of skills while out of their comfort zone, they will experience impactful growth. As you encourage your players to try new things, remember that positive reinforcement while players are out of their comfort zone enhances confidence in trying new skills and making progress.

CHOICES

The choices we make define who we are. It is the hope of any coach that players make choices that benefit the team. These choices can come on the court—making the extra pass, demonstrating discipline by not fouling, or taking a good shoot—or they can be off-court choices that impact the team—remaining academically eligible, arriving on time for practice, or getting enough sleep on game night.

You will never be around your players enough to know or influence all the choices they are making, so the best thing coaches can do is teach players to make and own their choices and be aware of the positive or negative consequences that come from them.

Put your players in decision-making positions and encourage them to reflect on the decision they made and the outcome. Are their choices moving them toward desired outcomes, or do they choose the path that only satisfies a short-term need?

When you recognize that a player has made a poor choice, it is important to hold them accountable and, if merited, apply a reasonable consequence. This must be the policy for players across the board. If you require players to maintain a certain grade-point average during the season and your star player dips below that threshold, hold him or her to the same consequence as you would any other player. Players should have the freedom of choice but not freedom from consequences. Teaching a player to make good choices and grow as a person is more valuable than any minute they'll spend on the court trying to win a game.

CREATING YOUR COACHING PHILOSOPHY

The philosophy of a coach is continually developed over time. Your coaching philosophy is shaped by your experiences with the game and the core values you want your program to embody.

Coaching philosophies can be influenced by or adapted from the coaching styles of mentors or other well-known, respected coaches, but it is important you make your philosophy relevant and your own.

Your coaching philosophy should include your standards and nonnegotiables—the core things for which you want to be known. Because your on-court principles may change each season based on team personnel, a coaching philosophy is value-based more than on-court execution-focused.

Follow these four principles to help identify and create your coaching philosophy:

ESTABLISH A SET OF CORE VALUES. List out your top three core values that you want associated with your team. Having a limited number of core values helps your players stay focused and develop meaningful connections.

BUILD YOUR PROGRAM AROUND YOUR CORE VALUES. Take time to think how you would implement each of your core values with your team. How will you teach the meaning of each value? Which examples will you give? What actions can you look for in practices and games to recognize and celebrate moments when players uphold the core values?

GIVE YOUR BEST EFFORT EVERY DAY AND ENJOY THE PROCESS. What does this mean to you as a coach? How do you determine enjoyment and personal fulfillment? How do you convince your players that effort and enjoyment are important?

YOU CANNOT ALWAYS CONTROL WHAT HAPPENS TO YOU IN LIFE, BUT YOU CAN ALWAYS CONTROL YOUR ATTITUDE. Reflect on the things you can and cannot control as a coach. Are you comfortable accepting the things you can't control? Give examples to your players of areas they cannot control on the court and areas they cannot control off the court. Ask players to reflect on an appropriate way to respond to these challenges and move forward.

ESSENTIAL COACHING BEHAVIORS

Understanding the principles of culture is one thing, but how do you put it all into play? Essential coaching behaviors are actions coaches take to demonstrate positive culture and amplify the four Cs.

These behaviors complement and catalyze individual skill and team development. They are core actions for every coach at every level of coaching.

USA Basketball highlights four essential coaching behaviors that coaches can adopt into their philosophy, thereby creating better basketball players and better people. For each behavior, we'll define the action, explain why it benefits development, and teach how to implement the action within your program.

COACHING BEHAVIOR 1: THE COMMUNICATION CIRCLE

WHAT. Gather your team together in a circle at the beginning or end of practices. While in the circle, talk to your players about the practice goal, reflect on practice effort, and ask critical-thinking questions for players to answer out loud, such as, "What is one thing you want to improve on at the next practice?"

WHY. Forming circles with your team creates connections. It allows coaches to preview and reflect on the practice and encourages players to contribute their thoughts and ideas.

HOW. Be consistent with the communication circle. Whether you choose to start or end practices with the communication circle, be consistent throughout the season to establish a trusted routine and buy-in from players. Communication circles encourage open, honest, and safe discussions. Challenge your players to open up based on the critical-thinking questions you ask. Include off-court questions such as, "What are you hoping to accomplish this week in school?" Or, "What is one thing no one knows about you?" These off-court questions allow coaches and teammates to get to know each other in a genuine way. Make sure the circle is uniform, with no player standing in front of another. Encourage players to use good eye contact as they share their thoughts and be good listeners.

COACHING BEHAVIOR 2: CATCH YOUR PLAYERS DOING SOMETHING WELL

WHAT. During practices and games, look to call out things that players are doing well more often than you correct behaviors. Make a conscious effort to watch for and acknowledge positive performance on the part of every player.

WHY. Building confidence in players requires a deep belief in their ability to get better. Calling out the things players are doing well, not just what they are doing incorrectly, demonstrates that belief to the player and makes them more apt to listen to constructive critique at appropriate times.

HOW. Be specific and authentic in your positive feedback. Merely saying good job to a player doesn't carry the same weight as explaining exactly what it is you like about something they did and why. Try to pinpoint exact actions to reinforce good habits, such as, "Good job chinning the rebound to keep the ball protected from opponents." Focus on the progress a player is making, not just performance. Not every player will compete at the same level, but every player can get better. By focusing on the ways every player is improving, you can help all players, not just the elite ones, build their confidence. Select your words wisely. Using a phrase such as, "I see you," can actually push you as a coach to look for things you want to call out. Set a personal goal for how many times you are going to say, "I see you," in practice or in games, so you are specifically aware of how often you call out the good things your players do. This also can be beneficial to set a specific "I see you" goal for a player whom it might not be as easy to catch doing something well.

COACHING BEHAVIOR 3: COACH WITH QUESTIONS AND SOUNDBITES

WHAT. Avoid the coaching tendency to overexplain things. Be concise in your instruction. Instead of telling players what to do, help them solve issues by asking questions to encourage them to figure things out themselves.

WHY. Asking questions makes players engage the parts of their brain that contribute to a deeper understanding of what is going on and deeper involvement in learning. Players have a better sense behind the "why" they are doing things on the court instead of just running through motions. Responding to questions also triggers the brain function that helps us manage our stress level. When we have to think about an answer, we calm down our otherwise activated stress response, something that can be beneficial to control during competition.

HOW. Train your first instinct to be listening when you interact with a player. When you open up a huddle or speak with a player coming off the court, ask questions to encourage players to provide answers and make yourself listen, such as, "What do you think?" Or, "What did you see out there?" Questions should also be used outside of practice or game settings. Check in with your players before practice starts to ask about their day and how they are feeling, which will help you tailor your approach that day to get the most out of them. You also can check in with players about how they are doing with a specific skill. Knowing where you think a player is versus how far along they think they are can provide key insight on how to continue with their development. A good ratio is to ask three questions for every one instruction you give your players. Do your best to be efficient and effective with your speech. Don't speak to simply feel better that you got out all you had to say. Coaching in paragraphs doesn't work well because very little of the information will be retained by players. Instead, use impactful soundbites to emphasize main teaching points, and then back up those soundbites with questions.

COACHING BEHAVIOR 4: CRITICAL COACHING MOMENTS—THE "TRY" AND "WHY"

WHAT. Critical coaching moments are those practice and game situations where the actions of a coach make a player reflect on their satisfaction or disapproval of the player's decision. How a coach behaves in critical moments, such as game substitution or play calls, will determine how willing a player is to take another risk in the future.

WHY. When you celebrate the act of trying, it encourages others to have a healthy relationship with risk taking, which is the only way to learn. Coaches often provide feedback to players on what to do and how to do it, but coaches who share the "why" are building the true foundation for a player to further develop. This strong foundation allows players to feel good about their actions and decisions. It also promotes a deeper understanding and helps to prevent young people from taking the coach's actions personally. Remember, as coaches we need our players to try in order to get better.

HOW. When a player tries something new, shows a new level of effort, or makes a great decision, recognize that action with authentic celebration. Be calibrated in your praise, so it comes across genuine, but do not glaze over these opportunities to celebrate "try" moments. When players do make mistakes, as they undoubtedly will, find ways to help them overcome their mistakes in a healthy manner. Helping players to let go of their mistakes and move forward allows them to accept that mistakes are a critical part of learning. Always share the "why" with your team, and don't assume they see the mistake or outcome the same way you may. Model humility by admitting your own coaching mistakes to create a culture in which mistakes are connected to taking risks and where risks are rewarded.

TYING IT ALL TOGETHER

The matrix below demonstrates the value of the essential coaching behaviors and how these four actions allow coaches to enforce the four Cs of culture. Each coaching behavior has a unique way to incorporate the critical pillars of culture to help you build a strong foundation for team growth.

COACHING BEHAVIOR 1: THE COMMUNICATION CIRCLE

COMMUNICATION	COMPETITION	COMFORT ZONES	CHOICES
Encouraging players to express themselves builds communication habits.	Investing in player voices shows players they matter. When they matter, they are more confident to take risks and compete.	Consistency and predictability create safe spaces for young people to go outside of their comfort zone.	Circles provide a built-in opportunity for players to reflect and talk about their choices, good and bad

COACHING BEHAVIOR 2: CATCH YOUR PLAYERS DOING SOMETHING WELL

COMMUNICATION	COMPETITION	COMFORT ZONES	CHOICES
When a player knows their coach is paying attention to the things they are doing well, they are more confident communicators about strengths and areas of improvement.	Players who are supported and have positive choices reinforced are more confident and resilient in competition.	Players who feel seen and supported are more likely to take risks and venture outside of their comfort zone.	Choosing to highlight the good choices players make positively reinforces those behaviors, so we see them repeated.

COACHING BEHAVIOR 3: COACH WITH QUESTIONS AND SOUNDBITES

COMMUNICATION	COMPETITION	COMFORT ZONES	CHOICES
Asking questions shows the coach is invested in what the players have to say and encourages their voice, leading them to communicate more.	Scaffolding questions help drive learning and the confidence needed to perform under pressure.	When players know their voice matters, they are more comfortable going outside of their comfort zone.	Answering questions provides practice at thinking through the possible outcomes of choices, so players get better at making decisions

COACHING BEHAVIOR 4: CRITICAL COACHING MOMENTS—THE "TRY" AND "WHY"

COMMUNICATION	COMPETITION	COMFORT ZONES	CHOICES
Engaging with a player during critical moments helps them practice communication. Focusing on the "try" and "why" helps players be less defensive in those moments.	Trying new things when it counts is how we improve the "try" and "why." Create an environment that supports players in doing that.	Knowing that a coach is supportive of players trying new things allows them the freedom to go outside of their comfort zone.	When players take more risks, because they know their coach supports the "try," more teaching and learning moments are created. Explaining the "why" helps players develop a deeper understanding of the game.

USA BASKETBALL PLAYER DEVELOPMENT CURRICULUM

INTRODUCTION TO THE PLAYER DEVELOPMENT CURRICULUM

The USA Basketball **Player Development Curriculum** has been established to guide players and the people who coach them through a level-appropriate system of basketball development. Using scientific guiding principles developed by coach educators Istvan Balyi and Richard Way and found in their book *Long-Term Athlete Development* (2013), USA Basketball has designed a practical, functional, and sequential development model to properly impart the game to a player.

The **Player Development Curriculum** consists of four levels of development: **Introductory**, **Foundational**, **Advanced,** and **Performance**. Each level takes the player through progressive development techniques based on their mastery of basketball and movement skills, as opposed to their age, grade in school, or physical attributes. This mastery-of-skills approach allows the player to develop physical literacy, learn basketball vocabulary, and acquire the movement confidence needed to optimize their basketball potential.

As explained in the sections that follow, the **Player Development Curriculum** incorporates seven stages of long-term athlete development: Active Start, Fundamentals, Learning to Train, Training to Train, Training to Compete, Training to Win, and Basketball for Life. Although the curriculum removes age from the skill-learning process, the long-term model provides age recommendations to demonstrate scientifically proven learning capabilities. USA Basketball incorporated these age recommendations in creating the curriculum levels to show how the levels translate to real learning environments.

Through the long-term athlete development model, the **Player Development Curriculum** addresses the topic of proper practice/training-to-competition ratios. USA Basketball has defined competition as the act of competing against another team, or imparting team strategies to prepare to compete against another team. Practice or training is defined as all activity related to a player's individual skill development. Based on these definitions, the diagram on the next page provides a summary of the four levels of development and USA Basketball's stance on practice/training-to-competition throughout the four levels.

As you continue through the curriculum and better understand the skills and drills that define each of the four levels, focus on correctly identifying the level or levels which best fit a player's ability. It is important to note that a player may be at the Advanced Level for one skill, but at the Foundational Level for another skill. Begin with the simplest drills to first assess a player's performance. Mastery of the drill merits progression to the next drill, and that progression can be rapid as long as it is justified. Misevaluation of a player's ability, especially for younger players, can lead to frustration if drills are constantly too challenging and could increase the likelihood of abandonment of the sport.

USA BASKETBALL

PLAYER DEVELOPMENT CURRICULUM

1 — INTRODUCTORY
Learn fundamental movement skills and build overall motor skills. Participation once or twice per week in basketball but daily participation in other sport activity is essential for further excellence. Group-skill competitions recommended throughout the level. Introduction to team principles/concepts ONLY; avoid actual 5-on-5 competition until fundamentals are further developed.

2 — FOUNDATIONAL
Learn all fundamental and basic basketball-specific skills; establish building blocks for overall basketball skills. Seventy percent of time is spent on individual fundamental training, and only 30 percent of the time is spent on actual game competition. Teach position concepts, but DO NOT assign player positions at any point in the level. Divide actual competition between special games (1-on-1, 2-on-2, 3-on-3, skill games) and 5-on-5 play, trying not to focus on actual 5-on-5 competition until later in the level.

3 — ADVANCED
Build the aerobic base, build strength toward the end of the level, and further develop overall basketball skills. Build the "engine" and consolidate basketball skills. Early in the level, 60 percent of the time is spent on individual training and 40 percent is spent on competition, including 5-on-5 play, special games (1-on-1, 2-on-2, 3-on-3, skill games), and team-oriented practices. Later in the level, depending on mastery of skills, the switch can be made to a 50:50 training-to-competition ratio and positions can be assigned.

4 — PERFORMANCE
Maximize fitness and competition preparation as well as individual and position-specific skills. Optimize the "engine" of skills and performance. Training-to-competition ratio in this phase shifts to 25:75, understanding that the competition percentage includes team-oriented practices and other competition-specific preparations.

USA BASKETBALL LONG-TERM ATHLETE DEVELOPMENT MODEL

(Concepts developed by coach educator Istvan Balyi and adapted by USA Basketball)

The stages that follow serve as building blocks for the four levels of development in the USA Basketball Player Development Curriculum. Each stage is incorporated into the appropriate level, and that level is identified in parentheses. In some instances, levels incorporate multiple stages to account for the various types of players throughout a program.

As you review, it's important to note that USA Basketball considers competition as the act of competing against another team, or imparting team strategies to prepare to compete against another team. Conversely, USA Basketball considers training to include all activity related to a player's technical skill development. Therefore, the recommended training-to-competition ratios listed throughout the guide reflect those considerations.

STAGE 1: ACTIVE START

(Found in USA Basketball Introductory Level)
Approximate Age: 0–6 years old

OBJECTIVES: *Starting at infancy, provide opportunities for children to be physically active each day within a safe, fun environment. Physical activity through play is an essential part of a child's development. Activity should incorporate fundamental movement skills throughout the four environments that lead to maximizing a child's physical potential:*

> *In the water: Swimming*
> *On the ground: Basketball (dribbling)*
> *In the air: Gymnastics*
> *On ice and snow: Sliding (skiing, skating)*

STAGE 2: FUNDAMENTALS

(Found in USA Basketball Introductory & Foundational Levels)
Approximate Age: 6–9 years old

OBJECTIVES: *Learn all fundamental movement skills (build overall motor skills). Participation once or twice per week in basketball, but daily participation in other sport activity is essential for further excellence. Special game competitions recommended throughout the phase. Introduction to 5-on-5 principles/concepts only in late phase, avoiding actual 5-on-5 competition until fundamentals are further developed.*

STAGE 3: LEARNING TO TRAIN

(Found in USA Basketball Foundational Level)
Approximate Age: 8–12 years old

OBJECTIVES: *Learn all fundamental and basic basketball-specific skills (build overall sports skills). A 70:30 training-to-competition ratio is recommended. Divide actual competition between special games and 5-on-5 play, trying not to focus on 5-on-5 competition until later in the phase.*

STAGE 4: TRAINING TO TRAIN

(Found in USA Basketball Advanced Level)
Approximate Age: 12–15 years old

OBJECTIVES: *Build the aerobic base, build strength toward the end of the stage, and further develop basketball skills (build the "engine" and consolidate basketball skills). Recommend 60:40 training-to-competition ratio. The 40 percent competition ratio includes 5-on-5 competition, special game competition, and team-oriented practices.*

STAGE 5: TRAINING TO COMPETE

(Found in USA Basketball Advanced & Performance Levels)
Approximate Age: 14–17 years old

OBJECTIVES: *Optimize fitness preparation as well as basketball, individual, and position-specific skills (continue to maximize the "engine" of skills and performance). The training-to-competition ratio now changes to 50:50. Fifty percent of available time is devoted to the development of player technical/tactical skills and fitness improvements, with the other 50 percent devoted to 5-on-5 competition and team-oriented practices.*

STAGE 6: TRAINING TO WIN

(Found in USA Basketball Performance Level)
Approximate Age: 17+ years old

OBJECTIVES: *Maximize fitness preparation and basketball, individual, and position-specific skills (goal is to optimize the "engine" of skills and performance). Training-to-competition ratio in this phase shifts to 25:75, understanding that the competition percentage includes team-oriented practices.*

STAGE 7: BASKETBALL FOR LIFE

(Found in All USA Basketball Levels)
The Retirement/Retention Stage

OBJECTIVES: *Retain athletes for recreational play, coaching, administration, officiating, and other basketball-related activities.*

APPLYING THE PROGRESSIVE COACHING METHOD TO BASKETBALL

WHAT IS PROGRESSIVE COACHING?

Progressive coaching is the teaching philosophy that focuses on engaging students individually and engaging groups in an activity. In the case of basketball, teaching occurs with individual athletes as well as teams in basketball-related activity. The philosophy behind progressive coaching is to challenge and engage each player individually in order to achieve the best results. If the philosophy is applied to every player, coaches will see marked improvement in players and the entire team. It is important that the goals for each player are challenging, attainable, and allow the athlete to keep building on a particular skill.

To best implement progressive coaching with your team, you must first understand the individual strengths and weaknesses of each of your players. Once this baseline measurement is set, you will be able to set goals with each player and develop a plan to help them reach their goals. Understanding the goals of each player also will help in developing drills for a practice.

Equally important to individual goals is the establishment of team goals to give the group something to collectively strive toward. Ensure that the goals are attainable, and challenge your team to build toward those goals each and every practice and game. For example, at the beginning of the season, a team goal may be to run an efficient fast break after a rebound. Build to this goal by first mastering how to secure a rebound, how to pivot, and then how to outlet the ball. Keep your training process-driven by ensuring that your players are mastering each step before taking the next one.

WHERE DO I BEGIN?

There are many different components to the game of basketball. In the Player Development Curriculum, USA Basketball separates skills into eight categories, including **Ball Handling & Dribbling, Footwork & Body Control, Passing & Receiving, Rebounding, Screening, Shooting, Team Defensive Concepts, and Team Offensive Concepts**. Each player in a group will have their strengths and weaknesses, and rarely will all players be on the same level in all skill categories. Also, there are many different levels of teams that you may find yourself coaching. Recreation programs, school teams, travel teams, college programs, and even professional teams all are comprised of players learning at different levels. Both the level of basketball and each player's skill set determines how you will coach and manage your group throughout a season.

As a coach, the first task is to evaluate each one of your players as well as your team as a whole. The best way to accomplish this is to establish and document a baseline of skills. This measures what your players can or cannot currently do on the basketball court. Again, measurements will vary depending on the level of play. Once you have established a baseline, you can begin to set goals for your players and team. Based on this information, you can begin to establish a proper training plan for the season.

EXAMPLE

Today, I begin my first day coaching a group of eight-year-olds through a local recreation league. Many of the players have never played on teams other than in physical education class at school. First, I must evaluate the level of my players before designing drills. The first skill I am going to assess is triple threat. I am looking to see if players know how to stand in the triple-threat position.

After completing the stance drill, I see that 80 percent of my players are in the proper triple-threat stance. Then, I can move on to a different drill that builds on these fundamentals, instead of working on a skill that the players already know how to do. At the same time, I will need to set aside extra time or assign an assistant coach to work with the other 20 percent of players to teach them the proper stance (see diagram).

DECISION-MAKING

There are several different decisions a coach must make while developing players in basketball. For example, "How many drills should the team do before I know they understand a specific skill?" "What do I do if a player is too good for the drills I am doing?" "What do I do if a player does not have the fundamentals required to complete the drills I am asking them to do?" USA Basketball offers up a few recommendations.

HOW MANY DRILLS SHOULD THE TEAM DO BEFORE I KNOW PLAYERS UNDERSTAND A SPECIFIC DRILL?

There are many different elements that should be considered. The first consideration is based on the level of the team. For example, a high school team may spend less time on triple threat than a middle school basketball team. A high school team may use one or two of these drills to reinforce fundamentals, but then quickly will move to more difficult skills. Conversely, middle school coaches may start on skills they find to be too advanced for the team but could revert back to teach the fundamentals of that particular skill.

The Player Development Curriculum offers several sample drills for each skill to ensure that players have an understanding of the particular skill. Ultimately, the coach will decide the type and amount of drills that are necessary before moving on to the next skill. For example, in the illustration below, the coach has decided to complete all three "Triple Threat Skill" drills and only two "Stationary Dribble Skill" drills before moving on (see diagram).

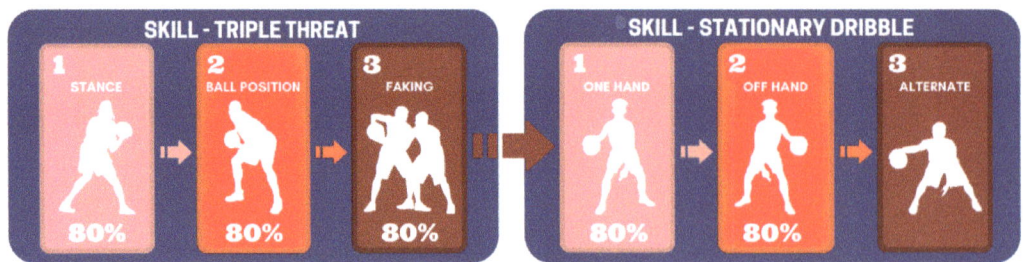

DIFFERENTIATION

As a coach, you will see that players range in their abilities in different aspects of the game. Differentiation is simply modifying a skill or a drill in order to challenge or meet the needs of your players and team. For example, you may have a player that is demonstrating skills above or below the majority of the group. While planning training, it is important to offer different drills within each skill that both challenge and enhance the skills of each player. This may be done at practices through individual stations, or perhaps it requires extra training outside of the group environment, such as after practices or within private training.

Often, coaches realize the level of the team may be inappropriate for a player. You may find yourself coaching a player who is too far below or too far above the skill set of the group. As a coach faced with either type of player, and after exhausting your options to develop that player, it may be necessary to recommend that the player join a program that can better enhance development. For example, this could involve recommending a more basic level program for a skill-deficient player, or suggesting a more competitive program for the player who is advanced in his or her skills.

PLAYER DEVELOPMENT CURRICULUM: LEVEL ONE

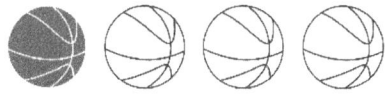

INTRODUCTORY LEVEL
FOUNDATIONAL LEVEL
ADVANCED LEVEL
PERFORMANCE LEVEL

INTRODUCTORY LEVEL
OFFENSIVE PRINCIPLES: BALL HANDLING & DRIBBLING

GENERAL OVERVIEW: *Ball handling and dribbling are of paramount importance. These two skills allow the basketball to be advanced legally throughout the court of play. At the Introductory Level, ball handling and dribbling take on the most basic form, allowing players to become familiar with the basketball.*

SKILL 1

HOW TO HOLD A BASKETBALL

- Teach young players to hold the basketball with two hands, one on each side of the basketball.
- Players should spread their fingers, with their thumbs pointed up at waist level.
- Give young players a sense of confidence handling the basketball.

POINTS OF EMPHASIS

- Slight knee bend.
- Strong grip on each side of basketball.
- Head up.
- Spread fingers, thumbs up.

SKILL 2

FAMILIARITY WITH THE BASKETBALL

- In this skill, the player will become acquainted with the basketball by moving it from hand to hand, controlling it through all movements.
- It is important to ensure that the player is confident handling the basketball while remaining stationary.
- Once players become consistent with this movement, they can begin to move the basketball with greater speed from hand to hand.
- Have the player create a popping sound with the basketball against the hand as speed increases.

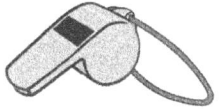

POINTS OF EMPHASIS

- Slight knee bend.
- Control of basketball from hand to hand.
- Head up.
- Spread fingers, thumbs up.

SKILL 3

TRIPLE-THREAT POSITION

Players who have become acquainted with the basketball are able to hold and move the basketball correctly. As soon as this occurs at the Introductory Level, it is important to introduce the concept of proper basketball positioning. This particular position is known as the "triple-threat" stance, which got its name from the idea that when players first receive the basketball, they are a "threat" in three different ways on the court: dribbling, passing, and shooting. Every aspect of basketball, from an offensive standpoint, centers around this stance.

- This skill can be taught as a group where each player has a basketball.
- Following an explanation and demonstration by the coach, players can hold the triple-threat position while coaches make proper adjustments to the stance.
- Players should be in a balanced basketball stance with the basketball just above the waist.
- Hand placement should be such that a shot can be taken from the position.
- Hands should resemble a large, spread-out T as formed with the thumbs.
- Later in the level, as players improve, it is important to emphasize using the pads of the fingers to hold the basketball.

POINTS OF EMPHASIS

- Balanced basketball position.
- Basketball at waist level of shooting hand.
- Hands positioned properly to shoot (T formation).
- Foot on same side of shooting hand positioned slightly in front of other foot.
- Head up.

SKILL 4

STATIONARY BALL HANDLING: THE FIRST DRIBBLE

At this level, dribbling the basketball for the first time can be an exciting moment. Teaching proper technique from the beginning is a critical element to instilling confidence in the player. Confidence determines a player's desire to continue playing the game.

- To teach the proper technique of dribbling, players will start in the triple-threat position, with the basketball placed at the waist, on the side of the player's shooting hand.
- The basketball should be dribbled in a controlled manner, rather than "slapped" at.
- The hand will push through the basketball with wrist movement (similar to a follow-through in shooting).
- Once the basketball returns from the ground to waist level, the player's hand will stop the basketball and begin the process of pushing downward through the basketball again.
- At this level, players should begin working on the nondominant hand as well.
- Coaches can instruct players to dribble a certain number of times, then catch the basketball in a triple-threat position, keeping track of how many times this is completed properly. Challenge players to do better than their own previous "record" each time. Fun, individual games such as these will keep players engaged and enjoying the process.
- Later in the level, as players improve, they should be encouraged to use their finger pads to control the basketball while dribbling. This is an important concept to introduce, as the way that the basketball rests in the hands is consistent for ball handling, dribbling, passing, receiving, and shooting. Once the technique is learned, it is important for players to learn how to control the dribble so that it stays at or below the waist level, while they keep their head up.

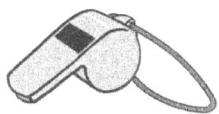

POINTS OF EMPHASIS

- Balanced basketball position throughout the entire process.
- Controlled dribbling (no slapping).
- Hand pushes through the basketball; downward wrist movement.
- Use both hands equally.
- Later in level: Use finger pads to control basketball.
- Later in level: Dribble no higher than waist level.
- Later in level: Head up.

SKILL 5

DRIBBLING TO ADVANCE THE BASKETBALL

This is the first step in learning how to advance the basketball up the floor using the dribble. Begin the process while walking, progress to a jog, and finish with a sprint.

DRILL: DRIBBLING IN A LINEAR PATH

Begin by teaching players how to dribble in a linear path. To make sure players are traveling in a straight line, coaches may use the painted lines on a gymnasium floor.

- Coaches will have players start in a triple-threat position, with the basketball placed at the waist, on the side of the player's shooting hand.
- Players should begin walking in a straight line while dribbling the basketball with their shooting hand.
- Players will need to adjust their hand positioning so that it is placed slightly behind the top of the basketball to account for the forward motion. If players keep their hands directly on top of the basketball, the basketball will not travel with them.

- The hand placement will be different based on the speed the player is traveling. Exploration will help players become familiar and comfortable with proper hand placement as they progress.
- Encourage players to dribble with their heads up by having players call out the number of fingers a coach is holding up at the other end of the floor. Further, players should be encouraged to keep the basketball at or below waist level while dribbling.
- The same dribbling concepts taught previously should be reinforced in this drill.

POINTS OF EMPHASIS

- Controlled dribbling (no slapping).
- Hand placement on basketball.
- Hand pushes through the basketball; downward wrist movement.
- Use both hands equally.
- Dribble no higher than the waist.
- Head up.

DEFENSIVE PRINCIPLES

GENERAL OVERVIEW: *At this level, due to the physical and psychological development of young players, teaching defense on the basketball is neither applicable nor recommended. Place emphasis on gaining confidence with the basketball rather than defending it. For reference, however, the defensive stance is first introduced to this level in the section entitled Footwork & Body Control.*

INTRODUCTORY LEVEL
OFFENSIVE PRINCIPLES: FOOTWORK & BODY CONTROL

GENERAL OVERVIEW: *Footwork and body control are important at all skill levels but should be emphasized especially at this level for the younger player. Footwork and body control are the foundation for all skills taught in basketball.*

SKILL 1

STOPPING AND LANDING

Coaches should teach players to stop and land with good basketball position for proper balance. The knees should be slightly bent, the head should be up, the hands should be above the waist, and the head should balance at a midpoint between the knees.

 ## POINTS OF EMPHASIS

- Slight knee bend.
- Feet wider than the shoulders.
- Head up.

SKILL 2

PIVOTING

This skill teaches pivoting for the young player.

- To make a pivot, pick one foot that will not move forward or backward; it will only spin. This foot is now "planted" and becomes the pivot foot.
- The other foot can move so that the body may swivel and turn accordingly.

 ## POINTS OF EMPHASIS

- Pivot foot stays planted.
- Swivel body while staying low.

SKILL 3

RUNNING, PIVOTING, AND BODY CONTROL

Here, the young player will become acquainted with running properly, stopping and landing, and learning how to pivot. In this skill, do not be concerned with the direction of the pivot.

- The stopping and landing position from Skill 1 is necessary to perform the pivot.
- Make the pivot with one foot turning and push off with the other foot so the body turns 180 degrees.
- After the pivot, players should begin to run in a direction specified by the coach. When running, arms should be bent so the forearm and the upper arm form a 90-degree angle. The faster the arms move, the faster the player runs.
- Coaches should select a spot on the floor as a target for the players. Once they reach that spot, instruct them to perform a jump stop while maintaining good balance.
- Make sure players use proper form while running.

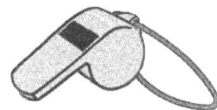

POINTS OF EMPHASIS

- Slight knee bend with feet wider than the shoulders.
- Pivot on one foot, turning the body 180 degrees.
- Arms at a 90-degree angle.
- Jump-stop with good balance, avoid falling forward.

DEFENSIVE PRINCIPLES

GENERAL OVERVIEW: *At this level, due to the physical and psychological development of young players, only stance and initial movement of the body are introduced. Additionally, no offensive players are used; the only focus should be on the footwork and body control needed on defense.*

SKILL 1

PROPER STANCE

The proper defensive stance should be introduced at this level. This will give the young defender the ability to move in all directions.

- A player's feet should be set wider than the shoulders.
- The hands should be above waist level.
- The chin should be up, and the head should be positioned above the knees and not leaning forward.

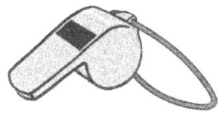

POINTS OF EMPHASIS

- Back should be straight, chin up.
- Toes pointed straight.
- Hands above the waist.
- Slight knee bend.

SKILL 2

INTRODUCING INITIAL LATERAL MOVEMENT

Introducing movement to the young defensive player should be a slow process, making sure the footwork is executed correctly. Emphasizing the proper basketball stance or position is essential to ensure that movement can be done quickly and with body control.

- Remind players to use the stance described in Skill 1.
- Once in the proper stance, instruct players to move in a particular direction. Since this is defensive movement, make sure players are sliding, not crossing their feet or running sideways.
- Encourage players to move the foot nearest to the direction they are sliding first, and then push off with the other foot. Their feet should not come together after completing the slide.
- Feet should be pointed in the direction of the slide.

POINTS OF EMPHASIS

- Hands above the waist.
- Slight knee bend.
- Point the foot in the direction of the slide. Push with the opposite foot.
- Do not bring feet together after the slide.

INTRODUCTORY LEVEL
PASSING & RECEIVING
OFFENSIVE PRINCIPLES: PASSING

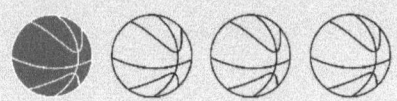

GENERAL OVERVIEW: *Passing and receiving are important abilities to develop. As with ball handling and dribbling, these two skills allow the basketball to be advanced legally through the court of play. At the Introductory Level, passing and receiving take on the most basic form.*

SKILL 1

PASS TO COACH

Once the player learns how to hold the basketball properly (see Introductory Level Ball Handling & Dribbling), the player can begin learning how to pass the basketball.

DRILL 1: TWO-HAND BOUNCE PASS

- Begin with the player standing in relatively close proximity to the target until the player is comfortable with the skill.
- Standing with a slight bend in the knee (or in triple-threat position), hold the basketball at waist level with two hands, one on each side of the basketball. The thumbs should be pointed upward.
- Taking a step toward the target, which can be either a coach or a wall (not a teammate initially), the player will push through the basketball with both hands equally.
- Encourage players to step into the pass with one foot, while keeping the pivot foot stationary. They should end with their thumbs pointing to the ground. Some refer to this motion as emptying a bottle of water.
- The basketball should bounce three-quarters of the distance between the passer and the target, but do not instruct players about this initially.
- Rather, select a spot or line on the floor in front of the players that, when hit with the basketball, will cause it to bounce up to the target successfully.
- Instruct players to try to hit the chosen spot or line with the basketball until they are comfortable enough to gauge an appropriate distance for themselves.
- Emphasizing that players pass from waist level and push through the basketball is crucial, as many beginners will try to pass the basketball from over the head.
- Hold the position at the end of the pass, holding the follow-through (similar to shooting).

 **POINTS OF EMPHASIS**

- Slight knee bend.
- Thumbs up to thumbs down (empty bottle of water).
- Step into pass toward target.
- Push through pass from waist level.

- Hit line on floor, three-quarters of the distance to the target.
- Hold follow-through.

DRILL 2: TWO-HAND CHEST PASS

Initial player positioning is similar to the positioning described in the prior drill.

- The player should begin with a slight bend in the knee, holding the basketball at waist level with two hands, one on each side of the basketball, and the thumbs pointing upward.
- The player will then take a step toward the coach or target, push through the basketball with both hands equally, and pass the basketball in the air to the target.
- The thumbs will end downward, creating a backspin on the basketball in flight.
- Encourage players to step into the pass with one foot, while keeping the pivot foot stationary.
- Once a pass is completed, players' hands should be pointing directly at their target.
- As players improve, encourage them to pass the basketball through the target, creating a straight line in the trajectory, rather than a lob.
- Begin close in distance to create good habits and technique from the start.

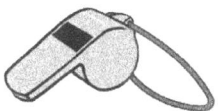

POINTS OF EMPHASIS

- Slight knee bend.
- Thumbs up to thumbs down (empty bottle of water).
- Step into pass toward receiver.
- Push through the pass from waist level.
- Straight trajectory, no lob.
- Hold follow-through.

SKILL 2

BOUNCE PASS TO TEAMMATE

As players improve, they will start to use proper passing techniques on a consistent basis. Once this happens, players can begin learning to make bounce passes to a teammate, instead of just to a coach or a wall.

DRILL 1: TWO-HAND BOUNCE PASS

- The player passing the basketball should begin in triple-threat position, facing a teammate, and should complete the two-hand bounce pass introduced before with the teammate as the target.
- The teammate receiving the basketball should provide a two-hand target around waist level for the pass to arrive. This player should catch the basketball on a two-foot jump stop, and immediately establish a triple-threat position.
- Players will then switch passing and receiving roles.
- At this point, players can also begin to communicate with one another, calling for the basketball and vocalizing to whom the basketball is being passed.

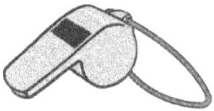

POINTS OF EMPHASIS

- Triple-threat position to start and finish.
- Step into pass, toward receiver.
- Push pass from waist level (strong passes as skill is learned).
- Proper follow-through, toward line on floor.
- Receiver provides two-hand target, catches on jump stop.

DRILL 2: ONE-HAND BOUNCE PASS

Once players become comfortable with the two-hand bounce pass, advance to a one-hand bounce pass.

- The general fundamentals remain the same with the triple-threat position, momentum and footwork stepping toward the target.
- Hand positioning on the basketball will be slightly different. The hand completing the pass will relocate from the side of the basketball to directly behind the basketball, with the wrist flexed backward, creating a T formation with the thumbs.
- The opposite hand, or guide hand, will remain on the side of the basketball for control.
- Players will step forward and push through the basketball with the hand behind the basketball, pushing four fingers toward the floor, pointing the fingers directly at the floor during the follow-through.
- Encourage players to use both hands to pass, while stepping into the pass with one foot, keeping the pivot foot stationary.
- Players receiving the basketball should maintain the same fundamentals described earlier.

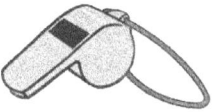

POINTS OF EMPHASIS

- Triple-threat position to start and finish.
- Step into pass, toward receiver.
- Push pass from waist level (strong passes as skill is learned).
- Proper follow-through, toward line on floor.
- Receiver provides two-hand target, catches on jump stop.

SKILL 3

CHEST PASS TO TEAMMATE

As players improve, they can begin learning to make chest passes to a teammate.

DRILL 1: TWO-HAND CHEST PASS

The mechanics of the two-hand chest pass are similar to those of the two-hand bounce pass described before.

- Begin in triple-threat position, facing a teammate, with appropriate distance between the two. This allows for a successful chest pass to be completed with two hands while maintaining proper technique.
- Again, the teammate receiving the basketball should provide a two-hand target around waist level for the pass to arrive. This player should catch the basketball on a two-foot jump stop, and immediately establish triple-threat position.
- Encourage communication between the two players.

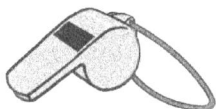

POINTS OF EMPHASIS

- Triple-threat position to start and finish.
- Step into pass, toward receiver.
- Push pass from waist level (strong passes as skill is learned, no lobs).
- Proper follow-through, toward teammate.
- Receiver provides two-hand target, catch on jump stop.

DRILL 2: ONE-HAND CHEST PASS

As for the one-hand chest pass, the main difference from the two-hand chest pass is hand placement on the basketball.

- The hand that is making the pass will shift directly behind the basketball, flexing the wrist backward, with the guide hand remaining on the side, creating a T formation with the thumbs.
- While stepping toward the target, push through the basketball, snapping the wrist to create a follow-through pointed directly at the teammate.
- Encourage players to make strong passes without lobs when first learning to pass. Especially at this young age, develop players to use both hands equally, stepping into the pass with one foot while keeping the pivot foot stationary.

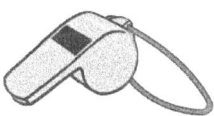

POINTS OF EMPHASIS

- Triple-threat position to start and finish.
- Step into pass, toward receiver.
- Push pass from waist level (strong passes as skill is learned, no lobs).
- Proper follow-through, toward teammate.
- Receiver provides two-hand target, catch on jump stop.

OFFENSIVE PRINCIPLES: RECEIVING

SKILL 1

INDIVIDUAL RECEIVING

Players should be taught to catch the basketball with their hands, rather than to corral it with their chest and arms. The younger players' instinct will be to corral the basketball, rather than extend their hands to catch it. It is important to correct this behavior before a bad habit or improper technique is formed.

DRILL 1: CATCH OWN DRIBBLE

- To begin the process, have players dribble the basketball, working on catching the basketball at the peak of the dribble.
- Players should work on catching the basketball with two hands, one on each side of the basketball.
- Once the basketball is caught, players' heads should be up, and they should be positioned as discussed in Skill 1: How to Hold a Basketball of the section entitled Ball Handling & Dribbling (page 43).
- Encourage players to control the basketball (hold it instead of immediately dribbling again) with the catch. They should use a strong grip, keeping their fingers spread and their thumbs up.

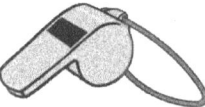 **POINTS OF EMPHASIS**

- Reinforce positioning from How to Hold a Basketball (page 43).
- Catch with two hands at peak of dribble.
- Control basketball on catch (strong grip, spread fingers, thumbs up).

DRILL 2: CATCH OWN PASS OFF WALL

Once players become comfortable catching their own dribble, have them catch a return pass off of the wall.

- Players should complete the initial pass against the wall so that they control the velocity of the basketball, making the experience less intimidating to start.
- Begin with the player making a two-hand bounce pass against the wall, sending the basketball back toward the player.
- The basketball will bounce once first, then the player can work on catching the basketball.
- When learning to catch a pass, players should create a W with their hands; the middle point of the W is formed with the thumbs. The W will encourage players to position their hands closer together, while also gaining an understanding that the hands are positioned behind the basketball in order to stop its momentum.
- Once the player gains confidence with this skill, the player may advance to making a two-hand chest pass against the wall. This will send a stronger bounce pass back to the player.
- Continue working with players to ensure they are using the W to catch and receive the basketball with control.

POINTS OF EMPHASIS

- Reinforce positioning from How to Hold a Basketball (page 43).
- Catch with two hands.
- Control basketball on catch (strong grip, spread fingers, thumbs up).
- Make a W with hands, spread fingers.

SKILL 2

CATCH PASS FROM COACH

DRILL 1: CATCH BOUNCE PASS

- Begin by having the player in a balanced stance with a slight knee bend, with hands up creating a W at chest level, ready to receive the basketball.
- The coach will then deliver a two-hand bounce pass to the player, putting the basketball as close to the player's W target as possible.
- Work with players to receive the basketball with both hands, controlling it on the catch, and immediately establishing a triple-threat position.
- As players gain confidence, coaches can vary the velocity and the location of the pass, requiring players to move their hands to catch the basketball.

POINTS OF EMPHASIS

- Slight knee bend.
- Create W target with hands.
- Catch with two hands.
- Control basketball on catch.
- Triple-threat position after catch.

DRILL 2: CATCH CHEST PASS

- After the player becomes comfortable catching a bounce pass, the player may advance to receiving a chest pass from the coach.
- Once the basic skill is learned, vary the speed and location of the passes to continue challenging the player.
- Be diligent about making sure players keep the basketball at waist level, away from their faces.

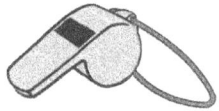

POINTS OF EMPHASIS

- Slight knee bend.
- Create W target with hands.
- Catch with two hands at waist level.
- Control basketball on catch.
- Triple-threat position after catch.

SKILL 3

CATCH BOUNCE PASS AND CHEST PASS FROM TEAMMATE

After players become comfortable catching passes from a coach, they may begin working with a teammate to continue developing passing and receiving skills.

- The teammate receiving the basketball should provide a two-hand W target for the pass at waist level. This player should catch the basketball on a two-foot jump stop, and immediately establish a triple-threat position.
- As the skill is learned, players can begin to vary the tempo used to pass back and forth to one another.
- Further, teammates can begin communicating to each other as they pass and receive the basketball.
- Finally, coaches should work with players to move their bodies in front of the basketball if it is passed outside of the frame of the body. This is the beginning stage of teaching players to move to meet a pass, and these are great habits to begin developing at a young stage.

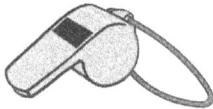

POINTS OF EMPHASIS

- Slight knee bend.
- Create W target with hands.
- Catch with two hands.
- Control basketball on catch.
- Triple-threat position after catch.
- Later in level: Vary tempo.
- Later in level: Player communication.
- Later in level: Move to meet pass.

DEFENSIVE PRINCIPLES

GENERAL OVERVIEW: *At this level, due to the physical and psychological development of young players, defending the pass is neither applicable nor recommended. Place an emphasis on building players' confidence with the basics of passing and receiving the basketball before introducing defense.*

INTRODUCTORY LEVEL

OFFENSIVE PRINCIPLES: REBOUNDING

GENERAL OVERVIEW: *While rebounding is an important aspect of the game, at this early stage, players must begin by simply learning how to grab the basketball with both hands. Therefore, coaches should focus on teaching the fundamental skills that assist with this, such as body control, running, stopping, and jumping.*

SKILL 1

SNATCHING THE BASKETBALL

Teach young players to jump and grab, or snatch, the basketball with both hands. This is the main skill to develop in younger players.

- Players should extend both arms fully above their heads and grab the basketball with both hands, pulling it toward them in a hard, downward motion.
- The basketball should be brought down to chin level, with players' elbows out to protect the basketball.
- Players should be instructed to snatch the basketball from a standing-jump position, then a one-step-and-jump position.

 ## POINTS OF EMPHASIS

- Knees bent for maximum height on jump.
- Full extension of arms.
- Both hands on the basketball.
- Snatch basketball to the chin.
- Head and chin up as basketball is snatched.

DEFENSIVE PRINCIPLES

GENERAL OVERVIEW: *At this level, due to the physical and psychological development of young players, defensive rebounding is neither applicable nor recommended. Place an emphasis on developing players' body control and snatching skills before introducing contact and defensive rebounding principles.*

INTRODUCTORY LEVEL

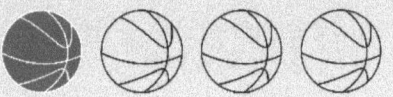

OFFENSIVE PRINCIPLES: SHOOTING

GENERAL OVERVIEW: *Shooting is a necessary fundamental to learn, as the objective of the game is to score the basketball. This may be the most important level for the proper development of a player's shooting mechanics. If improper habits are formed early in a player's development, they can be more difficult to correct later on. As a result, it is critical to emphasize proper shooting techniques at this stage, regardless of a player's strength or size.*

SKILL 1

BASIC SHOOTING MECHANICS

A basketball is not used in this skill to ensure strong habits are created prior to introducing one. The concepts below can be practiced in a group, facing an instructor, or circled around the three-point arc on a basketball floor. To teach the mechanics of shooting, it can be helpful to use the acronym BEEF, which stands for balance, elbow, eyes, and follow-through.

BALANCE

- To begin, feet should be comfortably set at or just wider than shoulder width apart. If feet are placed more narrowly, the player will likely be off balance.
- Toes should be facing forward, toward the basket or the instructor, with the same foot as the shooting hand positioned just ahead of the other foot.
- The proper distance "ahead" can be ensured by having players bring their feet together. The toe of the back foot should fit comfortably in the indentation of the arch of the front foot. Make sure players move their feet back to shoulder width apart after this foot alignment is determined.
- There should be a slight bend at the knees, the back should be straight, and the head should be over or slightly ahead of the rear end. If the head is too far forward, the player will not be properly balanced.
- Shoulders should be parallel, or "square" to the basket or instructor.

All of these elements combined will allow the shooter to be on balance. Coaches can slightly nudge the shoulders of players to test their balance while in this stance.

ELBOW

- At the initial stage of the shot, the elbow of the shooting arm should be next to the side of the player where the basketball will eventually be held in the "shooter's pocket." The elbow should not be out to the side at this stage because it will not allow for a smooth lift through the process of the shot.
- As the player begins the shooting process by raising the arm, the elbow should remain in alignment with the toe and knee of the shooting hand. The elbow will be in a U, not V, shape as the shooting hand is lifted.
- It is important to stress that the elbow should remain vertical. If the elbow is allowed to "chicken wing" outward, the shot will be more of a push. Once a basketball is introduced later, this improper technique would cause a flat trajectory as the basketball goes through the air, rather than an arched one.

EYES

- Although this skill does not involve using a basketball, it is important to instruct players as if it does, in order to prepare them for future lessons. When players use a basketball in later skills, many will want to watch its flight through the air. This is not ideal, as it can impact the mechanics of the shot and leave the basketball short.
- Once the shooting motion begins, players' eyes should be focused and locked on the rim of the basketball hoop. There is much discussion on whether the best focal point is the front, middle, or back of the rim, but the exact location is not the most important—the consistency is. Once players pick a place on which to focus, they should look at the same place for every shot.
- Emphasize that players should keep their eyes on the spot that they select for a few seconds after completing the shooting motion. This is a key habit to form without a basketball because once one is introduced, players will already be accustomed to focusing on their selected spot from the time the shooting motion begins, until the basketball goes through the hoop.

FOLLOW-THROUGH

- The follow-through may be the most important element in learning to shoot the basketball. Consistency is the key for all elements of the shot, but especially for the follow-through. As the "basketball" is in flight, instruct players to hold a strong and proper follow-through position for a few seconds to allow the "basketball" to reach the rim.
- As for technical placement of the shooting arm, the elbow should end just in front of the ear to create the correct amount of arc on the shot, and the wrist should snap forward and down, which will create a backspin once a basketball is used. The backspin is important, as it will give the basketball a chance to bounce on the rim, resulting in what many call a "shooter's roll."
- When the wrist is snapped for the follow-through, a player's first four fingers should end up pointing toward the floor. The middle finger will be the last finger that touches the basketball during the follow-through process. For players who learn from visual cues, it may help to have them pretend they are standing on their tiptoes trying to grab a cookie out of a jar above their head.
- Young players should freeze in this position, as if they are posing for a picture for a few seconds after the shooting motion ends to let the "basketball" hit the rim. At this point, the shot is finished.

 # POINTS OF EMPHASIS

- Focus on details of mechanics without a basketball.
- Use BEEF concepts.
- Create good habits from the beginning by breaking down each element.

SKILL 2

SHOOTING FROM A POSITION ON THE KNEES

A basketball should be introduced at this point in the level, but players will not be working with a basketball hoop quite yet.

DRILL 1: ON ONE KNEE, SHOOTING TO SELF WITH ONE HAND

- To begin developing a comfort level with the mechanics of the shot, isolate the upper body by having players start on their knees with a basketball. Begin teaching the form with the shooting hand only, as the guide hand can be challenging at this age due to the strength and size of young players.
- Start with the player on one knee, with a straight back, and squared to a target. The knee that players put their weight on should be the one opposite their shooting hand. In other words, players who shoot with their right hand should kneel on their left, with the right knee out in front of them. Coaches should watch players carefully to ensure they are not rocking in any direction throughout this exercise.
- In this position, players will hold the basketball out in front of them at waist level, with the shooting hand underneath the basketball and the guide hand behind the back. The basketball should be placed on the pads of the fingers, allowing a little bit of light to show between the basketball and the thumb.
- Once players have the appropriate grip, instruct them to move the basketball from the waist up to shoulder level, turning the wrist in the process so their fingers end up pointing backward. This helps players work on movement control and teaches the importance of using finger pads.
- The elbow should now be in a U shape, parallel to the knee of the shooting hand, with the wrist cocked backward. Make sure players maintain correct basketball positioning, so that a trace of light can be seen through the basketball. Pause briefly at this position to make any corrections before allowing players to begin the upward shooting motion.
- At the end of the shooting motion, the elbow should be slightly ahead of the ear and the middle finger should guide the follow-through, ending with four fingers pointed toward the floor as if grabbing a cookie out of a jar above the head.
- The eyes should remain on the target until the basketball hits the ground. Ideally, if the follow-through creates the correct backspin, the basketball will spin back to the shooter after bouncing off of the ground so that the shooter can grab the basketball without having to move.
- Coaches should be aware that players just learning this skill will not be accurate with the trajectory of the basketball. Ensure players do not hit themselves in the head, as many times the basketball will travel directly upward.

 **POINTS OF EMPHASIS**

- Focus on details of mechanics.
- Control basketball when raising from waist to head level.
- Basketball rests on finger pads, not palm.

DRILL 2: ON ONE KNEE, SHOOTING TO SELF WITH TWO HANDS

- As players become comfortable with one hand, they can begin using two hands by incorporating the guide hand. The "guide hand" should remain just that, a guide.
- At this level, players have a tendency to want to shoot with two hands, pushing the basketball rather than shooting it. The guide hand should be placed on the side of the basketball, creating a wide, spread-out T with the thumbs on the basketball.
- Have the players repeat the exercise above, adding the guide hand. This hand will remain on the side of the basketball to assist with control as the player raises the basketball from the waist to the head.
- At this point, the guide hand will stop and allow the shooting hand to complete the follow-through. However, the guide hand is part of the follow-through and should remain around head level until the basketball hits the ground. It is important to encourage the proper use of the guide hand prior to shooting on a basket to avoid creating bad habits.
- Once players use their guide hand properly from one knee, instruct them to begin on both knees, seated with their rear end on their heels. From this position, they should perform the same arm movements, and rise from the seated position to a kneeling, upright position as they shoot the basketball. This will help simulate the motion of the shot from a standing position.

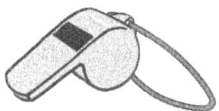

POINTS OF EMPHASIS

- Focus on details of mechanics.
- Control basketball when raising from waist to head level.
- Ensure proper technique using one hand before moving to two.

SKILL 3

SHOOTING FROM A STANDING POSITION

DRILL 1: SHOOTING TO SELF WITH ONE HAND

- The feet should be properly spaced and balanced as discussed in Skill 1, and the shoulders should remain squared toward a target.
- Players should hold the basketball at the waist with the shooting hand under the basketball. Begin the same process as detailed above, ending with a solid follow-through.
- Introduce the use of the legs in conjunction with the upper body at this point. Initially, players should not jump; instead, they should rise slightly onto the balls of their feet.
- Using the legs will result in a stronger shot, and allow there to be more of an arc in the basketball's trajectory through the air than when players are on their knees.
- An appropriate backspin will cause the basketball to bounce directly back to the player without having to move to catch it.

POINTS OF EMPHASIS

- Focus on details of mechanics from beginning to end.
- Legs should work in conjunction with upper body.
- Basketball rests on finger pads, not palm.

DRILL 2: SHOOTING TO SELF WITH TWO HANDS

- Once the player becomes comfortable with one hand, begin using both hands. Again, focus on the guide hand being just a guide.
- As players improve, challenge them to have the basketball hit the same spot on the floor, creating consistency in the shot.
- An appropriate backspin will cause the basketball to bounce directly back to the player without having to move to catch it.
- As this skill involves both hands on the basketball, coaches should feel free to combine it with other skills, such as receiving. For example, as the basketball travels back toward the player after a shot attempt, encourage the player to receive the basketball on a two-foot hop, placing the basketball in the shooting pocket in a triple-threat position. From there, continue with another two-hand shot attempt.

POINTS OF EMPHASIS

- Focus on details of mechanics from beginning to end.
- Legs should work in conjunction with upper body.
- Create solid comfort level with one hand before moving to two.

DRILL 3: SHOOTING AGAINST A WALL WITH ONE HAND

- Next, have players begin shooting the basketball toward a target. Initially, use a wall for this purpose.
- Instruct players to stand approximately five feet away, facing the wall. Make sure they are squared to the wall and in a balanced stance. Players should use the same motion learned above to shoot the basketball to themselves.
- Coaches should be aware that once targets are introduced, players often focus on hitting the target at the expense of proper technique. Take care to reinforce correct mechanics at this stage.
- One of the more important mechanics is the follow-through. Remind players that the elbow should be just in front of the ear, creating the appropriate arched path as the basketball goes through the air.
- As players improve, provide an exact location on the wall directly in front of them that they should try to hit with consistency.

POINTS OF EMPHASIS

- Focus on details of mechanics from beginning to end.
- Focus on proper follow-through.
- Reinforce correct mechanics.

DRILL 4: SHOOTING AGAINST A WALL WITH TWO HANDS

- Once the player becomes comfortable with one hand, begin using both hands. Again, focus on the guide hand being just a guide.
- As players improve, challenge them to have the basketball hit the same spot on the wall, creating consistency in the shot.
- As this skill involves both hands on the basketball, coaches should feel free to combine it with other skills, such as receiving. For example, as the basketball travels back toward the player after a shot attempt, encourage the player to receive the basketball on a two-foot hop, placing the basketball in the shooting pocket in a triple-threat position. From there, continue with another two-hand shot attempt.

POINTS OF EMPHASIS

- Focus on details of mechanics from beginning to end.
- Focus on proper follow-through.
- Encourage consistency as comfort level progresses.

SKILL 4

SHOOTING FROM A POSITION ON THE GROUND

This skill is recommended if a player struggles with the mechanics of the follow-through. When a player is lying on the ground, it isolates the shooting arm and allows the player to focus solely on this aspect of the shot.

- Instruct the player to lie on the ground, facing up. A coach or instructor should stand above the player.
- The basketball should be placed on the pads of the player's fingers and held above the head with the shooting hand only. The arm should be slightly bent, creating a U with the elbow. Make sure the player keeps the elbow tucked into the side of the body.
- From this position, have the player begin the shooting motion. The wrist should snap, resulting in four fingers pointed toward the floor. The basketball should travel straight up toward the coach and return to the hand.
- With this vantage point, the player can easily see the rotation of the basketball, making sure backspin has been created.
- Once the player becomes comfortable with one hand, begin using both hands. Again, focus on the guide hand being just a guide.

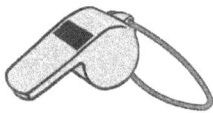# POINTS OF EMPHASIS

- Basketball placement on finger pads.
- U created by elbow.
- Snap wrist, four fingers to the floor.
- Backspin.

SKILL 5

SHOOTING ON A BASKETBALL HOOP

Once the player has established a solid set of mechanics for a shot, the basketball hoop may be introduced. At first, it may be beneficial to use a hoop that is lower than a standard basketball hoop, especially if the player does not have the strength or size to shoot properly on a ten-foot basket.

DRILL 1: SHOOTING ON A BASKETBALL HOOP WITH ONE HAND

- Using only the shooting arm, begin working through the mechanics detailed in drills before.
- The goal should continue to be creating good habits, not compromising form to make a basket.
- Encourage players to keep their eyes focused on the same spot on the rim for each shot attempt.
- Emphasize that the middle finger of the shooting hand should be the last finger to touch the basketball during the follow-through.
- Hold the follow-through until the basketball hits the ground. At this level, encourage and reinforce proper mechanics rather than the number of made shots.

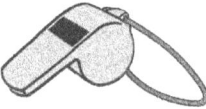# POINTS OF EMPHASIS

- Focus on details of mechanics from beginning to end.
- Encourage proper mechanics rather than made shots.
- Focus eyes on same spot on the rim.

DRILL 2: SHOOTING ON A BASKETBALL HOOP WITH TWO HANDS

- Once the player becomes comfortable with one hand, begin using both hands. Continue reminding players that the guide hand is just a guide.
- Further, make sure players use their upper and lower bodies together. This will be important later in the growth of the shooter to create range on the shot.

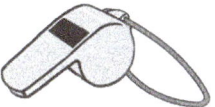 ## POINTS OF EMPHASIS

- Focus on details of mechanics from beginning to end.
- Encourage proper mechanics rather than made shots.
- Upper and lower body work together.

INTRODUCTORY LEVEL
TEAM DEFENSIVE CONCEPTS

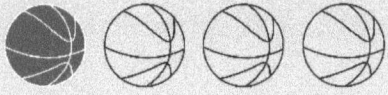

GENERAL OVERVIEW: *Once your players understand and can properly execute the individual defensive skills, the coach can begin organizing them together into defensive team concepts. The primary defensive objective in basketball is to stop the opponent from scoring. At this level, we are concerned with proper stance and the ability to guard one offensive player.*

SKILL 1

UNDERSTAND DEFENDING ONE OFFENSIVE PLAYER

- This level will stress the importance of just guarding or defending one offensive player with and without the ball.
- The help-side defensive concept is not introduced at this level, as the young player needs to develop on-ball defense in a 1-on-1 situation.
- Start out with the defender working to be in a position between the offensive player and the basket in a 1-on-1 situation.
- Start the offensive player at the top of the key without the basketball. Rule for the offensive player is move and try to get to the baseline between the lane lines without getting touched by the defender.
- Progress to the coach, who will dribble the ball from the top of the key to the basket with the defender in a good stance staying in front of the coach.
- The drill then can be done 2-on-2 or 3-on-3, where each of the offensive players has a ball starting at a spot on the court. One offensive player starts dribbling to the basket with the defender staying between the ball and the basket. The next offensive player will start on coach's command.
- Extend the drills to full court—have the offensive player without the ball use V-cuts starting at one baseline and go to the opposite baseline. The defender stays an arm's length from the offensive player using drop steps when the offensive player changes direction.

 ### POINTS OF EMPHASIS

- When playing the 1-on-1 tag game, the defender keeps distance with the offensive player in front until the defender decides to make a tag.
- The defender needs to keep a good stance when trying to stay in front of the offensive player.
- The defender should keep one foot ahead of the other foot when in a stance guarding the dribbler.
- The defender should try to keep the hand down to discourage the crossover dribble—same hand down as the top foot.
- Have a rule for the defender when playing the offensive player with the ball to not reach for the ball and keep an arm's-length distance.
- Eyes should be kept on the waist of the offensive player and not on the ball or the head of the offensive player.
- The offensive player must stay on one-third of the court when moving with V-cuts the full length of the court.

INTRODUCTORY LEVEL
TEAM OFFENSIVE CONCEPTS

GENERAL OVERVIEW: *Once players understand and can execute the individual skills explained in this level, coaches may begin providing instruction on offensive tactics. The primary objective on offense, scoring, is achieved most easily when the basketball is moved effectively between the players on the court. At this level, coaches should focus on teaching players how to be aware of where their teammates are on the court during various offensive scenarios.*

SKILL 1

PROPER FLOOR AND PLAYER AWARENESS

The most important concept when coordinating an offensive attack is to maintain balance on the court. To do this, it is crucial that players learn how to be aware of where their teammates are around them.

- At this level, start with three players standing inside the lane.
- On command, the players must spread out inside the three-point line, making sure they are aware of where their teammates are located. As players improve, increase the number on the court to four, and then to five players at a time.
- The progression for proper floor and player awareness is to have the players switch places with a teammate on command by the coach.
- Once the players are spread out, the coach will pass the basketball to one player and the players should be able to pass the basketball to their teammates easily if they are properly spread out.

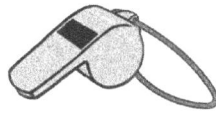 ## POINTS OF EMPHASIS

- The players must be twelve feet apart from each other, which is the width of the foul lane.
- Have the players throw air passes to each other and then bounce passes while they are in the proper floor positions.
- When the players switch positions on the court, the player who just passed should communicate the change of position with the teammate by a raised hand or by calling change.
- The coach can call out a certain number of passes, and then the player who has the basketball will shoot.

SKILL 2

RECOGNIZING SPOTS ON THE FLOOR

- Once players are aware of where their teammates are located, the coach can teach the areas of the half court—baseline, wing, high post, low post, top of key.
- Set a basketball down in each of the five areas on the floor: baseline, wing, top of key, low post, high post. Starting at the baseline with five players, each player runs to an area and stands next to the basketball. Repeat until all players have had a chance to run to all spots.
- Next, using the same starting process, call out certain areas of the court and players must run to fill those spots. Players will pick up the basketball and get into triple-threat position. For this part of the drill players will not shoot the ball. Coaches should start by calling out one spot and then work up to calling out all five spots in succession.
- The same drill can start at half court with five lines. In this variation, the front player in each line will fill in one of the areas on the floor when prompted by the coach.
- For this drill, players will sprint to the area called, pick up the basketball, and shoot it. It would be best to use an additional coach to serve as a rebounder to keep the drill moving.
- A final variation of the drill at this level would incorporate passing. Once prompted, the first player in each of the five lines would sprint to an area but not pick up the basketball. The coach would then call out one of the spots. The player in that spot would pick up the ball and get into triple-threat position. The coach would then call out a spot for that player to pass the basketball to. The player who receives the pass would then take a shot.

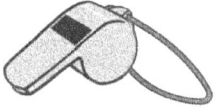 ## POINTS OF EMPHASIS

- Insist that players remain in the spot and not in between spots.
- Remind all players to get into triple-threat position, facing the basket at all times.

SKILL 3

INBOUNDING THE BASKETBALL

- When inbounding the basketball at this level, the passer must make a pass to the player moving to the basketball. At this level, players moving away from the basketball should not receive the pass.
- To avoid crowding, the players should have balanced spacing. Encourage two players moving to the basketball and two players moving away from the basketball.
- Emphasize movement by having players exchange places with a player in another area. This encourages teamwork and spacing to become an open receiver for the passer.
- Teach the passer to use a prompt to start the motion of the other players. Slapping the ball or shouting "go" are great cues to start.

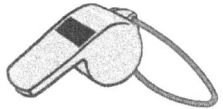

POINTS OF EMPHASIS

- Slap the ball or shout "go" to start motion.
- Keep proper spacing; avoid crowding.
- Receiving players must come to the ball.
- All players should have hands ready to receive.

SKILL 4

SPACING

- It is important for young players to understand that spacing on the court is important for team basketball.
- Coaches may begin teaching this concept to players at the Introductory Level by using markers (cones or discs) on the court. The markers should be spread out approximately twelve to fifteen feet apart. Players will sprint to a marker on command.
- Continue the drill with the players sprinting to a new marker on command of the coach.
- For variation, give players a marker and start them lined up at the baseline. The first player in line will place the marker anywhere on the court and stand by it. The next player in line will space their marker about twelve to fifteen feet from the first marker. Follow until all players are completed.
- To show the importance of spacing, have players pass a ball to the nearest teammate. Next, have players try to pass a ball to a teammate much farther away. Highlight that shorter passes are easier, and longer passes are more difficult.

POINTS OF EMPHASIS

- Demonstrate to players a twelve-to-fifteen-foot distance.
- Encourage sprinting to spots.
- Emphasize short passes; discourage long passes.

SKILL 5

TRANSITION FROM DEFENSE TO OFFENSE

At this level, transition from defense to offense is about proper spacing and knowing the spots on the floor.

- Place cones at the top of the key at both ends to mark off five distinct areas of the court: two outside lanes, two inside lanes, and the middle lane. Four cones should be set up to show the five lanes.
- Start players in five lines at one end of the court. Without the basketball, and on command of the coach, have the first player in each line sprint to the opposite baseline while remaining in their lane.

- Players should rotate lines so that each player gets a turn running through each lane.
- Next, perform the same drill with basketballs. The middle lane dribbles the basketball while the outside two lanes pass a basketball back and forth while sprinting in their lanes.
- Next, have the middle lane pass the basketball back and forth with the inside lane players while sprinting down the court. The outside two players will dribble a basketball.
- Progress the drill with three players inside the middle lane running in a circle with their hands ready. The coach will pass the basketball to one of the players. This player will then dribble the basketball in the middle lane while the other two players sprint the outside two lanes to the other end. If appropriate, the sequence can end with a pass for a layup.
- Continue this drill using five players. One of the inside two players will sprint to the low-post area and the other will sprint to the high-post area. The dribbler should make a pass to the outside lane player, who will then pass to one of the post players up ahead of the sequence.
- The last phase in this transition should be the middle player dribbling to the top of the key while the other four run their lanes. Allow the dribbler to decide whom to pass to.
- Progress the drill until all players have had the opportunity to play all of the lanes.

POINTS OF EMPHASIS

- Players without the basketball stay slightly ahead of the ball.
- Sprint with hands ready and eyes on the basketball.
- Keep proper spacing between players.
- Emphasize short, accurate passes; discourage long passes.
- Rotate players through each lane multiple times, disregarding positions, height, and ability.

PLAYER DEVELOPMENT CURRICULUM: LEVEL TWO

INTRODUCTORY LEVEL

FOUNDATIONAL LEVEL

ADVANCED LEVEL

PERFORMANCE LEVEL

FOUNDATIONAL LEVEL OFFENSIVE PRINCIPLES: BALL HANDLING & DRIBBLING

GENERAL OVERVIEW: *Ball handling and dribbling are of paramount importance. These two skills allow the basketball to be advanced legally throughout the court of play. At the Foundational Level, ball handling and dribbling will develop such that players may engage in 2-on-2, 3-on-3, 4-on-4, and eventually 5-on-5 basketball.*

SKILL 1

TRIPLE-THREAT POSITION WITH A TEAMMATE

As a warm-up, this is a good way to continue building on overall ball-handling skills. Coaches will partner players up, lining them across the lane lines.

- Players will begin in the triple-threat position.
- Remind players that the shooting foot should be slightly ahead of the other, and stand in a balanced basketball position.
- The basketball should be held just above the waist, resting in the finger pads rather than on the palm of the hand; fingers should be spread out.
- The thumbs should form a large, spread-out T. Keep the head up, looking at the teammate standing across from the player.

From this triple-threat position, coaches will have players execute all three options from the stance: dribbling, passing, and shooting.

- For passing and shooting, the players will utilize their partner.
- For ball handling, emphasize the importance of using finger pads and controlling the basketball through every bounce.
- Coaches can start encouraging players to pound the basketball into the floor to ensure a solid feel of the basketball and gain confidence in the dribble.
- Players can begin creating the habit of protecting the basketball from an imaginary defender by front pivoting ninety degrees toward their partner and placing an arm bar at chest level for protection.
- Coaches can also have players dribble the basketball at varying heights to improve control. This will help increase the use and strength of finger pads and wrist action through the dribble.

POINTS OF EMPHASIS

- Balanced basketball position.
- Finger pad control.
- Wrist movements.
- Pound basketball.
- Arm bar for protection.
- Carry over principles from passing and shooting.

SKILL 2

STATIONARY BALL HANDLING

Stationary ball handling without a dribble is an efficient and fun way to help players increase their level of comfort when moving the basketball. Although many of the drills below are never executed in the game, they are still necessary to develop a player's confidence when handling the basketball under duress.

DRILL 1: STRAIGHT ARM TAPS

This works on finger pad control and arm strength through ball handling.

- Players will start by tapping the basketball as closely and quickly as possible from one hand to the next, straight out in front of them at chest level. This should be repeated over and over.
- Instruct players to use finger pads and wrist motion to make the basketball move back and forth successfully without dropping it.
- Players should have straight elbows while performing this drill, which isolates the fingers and wrists.
- After players have worked on the skill straight in front of them, have players adjust the basketball above their head, completing the same motion. Then move the basketball to the waist.
- Coaches can be creative moving the basketball position throughout the skill.
- Players will notice the importance of hand positioning in order to complete the drill at the different locations to ensure the basketball does not fall to the ground.

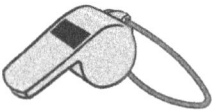

POINTS OF EMPHASIS

- Finger pad control.
- Wrist action.
- Elbows remain straight throughout all locations.
- Head up.
- Slight knee bend.

DRILL 2: AROUND THE BODY

This drill begins in an elongated stance with a slight knee bend. Using the finger pads to control the basketball is important. Coaches will also want to encourage players to keep their body still, rather than moving in a circular motion mimicking the path of the basketball.

- Players will rotate the basketball around the waist from hand to hand clockwise, not allowing the basketball to fall to the ground.
- Once players have worked on the clockwise motion, switch to counterclockwise.
- Players can then move on to performing the drill around the head and knees. Depending on ability, players may move the basketball around one knee, or both knees together.
- Coaches can create a pattern of movement as well.
- As players continue to improve, encourage them to perform the drill with increased speed, taking care to keep their head up.

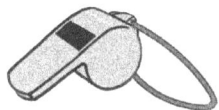

POINTS OF EMPHASIS

- Finger pad control.
- Slight knee bend.
- Head up.
- Learn mechanics first, speed second.
- Body still.

DRILL 3: AROUND THE KNEES

A coach can modify the drill above by instructing players to work the basketball in a circular motion around the knees, while moving their legs in and out of position. The basketball itself does not deviate from the circular path.

- Players will be slightly bent over for this drill, but remind them to keep their head up. They should also avoid moving their upper body. Many times during this drill, players move their back up in a "bobbing" manner. This should be discouraged.
- The footwork will begin with both feet together on one spot; let's call this spot "home base." After the basketball travels around both legs together, the player will move the right foot straight backward. The basketball will then travel around the left knee only, which is still located on home base.
- Next, the player will move the right foot back to home base and complete a circle around both knees. After completing the circle, the player will move the left foot backward and away from home base, allowing the player to move the basketball around the right knee, only. Upon completion, the player will bring the left foot back to home base.
- The drill continues in this fashion alternating circles with the basketball around both knees, then one knee, then both knees again, followed by the other knee and so on.

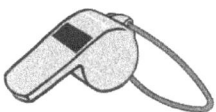

POINTS OF EMPHASIS

- The legs move, not the basketball.
- Head up.

- No bobbing motion with body.
- Finger pad control.
- Learn skill first, speed second.

DRILL 4: FIGURE 8

With the player in a position similar to a defensive stance, the player will circle the basketball through and around the knees in order to make a figure-8 path with the basketball.

- To begin, teach the figure 8 by going through the "front door." The first motion with the basketball should go through the middle of the legs from the front of the body to the back.
- Once the player has learned this, coaches can reverse the direction and go through the "back door." This motion is a bit more challenging due to the player having to cup the basketball on the backside to perform the drill correctly.

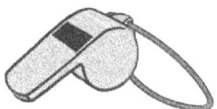 **POINTS OF EMPHASIS**

- Finger pad control.
- Head up.
- No bobbing motion with body.
- Learn skill first, speed second.

DRILL 5: EGGBEATER

This will help increase general hand speed, coordination, and timing with the basketball.

- Instruct players to begin in a defensive stance.
- Place the basketball between the legs at the knees. The knees should not touch the basketball. Instead, the basketball should be held with the right hand in front of the body and the left hand behind the body.
- Next, the player will gently toss the basketball up between the legs and quickly switch the positioning of the hands and catch the basketball. If completed properly, the basketball is now being held between the legs by the left hand in front and the right hand behind the body. The basketball should not be allowed to hit the ground.
- The drill continues with the constant switching of the hands, while not allowing the basketball to hit the ground.

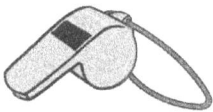 **POINTS OF EMPHASIS**

- Balanced, defensive stance.
- Head up.
- Finger pad control.
- Quick hand movements.

DRILL 6: FRONT TO BACK

The front-to-back skill is the same concept, but requires different hand placement.

- Players will be in the same stance with the basketball between the legs. This time, however, both hands will hold the basketball in front of the body.
- To execute this drill, players will gently toss the basketball up between the legs and catch it with both hands behind the legs before it hits the ground.
- The basketball will move from front to back slightly with the hands following. Again, the objective is to quickly move the hands and catch the basketball without allowing it to touch the ground.

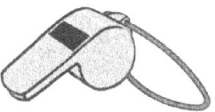

POINTS OF EMPHASIS

- Balanced, defensive stance.
- Head up.
- Finger pad control.
- Quick hand movements.
- Toss the basketball slightly upward to allow time for switching.
- No bobbing motion with body.

SKILL 3

STATIONARY BALL HANDLING; ADD A DRIBBLE

Stationary ball handling with a dribble is another efficient and fun way to help players increase their level of comfort when moving the basketball. Again, although many of the drills below are never executed in the game, they are still necessary to develop a player's confidence when handling the basketball under duress.

DRILL 1: WALL DRIBBLING

Dribbling the basketball against a wall is a great way to help develop basketball control, body strength, and confidence using the finger pads.

- Here, players line up directly in front of a wall and dribble the basketball as quickly as possible against the wall at shoulder height.
- Coaches can have the players move slowly in both lateral directions, controlling the basketball with motion.
- Lastly, the coach can have players draw shapes with their dribble and ultimately improve to the point where they are signing their names in cursive on the wall. It is a fun way to develop confidence handling the basketball.

POINTS OF EMPHASIS

- Keep elbow directly under wrist.
- Finger pad and wrist motion.
- Placing of hand on basketball to assure basketball does not fall to ground.
- Quick, hard, and controlled dribbles.
- On movement, basketball should stay close to wall.

DRILL 2: RHYTHM DRIBBLE

This skill is called the "rhythm dribble" because of the rhythm that can be heard when completed properly.

- Instruct the player to begin in the same starting position as the eggbeater: in a defensive stance with the right hand in front and left hand behind.
- Player will then drop the basketball, allowing it to bounce one time while switching hands.
- After the switch, the left hand should be in front and the right hand will be behind.
- Next, the player will move the basketball in a full circular motion starting with a backward motion from right to left, without the basketball traveling through the front door.
- Once the basketball comes back to the starting point with the right hand in front and the left hand behind, the player will start the drill again.
- Switch directions once the drill is learned.

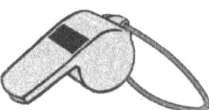
POINTS OF EMPHASIS

- Establishing the rhythm of the skill.
- Control of basketball.
- Body control, no bobbing motion
- Head up.
- Learn drill first, then work for speed.

DRILL 3: FIGURE-8 DRIBBLE

To begin, the player should start in a balanced, defensive stance.

- The player will begin the figure-8 motion, as discussed earlier, using a dribble this time.
- Using a dribble, it is easiest to begin teaching that the player move the basketball through the back of the legs ("the back door"), rather than through the front door.
- Coaches can dictate the number of dribbles to be used to complete the figure-8 motion, ranging from four dribbles to as many as the player can possibly get in.
- Once the player gets comfortable with the dribble figure 8 through the back door, have the player switch directions to the front door.

- For players who excel at the figure 8 with two hands, coaches can challenge players to complete the same motion with only one hand. It is easiest to again teach this skill by first going through the back door, then changing to the front door.

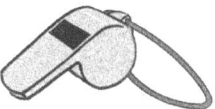

POINTS OF EMPHASIS

- Controlled dribble, close to legs for efficiency.
- Finger pad control and wrist movements, especially if low maximum dribbles.
- Head up.
- Body control through movement; no bobbing.

DRILL 4: SINGLE-ARM PENDULUM DRIBBLE—FRONT

The goal is for the basketball to travel from knee to knee at a minimum, in front of the body. The hand should completely turn over in order to catch and change the direction of the dribble.

- Starting in a balanced, comfortable defensive position, the player will dribble the basketball with one hand in the motion of a V in a pendulum-type pattern.
- Encourage players to maintain a stable position below the waist, not allowing the knees to buckle in either direction with the movement of the basketball.
- To challenge the player even more, coaches can have players complete one pendulum swing and then cross over to the other hand. Players can continue this pattern, working on both hands and a crossover dribble at the same time.
- Increase speed as the drill progresses.

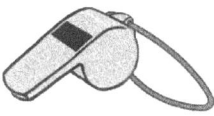

POINTS OF EMPHASIS

- Hard, controlled dribble.
- Turn the hand over from movement to movement.
- Cover distance with the basketball.
- Control of the body throughout the motions.

DRILL 5: SINGLE-ARM PENDULUM DRIBBLE—SIDE

Once the pendulum in front is learned, coaches can move to a pendulum dribble along the side of the body.

- Instruct the player to begin in a balanced, comfortable defensive position.
- Perpendicular to the shoulder line, the player will dribble in a V formation. Ideally, the hip serves as the midpoint of the pendulum, swinging forward and backward.
- Hand should turn completely over to achieve the appropriate motion extending as far as possible front and back.
- A clean, straight line with the dribble is ideal. Players may use the lines painted on the floor as a guide.

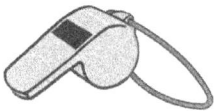

POINTS OF EMPHASIS

- Hard, controlled dribble.
- Turn the hand over from movement to movement.
- Cover distance with the basketball.
- Control of the body throughout the motions.

DRILL 6: DOUBLE-ARM PENDULUM DRIBBLE—FRONT

- After one hand is learned, challenge players to use two hands in the front, creating a crossover dribble.
- Players will make the same V motion with the basketball from hand to hand.
- As players improve, instruct them to pound the basketball under control with increased speeds.
- Further, coaches can progress players to make the same, hard dribbling V motion between their legs. Pivot so the chest is pointed directly at one of the knees to create the same angle of dribble. To switch directions, move the chest so it is pointed directly at the other knee.

POINTS OF EMPHASIS

- Hard, controlled dribble.
- Cover distance with the basketball.
- Control of the body throughout the motions.

DRILL 7: BEHIND THE BACK

To begin learning how to dribble the basketball behind the back, players should first begin by dribbling the basketball in a V motion, similar to a crossover, behind the body instead of in front. Ideally, the dribble will follow the exact shoulder line of the player.

- Coaches can use lines painted on a gymnasium floor to help achieve these types of dribble lines.
- As players improve, encourage them to keep their head up.
- Rather than look at the basketball, instruct players to look at the shadow that the basketball casts on the floor.
- Once the drill is learned, begin working on pounding dribbles and increased speed.
- Once the V motion is learned, coaches can work on having the player wrap the basketball around the back. The player will take one dribble at the side of the body, and then wrap the basketball around the body, allowing it to bounce by the opposite hip.

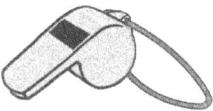

POINTS OF EMPHASIS

- V motion with basketball.
- Body control.
- Head up.
- Clean lines with dribble motion.
- Slight knee bend.

SKILL 4

DRIBBLING ON THE MOVE

This is designed to teach players various types of dribbles that will advance the basketball while they are being defended. Learning to handle the basketball is critical to every player's development, regardless of position or size. Every player will need to dribble the basketball at some point!

DRILL 1: SPEED DRIBBLE

The speed dribble is used most often in the open court when transitioning from defense to offense. The objective of the speed dribble is to advance the basketball as quickly as possible, pushing the basketball out in front of the body.

- Begin by lining players up at one end of the court in a triple-threat position.
- On the whistle, have players advance the basketball straight up the floor in the dominant hand as quickly as possible to the other baseline, ending in a jump stop and triple-threat position.
- Coaches should encourage players to increase their speed while still controlling the basketball. Players will likely dribble the basketball by their shoulders the first time in an attempt to move quickly.
- Continue to encourage control and speed in a healthy combination, keeping the basketball a little above waist level.
- After players become comfortable with using the dominant hand, move to the use of the nondominant hand. Once that is comfortable, have players move up the floor in a straight line, alternating hands.

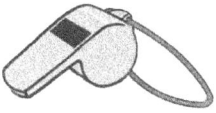

POINTS OF EMPHASIS

- Head up.
- Run in a straight line for efficiency.
- Dribble basketball no higher than just above the waist.
- Healthy balance of control and speed.
- Correct dribbling mechanics.

DRILL 2: CROSSOVER DRIBBLE

The crossover dribble can be used to simply change directions or sides of the floor, or to attack a defender.

- Again, players will start on the baseline in a triple-threat position.
- A player will take two dribbles to the right, cross over, and head back to the left, creating a zigzag-type motion.
- When crossing over, it is important to plant the outside foot in front of the body and push off with that foot in order to change directions.
- The opposite foot will cut in the new direction, most effectively near the defender's foot out in front.
- The body should be positioned low throughout the move to enable the player to explode out of the crossover.
- The crossover dribble itself should be low and tight to the body, not allowing the defender's hands to interfere with the dribble.
- Once players complete the crossover, instruct them to immediately get the basketball on the outside of the body to protect it from a defender.
- Encourage change of speed and change of direction for an efficient and effective crossover move. It is best to learn the skill without a defender present to gain confidence before performing the drill against a live defender.

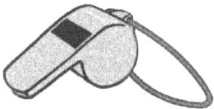 **POINTS OF EMPHASIS**

- Low dribble, tight to body on crossover.
- Plant outside foot to push off.
- Efficient footwork coming out of crossover.
- Change of speed, change of direction.
- Head up.

DRILL 3: RETREAT-CROSSOVER DRIBBLE

Once the crossover dribble is learned, coaches can introduce a retreat-crossover dribble. A retreat-crossover is used when players are in an uncomfortable situation, but still have a live dribble. A good example of this would be when a team traps the offensive player. The player will approach the trap, feel pressure, retreat using a backward dribble, then perform a crossover to escape the trap.

- For this drill, players will begin on the baseline in a triple-threat position.
- Players will take three dribbles to the right and plant on their back foot (right) with their left foot forward, protecting the basketball.
- Players will then slide directly backward (parallel with the sideline), taking two dribbles as they retreat.
- After the retreat, players will perform a crossover dribble and then attack to the left, out of the imaginary trap.
- The concepts for the actual crossover dribble will carry over from before.
- Again, once the drill is learned, change of speed and change of direction are critical in developing an effective retreat crossover.

POINTS OF EMPHASIS

- Protect the basketball on retreat.
- Efficient footwork coming out of crossover.
- Change of speed, change of direction.
- Head up.

DRILL 4: HESITATION DRIBBLE

The hesitation dribble can be used in a variety of ways, most commonly and effectively used to freeze a defender for a second, creating an opportunity for the offensive player to get by the defender.

- Players can start on the baseline in a triple-threat position.
- Player will take three speed dribbles, in a straight line, using the dominant hand. Imagining a defender in front of the player, the player will hesitate, or pause for a second, raising or freezing the defender.
- Following the hesitation, the player will explode forward out of the move, keeping the basketball in the dominant hand.
- It is most efficient for the player to use a direct step coming out of the move. For example, if the player were dribbling the basketball in the right hand, the step coming out of the move would be with the right foot. It is important to keep the hand on top of the basketball during the move to assure the player does not illegally carry the basketball.
- Coaches should be able to physically see a change in speed. The player should approach the move sprinting, pause, and then depart the move sprinting. There should be a clear, distinguished, and concise change in speeds to be most effective.

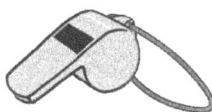

POINTS OF EMPHASIS

- Freeze defense.
- Changes of speed into, during, and out of move—most important, explode out.
- Hand on top of the basketball.
- Come out of move in straight line, foot directly next to defender's foot.

DRILL 5: HUMAN CONE DRIBBLING

Human cone dribbling is a fun method of teaching players how to dribble with obstacles in front of them.

- Coaches will evenly space the human cones in a direct line the length of the basketball court.
- Begin with the human cones standing straight up and down, not moving or reaching at the ball handlers as they pass.
- The player with the basketball will begin working through the cones using a speed dribble, alternating hands, circling the last human cone, and then returning.

- The player will give the basketball to the next person in line with the entire line moving forward one spot, while the player who just finished sprints to the last position in line and become a human cone.
- The next person in line will begin dribbling through the human cones.
- Coaches can also set the human cones up in a zigzag pattern, allowing players to work on the crossover dribble and other change of direction moves.
- Further, once players become comfortable with this skill, coaches can have the human cones reach at the basketball as the player passes, teaching players to protect the basketball with their arm bar and body.

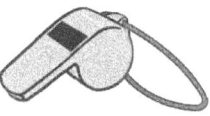

POINTS OF EMPHASIS

- Reinforce concepts from previous dribbling skills.
- Protect basketball from human cones.
- Head up.
- Speed and efficiency once skill is learned.

SKILL 5

DRIBBLING ON THE MOVE

The following three moves are more advanced and are best introduced after a healthy comfort level is established with the previous skills, to help alleviate frustration. All three of these drills can first be introduced with the player on the baseline in a triple-threat position. Moving forward, in a zigzag motion, players will end on the opposite baseline in a triple-threat position. The three drills can be used both to beat a defender off the dribble and to protect the basketball when changing directions.

DRILL 1: BEHIND THE BACK

To begin, it is recommended to teach the behind-the-back dribble on the move, in open court. The actual dribble will be executed just as taught in the stationary ball handling.

- Going into the move, the basketball will be dribbled next to the hip, wrapping it around the body, landing beside the opposite hip.
- A hard, controlled dribble prior to the wrap-around can make for an easier maneuver of the basketball behind the back, as it creates necessary momentum to complete the motion.
- Encourage the player to keep the body low entering into and exiting the move.
- Footwork can vary on the behind the back, but it is easiest to learn through a one-two step, rather than a hop.
- Once the basketball has worked its way to the other side of the body, encourage the player to protect the basketball by keeping it on the outside of and tight to the body.
- Once the skill is learned, continue to work on keeping the wrap-around as low and tight to the body as possible.

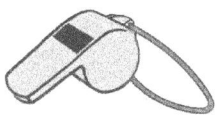

POINTS OF EMPHASIS

- Hard, controlled dribble leading into wrap.
- Wrap from one hip to other.
- Keep wrap close and tight to the body.
- Head up.
- Protect basketball coming out of move.
- Change of speed, change of direction.

DRILL 2: BETWEEN THE LEGS

Starting to the right, the player will take two speed dribbles and land on a jump stop. The shoulders should be perpendicular to the direction just traveled.

- To teach the move for the first time, have the player, once the jump stop is performed, turn the shoulders to be parallel with the direction just traveled.
- The chest should now be pointed toward the front knee (left).
- The basketball will then be dribbled between the legs, from the front door to the back door, catching the basketball in the left hand behind the body.
- Keeping the front foot (left) planted, move the back foot (right) forward in the new direction.
- Encourage the player to keep the basketball on the outside of the body after the completion of the move in order to protect the basketball.
- Once the drill is learned, continue to encourage change of speed, change of direction, and keeping the basketball low and tight for efficiency.

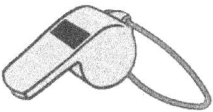

POINTS OF EMPHASIS

- Come to jump stop prior to starting move.
- Quick, low, and tight on the dribble between the legs.
- Low body positioning throughout the skill.
- Change of speed, change of direction.
- Head up.

DRILL 3: SPIN DRIBBLE

Similar to the between-the-legs dribble, the player will go into the spin dribble by jump-stopping after two speed dribbles, with the shoulders perpendicular to the direction just travelled.

- From this position, the player will dribble the basketball hard and controlled in front of the body, creating the necessary momentum leading into the spin.
- The player will then complete a 180-degree reverse pivot, quickly, with the front foot (left) being the pivot foot.
- Once the dribble leading into the spin is made, the basketball will somewhat be cupped in the player's hand, with the hand remaining on top of the basketball, at the waist level, close and tight to the body.

- From the start of the dribble until after the pivot, or spin, is complete, the basketball will remain in the same hand, switching once the player places it on the floor in front of the opposite hand.
- As soon as that happens, the player should ensure the basketball is on the outside of the body for protection.

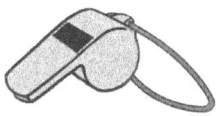

POINTS OF EMPHASIS

- Jump-stop leading into spin dribble.
- Hard, controlled dribble leading into spin.
- Quick, low pivot, creating the spin motion.
- Keep hand on top of the basketball through spin.
- Protect basketball coming out of spin with body.
- Change of speed, change of direction.
- Head up.

DEFENSIVE PRINCIPLES

GENERAL OVERVIEW: *At the Foundational Level, it is appropriate and necessary to begin developing skills for a player to successfully defend the basketball, better known as on-ball defense. On-ball defense is critical to learn both for personal success as well as within a player-to-player team defensive scheme. Below are several skills to begin introducing different mechanics and elements of on-ball defense.*

SKILL 1

STATIONARY ON-BALL DEFENSIVE MECHANICS

First, coaches should work on mechanics and defensive positioning around the basketball before introducing a moving offense. This will allow the first-time defender to gain confidence and a general understanding of on-ball defense.

- To begin, players will organize in groups of two, with one basketball between them.
- Spread groups out throughout the gymnasium.
- Coaches will then progress through a series of steps with the players, focusing on the details of footwork, hand placement, and fundamentals of the defensive stance throughout the skill.
- The proper stance entails the following:
    - Sit rear end back and low.
    - Straight back with head and chin up.
    - Toes pointed straight ahead.
    - Hands placed above the waist.
    - Slight knee bend.
    - Arm's length from player.
    - Eyes on offensive player's waist.
- To execute the footwork for a defending jab with a live offensive player:
    - Defender will react with a drop step to respect the offensive player's jab.
    - Stay low through the drop step, maintain the proper stance.
    - Keep eyes on offensive player's waist.

- Keep active hand high on the side of the jab or basketball while keeping the active hand low on the opposite side.
- Maintain arm's-length distance.
- If offensive player retreats, so does defensive player.
- The footwork for defending the dribble is as follows:
  - The initial step is the most critical in defending the dribble.
  - Point foot in direction of slide; push opposite foot.
  - Do not bring feet together after slide (if a wooden stick is placed between the legs of defender, just shorter than shoulder width, the player should not break the stick).
  - Maintain arm's-length distance.
  - High active hand on side of dribble, low active hand on opposite side.
  - Stay low before, during, and after dribble.
  - Slide should be at a slight angle, but not at a 180-degree angle, allowing direct drive to offense.
- Defending a change of direction dribble:
  - Stay low changing direction.
  - Big, urgent push off of back foot when changing direction.
  - Correct angles.
  - Stay low the entire time.
  - Switch hand positioning on direction change.
- Defending an offensive player after picking up the dribble:
  - Defender should immediately "belly up" to the player, closing all space between them.
  - Mirror basketball with the hands, trying to deflect the pass.
  - Offense is at a disadvantage, so avoid fouling.
- In order to defend a shot, players should keep the following in mind:
  - When a shot is taken, contest it with the high hand.
  - Immediately make contact with the offensive player, still allowing the player to land safely, to begin to box out.
  - Turn to face the basket, maintaining contact on the box out.
  - Keep the head and hands up in preparation for a rebound.

With the above in mind, the progression includes:

- Stance in reference to offensive player.
- Defending live dribble with jab step.
- Defending triple threat, jab step, then one dribble.
- Defending triple threat, jab step, one dribble, then pickup/shot.
- Defending triple threat, jab step, then two dribbles.
- Defending triple threat, jab step, two dribbles, then pickup/shot.
- Defending triple threat, jab step, one dribble one way, then one dribble the opposite direction, then pickup/shot.
- Defending any combination of the above through to pickup/shot.
- Coaches can progress through the above drills with various verbal or physical cues.
- Ensure that both directions are worked on and that all players work on defensive skills.
- Although it is best to focus only on defense to begin, coaches can eventually encourage offensive players to display proper footwork and basketball positioning.
- These are ways to continue raising the level of the drill through offense and defense, even though this is introduced primarily as a defensive skill.
- Encourage players to develop the habit of communicating early while running these drills. You should hear terms such as "ball" and "shot" through the course of these drills.

POINTS OF EMPHASIS

- Stance and footwork.
- Stay low and active with hands.
- Communication.

SKILL 2

CLOSEOUTS

Closeouts are a critical habit to begin forming early on. They enable the player to defend a shooter and penetrator at the same time, through the use of good body control and positioning.

- For example, a defender is standing in a proper help-side position; the player they are defending quickly receives the basketball five feet away from the defender. The defender is in a situation where they will need to use a closeout in order to effectively defend the immediate shot, along with the possibility of the offensive player penetrating.
- Player will execute a closeout by first sprinting three-quarters of the distance between the offensive player and original location.
- Sprinting this initial distance is critical, as it is urgent the defender arrive at the offensive player as quickly as possible.
- The last quarter of the distance, the player will begin to quickly "chop" their feet in a controlled manner.
- The weight and head of the defender should be thrown backward in order to control and slow the momentum created in the sprint.
- If the defender does not execute this part of the closeout, keeping their head down and momentum moving toward the offensive player, the defender will not have the ability to defend penetration upon arrival.
- In addition to throwing the head and weight backward, the arms should also raise above the head, discouraging the offensive player from shooting, in addition to possibly deflecting a potential pass.
- The defender should also stay low in stance while approaching the offensive player, allowing the defender the ability to slide laterally should the offensive player penetrate. It is important to remember the offensive player is live, and therefore has many options.

POINTS OF EMPHASIS

- Sprint three-quarters of distance.
- Controlled chop at one-quarter distance.
- Weight, head back.
- High hands.
- Stay low in stance.
- Arm's length distance.

DRILL 1: FOUR-ACROSS CLOSEOUTS

Players will begin by lining up in four lines across the baseline, the first four players standing in a defensive stance. Coaches will cue players to begin through a verbal or physical signal.

- Out of the defensive stance, players will sprint straight ahead to perform a closeout ending at the first free-throw line extended, or floor marking provided by coach.
- After the closeout is performed, the player should end in a defensive stance. The next group will step up to the baseline and sit in a defensive stance.
- Coach will use the same cue letting the players know to work on the next closeout; now two rows of players will be going.
- Original group will perform closeout at half court; the second group will perform closeout at the first free-throw line extended.
- Skill will be continued until all players make it to the opposite baseline, having executed four closeouts.

 **POINTS OF EMPHASIS**

- Sprint to closeout spots.
- Break down feet with short, choppy steps.
- Stay low in stance.

DRILL 2: LATERAL SLIDES

Once the previous drills are learned, coaches can challenge players by including lateral slides, simulating an offensive player penetrating.

- As players are closing out, coaches can point or provide verbal cues for the players to slide laterally right or left.
- It is best to work on the efficiency of one slide before moving to several. Encourage players to push off of the back foot, point the lead foot, and not cross feet. Reinforce concepts from before.
- Coaches can be creative in how the players move following the closeout, making players engage and react. After lateral slides become easier, coaches can also challenge the players to perform a drop step rather than a lateral slide, or a series of slides in combination.

Once players have learned the skill of closing out, coaches can focus on specific details to continue to challenge the player.

- For example, many players will take a negative step out of the defensive stance when asked to sprint forward. No different than a runner at a starting line for a race, the step backward takes away a valuable second and is not efficient, desired footwork.
- Further, in order to create a more urgent first step, encourage players to split their arms on the first movement. This creates a positive momentum and immediate push in the desired direction.
- The body will not go anywhere without the arms; they are just as important as the footwork. Create good habits from the beginning to help the player progress successfully through the sport.

POINTS OF EMPHASIS

- Reinforce emphasis from closeouts technique.
- No negative steps.
- Stay low.

DRILL 3: THREE-POINT LINE CLOSEOUTS

Once the previous closeout drills have been developed, relocate the drill to a different location on the basketball floor to allow players to develop an understanding of when and how to use closeouts in a live game situation. There are endless amounts of ways to achieve this, but below is an example:

- Two offensive players will be positioned on the wings; coaches (or players) will be positioned at the top of the key.
- Two defensive players will stand at midline, feet touching (this takes away the potential of a negative step on the start); on the pass (using two basketballs), defensive players will sprint to their respective offensive players using a closeout.

A simple progression is as follows:

- Closeout to defensive stance.
- Closeout to defending jab step.
- Closeout to defending one dribble penetration baseline.
- Closeout to defending one dribble penetration middle.
- Closeout to defending one dribble penetration baseline/middle to pickup/shot.
- Closeout to defending one dribble one way, then one dribble different direction to pickup/shot.
- Closeout to any combination, controlled.
- Closeout to any combination, live to score (later in level, limit offense to three dribbles).

POINTS OF EMPHASIS

- Control the body to gain confidence.
- Reinforce concepts from closeouts and slides.
- Focus on footwork, no negative steps.
- Stay low.

SKILL 3

FULL-COURT ZIGZAG

Coaches can utilize the full-court zigzag skill to begin teaching players how to defend the basketball in the open court. It is recommended to begin working technique without offense before playing any type of simulated live action in the full court. This skill has the potential to cause players to become frustrated when attempting to learn it, if not introduced properly.

DRILL 1: NO OFFENSE—ALL SLIDES

As mentioned, to begin it is best to work on footwork in a controlled manner without offense.

- Players will utilize one-third of the court lengthwise, allowing more players to be actively engaged at the same time.
- Players will slide at a forty-five-degree angle, simulating the angles an offensive player would dribble.
- After three slides, the player would drop step and slide in the other direction.
- Motion should be repeated the entire length of the floor, working on developing a solid foundation for the general skill.

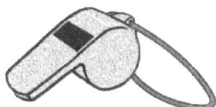 **POINTS OF EMPHASIS**

- Stay low with head up.
- Push off back foot, point lead foot.
- Forty-five-degree angle on drop steps.
- Do not cross feet or bring feet together.
- No negative steps.
- Proper hand placement both directions.

DRILL 2: CONTROLLED OFFENSE

Similar in nature to the drill above, the defensive player will work on basketball defense against a controlled offensive player.

- Here, the offensive player will take three slow dribbles one way, and then change directions.
- The defensive player will work on all of the concepts listed above.
- Focus on staying low, moving at forty-five-degree angles on drop steps, maintaining proper hand placement and staying arm's-length distance from the offensive player.
- The drill should first be learned at a slower pace, without the offense attempting to beat the defensive player.
- Once the drill is picked up, the offensive player can pick up the pace.

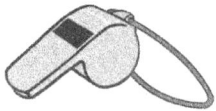

POINTS OF EMPHASIS

- Head on the basketball.
- Arm's-length distance.
- Eyes on waist of offensive player.
- Proper hand placement.
- Stay low.

DRILL 3: NO OFFENSE AND CONTROLLED PLAYER IS BEAT OFF DRIBBLE

If a player gets beat off of the dribble, it is important to understand the footwork that should be used to catch up and reestablish proper positioning.

- This drill should first be accomplished without an offensive player, then progress to a controlled offensive player.
- The quickest and most efficient way to catch up is to turn and sprint.
- However, the defensive player does not want to run directly next to the offensive player. Instead, the defender wants to pick a spot up ahead and beat the offensive player to that spot, mainly by using a better angle.
- Once the defensive player beats the offensive player to the spot, the defender will turn and immediately get into a defensive stance to stop the ball handler.
- From this position, the defender will begin sliding laterally again.
- Coaches can simulate this action by instructing players where to pretend the offensive player beats the defensive player. When an offensive player is introduced, this instruction is not needed.

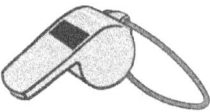

POINTS OF EMPHASIS

- Once beat, cross over toward new direction and sprint.
- Split arms to create momentum.
- Pick spot ahead, create better angle, and beat offense to spot.
- At spot, immediately turn and get in defensive stance to stop offense.
- Begin lateral slides; stay low.

DRILL 4: LIVE OFFENSE—NO SCORE

To simulate live-game action, coaches can allow offensive players to try to beat the defense to the other baseline, without allowing any shots.

- Instruct offensive players to try to beat the defense off the dribble.
- If successful, after two dribbles, offensive players can slow down and allow the defense to catch up and reset.
- From that position on the floor, the two players can play "live" again.

- As players improve, coaches can allow offensive players to try to beat the defensive player and reach the opposite baseline first. This is a good way to challenge the players without scoring.

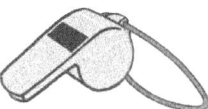

POINTS OF EMPHASIS

- Combine and reinforce concepts from progression.
- Keep arm's-length distance between offensive and defensive player.

DRILL 5: LIVE OFFENSE—SCORE

Once players are comfortable with the above drill on both sides of the basketball court, it is appropriate to allow players to attempt to score at the end of the zigzag drill.

- Instruct players they must stay on their third of the basketball court until reaching half court; then they must stay on their half of the court.
- This instruction is important so players working on the other side of the floor do not collide with one another.
- Encourage defensive players to play through until the end of the drill, including a box out and securing the rebound.

POINTS OF EMPHASIS

- Combine and reinforce concepts from previous drills.
- Play through until the end of the drill.
- Box out and secure rebound.

FOUNDATIONAL LEVEL
OFFENSIVE PRINCIPLES: FOOTWORK & BODY CONTROL

GENERAL OVERVIEW: *Footwork and body control are important in all levels. At the Foundational Level, these two skills will be developed through drills performed at a tempo closer to that of an actual basketball game, which requires changes in direction to happen more quickly.*

SKILL 1

PIVOTING

This skill advances a young player's ability to use proper footwork and body control when pivoting. It is important that players learn how to pivot correctly, as this is essential to a number of other skills, such as shooting and passing.

- Ensure that players are in good basketball position to start, with the chin up and the hands above the waist. Players should slightly bend their knees, and their feet should be at least shoulder width apart.
- Make the pivot by planting one foot so that it will not move forward or backward; this is the pivot foot. The other foot can move so that the body may swivel and turn accordingly.
- Instruct players to spin on the ball of the planted foot when they are pivoting and remain in good basketball position the entire time.
- Players may pivot 180 degrees in either direction. A "front pivot" is where the body turns forward, and a "reverse pivot" is where the body turns backward.

POINTS OF EMPHASIS

- Maintain good basketball position.
- Keep the chin up.
- Pivot on one foot using a front or reverse pivot.

SKILL 2

BODY CONTROL WHEN CHANGING DIRECTION/SPEED

Players who are able to change speed and direction will become more efficient in all aspects of their basketball game. Understanding how to vary speed and direction forms the basis for many other skills that players will learn at higher levels.

- Remind players to maintain proper basketball positioning when learning and practicing these skills, with the knees bent and the hands above the waist.

- In order to change direction, instruct players to push off of the foot opposite the direction they wish to travel. To travel to the right, push off of the left foot; to travel left, push off of the right. To travel backward, push off of the foot in front of the body; to travel forward, push off of the back foot.
- As players begin to travel in a new direction, they should turn their shoulders in the direction they wish to travel.
- To change direction efficiently, players must learn to push off of the appropriate foot quickly.
- It is important that players change speed when they change direction.

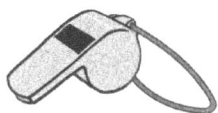

POINTS OF EMPHASIS

- Proper basketball positioning
- Push off the foot opposite the desired direction.
- Turn shoulders toward desired direction.
- Change speed when changing direction.

DEFENSIVE PRINCIPLES

GENERAL OVERVIEW: *At this level, the focus is on defensive stance. There will also be instruction on body movement, which will involve pivoting and performing drop steps while in the proper stance. To learn these skills, players will be engaged in defensive slide drills. Initially, drills will involve neither a player on offense nor a basketball, but as players become comfortable, those will be added in.*

SKILL 1

PROPER STANCE

The proper defensive stance should be introduced at the Introductory Level with continued progression throughout this level.

- Feet should be wider than the shoulders, hands above the waist, with the chin up and the head in a position above the knees, though not leaning forward.
- This will give the player the ability to move in all directions and allow the player to make the necessary pivots to become a good defender.

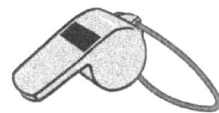

POINTS OF EMPHASIS

- The back should be straight with the chin up.
- Feet should be wider than the shoulders.
- Hands placed above the waist.
- Slight knee bend.

SKILL 2

360-DEGREE MOVEMENTS

When moving on defense, players should remain in the proper stance outlined in the Footwork & Body Control section of the Introductory Level (page 48). Footwork should be similar to that which is described in Foundational Level Footwork & Body Control Skill 2 of Offensive Principles (page 47).

- Defensive players should practice following the player on offense around the basketball court.
- Proper movement on defense requires the defender to slide in the same direction as the player on offense.
- In order to slide correctly, coaches should remind players of the footwork they learned in the Offensive Principles; they should be pushing off of the foot opposite the direction they wish to travel.
- Watch to make sure players are not bringing their feet together after sliding.
- It is important to consider spacing between offensive and defensive players at this level. Instruct defenders to stay within arm's length of offensive players.
- To help a defender follow an offensive player around the basketball court, encourage the defender to look at the offensive player's waist.
- When the offensive player changes direction, defenders should use a pivot to continue following the player on offense.

 **POINTS OF EMPHASIS**

- Proper defensive stance and footwork.
- Push off foot opposite desired direction of travel.
- Feet should not come together after slide.
- Pivot to change directions.

FOUNDATIONAL LEVEL
PASSING & RECEIVING
OFFENSIVE PRINCIPLES: PASSING

GENERAL OVERVIEW: *Passing and receiving are important abilities to develop to allow the basketball to be advanced legally throughout the court of play. At the Foundational Level, passing and receiving continues to work on efficiency and proficiency of the basics previously introduced, while also learning new skills and concepts that will be needed for game-like situations progressing forward.*

SKILL 1

STATIONARY PASSING

In addition to the new drills listed below, players at this level should continue working on improving chest and bounce passes, with both hands and one hand. Passes should be crisp with high velocity and accuracy, leaving the hand quickly and hitting the receiver's target with little movement needed. These two passes will be the foundation for all other passing skills learned, hence the importance of continuing to master the drills below.

The drills introduced at this level can initially be taught with two teammates passing to one another, both stationary.

DRILL 1: WRAP-AROUND BOUNCE PASS

The wrap-around bounce pass is most commonly used by perimeter players while executing a post entry pass. To teach this type of pass, begin with the hand motion, exaggerating it at first.

- With one hand, have the player rest the basketball on the finger pads with the palm facing upward.
- The player will then turn the hand over, 180 degrees, with the palm facing downward, passing the basketball on the bounce to the teammate.
- When beginning to learn this drill, have the player experiment with how the basketball bounces based on the spin the player puts on the basketball, as a result of the turning of the hand.
- Next, have the player add the guide hand, used only for control and protection into the pass.
- As the player gets comfortable with the guide hand and how the basketball spins back to the teammate, challenge the player to bounce the basketball outside of a painted line, that is just outside the direct line to the teammate, making the player use the spin to get the basketball back to the teammate.
- Further, a coach can stand directly in front of the player, making the player release the basketball outside of the body, again causing the player to use spin to execute the pass.
- As players improve, coaches can challenge passers to increase tempo, make crisp passes, and hit the target perfectly.

POINTS OF EMPHASIS

- Triple-threat position.
- Proper hand motion, creating proper spin back to teammate.
- Stay low throughout pass.
- Follow-through.

DRILL 2: WRAP-AROUND BOUNCE PASS (FOOTWORK)

- From a triple-threat position, first begin teaching a direct jab.
- If the player is passing with the right hand, a direct right jab step would be used, placing the right foot directly next to the left foot of the defender.
- The player will adjust the basketball to be released as far away from the body as possible, keeping the basketball away from the defender.
- Release the basketball low, turning the hand over, spinning the bounce pass back into the teammate's target. Hold the follow-through, pointing directly at the target.
- Keep the body low throughout the passing motion. The receiver will catch with two hands on a jump stop, immediately establishing a triple-threat position.
- Further, coaches should encourage equal use of hands and feet in the footwork, eventually moving to a crossover jab step to make the pass.
- With the crossover, focus on how the player is able to protect the basketball with the body, utilizing the proper footwork.

POINTS OF EMPHASIS

- Triple-threat position.
- Proper hand motion, creating proper spin back to teammate.
- Proper footwork.
- Stay low throughout pass.
- Follow-through.
- Receiver catches with two hands.

DRILL 3: OVERHEAD PASS

Overhead passes can be used in many situations, most commonly to quickly skip the basketball across the court, against a zone defense, or in the open court.

- Starting in a triple-threat position, the player will quickly bring the basketball above the head, with one hand placed on each side of the basketball, gripping it firmly with the elbows out.
- The player will use both hands equally to pass the basketball, while stepping toward the target.
- When making the pass, the hands should not travel back behind the head, as there may be a defender behind the player.
- The basketball should depart from just above the head, allowing for strength and a quick release.
- The hands should rotate through the basketball, following through with the thumbs rotating downward pointing directly at the target.

- Encourage the pass to be crisp, located just over the defense, without lobbing it.
- Continue to work on accuracy as the drill is practiced.
- The receiver should catch the basketball with two hands, on a two-foot jump stop establishing a triple-threat position.

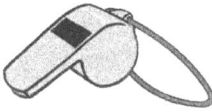

POINTS OF EMPHASIS

- Triple-threat position.
- Basketball just above the head, not behind.
- Quick release.
- Thumbs up, thumbs down.
- Step toward target, follow through directly at target.
- Receiver catches with two hands, two-foot jump stop.

DRILL 4: FAKE PASS

Defenders are taught to mirror and react to the basketball, making pass fakes valuable to an offensive player. The idea is to use a pass fake to get a defender to react in one direction, opening up a passing lane in a different direction. When playing against pressure defenses, coaches often use the phrase "fake a pass to make a pass."

- Staying with concepts of overhead passes learned before, have three teammates work together. This helps to provide a visual target for the passer when first learning to fake a pass.
- From a triple-threat position, the player with the basketball brings the basketball to just above the head and begins the motion of an overhead pass toward one of the teammates.
- The idea is to make the fake and general motion look realistic enough for a defender to react.
- Create momentum with the basketball moving forward, eyes on the target, pulling the basketball back to its original position.
- Once the fake is complete, step toward the other target and execute the pass.
- Have players execute all types of passes when learning pass fakes.
- If working on a fake bounce pass, the player should fake low, at the same height as an actual pass would be executed.
- Further, have players execute pass fakes without a third teammate. For example, if trying to complete a post entry pass, a perimeter player might fake an overhead pass; then execute a bounce pass.

POINTS OF EMPHASIS

- Realistic pass fakes.
- Eyes on target.
- Motion with basketball.
- Quick transition from fake to actual pass.

SKILL 2

PASSING WITH A PLAYER ON THE MOVE

In this scenario, it is imperative to pass the basketball ahead to where the teammate is running, not to where they are currently.

- The pass must be made in front of the running teammate. The runner should not have to break stride to catch the basketball. With experience, players will be able to gauge how far in front of each of their teammates the basketball needs to be thrown.
- Conversely, when passers are also moving, it is important that they take their own momentum into account, especially if the player receiving the basketball is stationary.
- The following drills present both scenarios.

DRILL 1: FOUR-CORNER PASSING

Using half of the basketball court, place four lines in each of the corners. Eventually, lines may be extended, but at this level shorter lines lead to successful execution of chest passes without compromising technique. Name two lines, diagonal from each other, as the movement lines and the other two lines diagonal from each other as the stationary lines. Each movement line will have one basketball.

- To begin, explain to players in the two movement lines that they will be in both the line they are currently standing in and the one diagonal from them throughout the drill.
- Players in stationary lines will remain in just their one line.
- Movement players will be looking to the line on their right when they run diagonally toward the other line.
- The first player in each movement line will make a pass to the first player in the stationary line to their right and then cut through the middle of the square in a straight line headed toward the opposite, diagonal line.
- As the player cuts, the receiver of the pass will pass the ball back to the cutter, hitting the player roughly in the middle of the square.
- The two cutters will catch the pass in motion and then pass it to the next player in line at the front of the diagonal line they are running to and then fill in at the end of that line.
- Players in the stationary lines are looking for a pass from the line to their left, passing back as the cutter cuts up the middle and then going to the end of their line.
- Once the drill is picked up, switch directions to the left. Then start the basketballs at the other two diagonal lines, flipping which two lines are stationary and which two are movement.
- This drill provides players opportunities to work on passing with all dynamics of stationary and moving targets, teaching players to understand momentum and the impact it has on passing.
- Encourage players to hit targets with accuracy, making crisp passes without breaking stride. Receivers should catch the basketball with two hands and communicate throughout the drill.
- Further, once the drill is learned, make sure players are making another pass immediately, rather than traveling with the basketball.

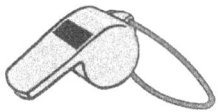

POINTS OF EMPHASIS

- Crisp, accurate passes.
- Hit player in stride; pass ahead of current location if in movement.
- Hit target.
- Receiver shows target and keeps head up while cutting through the middle.
- Do not travel between the catch and the pass.

DRILL 2: FULL-COURT PASSING LAYUPS

This drill progresses players to make appropriate passes within a shorter distance, making it more challenging. Coaches can also incorporate layups to integrate drill sets together.

- Six players will be stationary passers while remaining players line up under each basket.
- Spots for the six passers are four at the free-throw lines extended (with backs to sideline) and two at half court (in the middle of the floor back-to-back).
- Players will complete three passes, first to the near-side free-throw-line extended passer, then the middle passer, then the far-side free-throw passer, while advancing up the court to complete a layup at the opposite basket.
- The players shooting the layups will continue to do so for the allotted amount of time.
- Once that time is up, have the stationary players become the players shooting the layups and vice versa.
- Players that make the last pass leading to the layup should use a bounce pass with all other passes being chest passes.
- Continue to focus on players not traveling between the catch and the pass.

POINTS OF EMPHASIS

- Crisp, accurate passes.
- Hit the target.
- Bounce pass leading to layup.
- Catch with two hands.
- Clean catch; transition to pass quickly.
- Reinforce points of emphasis from layup section.

SKILL 3

PASSING WITH TWO PLAYERS ON THE MOVE

Understanding how to hit a moving target, while also moving, is an important skill, as players will constantly be in this situation. These drills will help players become comfortable with passing on the move.

DRILL 1: SIDE-CENTER-SIDE PASSING

Forming three lines on the baseline, have players move up the floor, three at a time, using the chest pass.

- The players will run in a straight line, staying even with one another, passing from the center to the side, back to center, over to the other side, and back to the center.
- Players will continue this pattern the length of the floor.
- If the players are just learning the drill, it is best to only complete passing down to the opposite baseline.
- If the players are comfortable with the drill, add a layup on the opposite end, with the player in the middle jump-stopping at the free-throw line and making a bounce pass to an outside player for the layup.
- Depending on the number of players involved, coaches can have the players return prior to the next group going, or simply have everyone complete the drill to the opposite end prior to returning.
- Encourage players to lead the teammate and not travel between the catch and the pass.

 **POINTS OF EMPHASIS**

- Crisp pass, no lobs.
- Hit target.
- Lead teammate; do not break stride.
- Do not travel between the catch and the pass.

DRILL 2: THREE-PLAYER WEAVE

Beginning in three lines on the baseline, three players will move up the floor together, weaving and passing to get to the opposite baseline, or shooting a layup to finish.

- With the basketball starting in the middle line, a chest pass will be made to one of the players on the wing.
- As passes are made, players should immediately follow their pass and run behind the player receiving the pass.
- Players receiving the basketball will pass across the floor to the opposite player, again, following their own pass behind the receiving player.
- The three players will work together in this pattern of passing and cutting up the entire length of the basketball court to the opposite end.
- Coaches can have players end at the opposite baseline or continue back without a break in the pattern. This is especially fluid if used following a layup.
- Further, coaches can dictate how spread out the lines are, varying the length of passes being made, based on what is appropriate for the players.
- As discussed above, encourage players to make crisp passes, leading the teammate while the receiving teammate takes care not to travel between the catch and the pass.
- Further, ensure players are moving up the basketball floor together, as many players first learning this drill tend to drift in the wrong direction. Coaches may even walk behind the group, giving them a visual of how they should be moving up the floor.

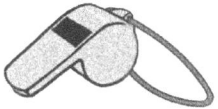

POINTS OF EMPHASIS

- Crisp pass, no lobs.
- Hit target.
- Lead teammate; do not break stride.
- Do not travel between catch and pass.

DRILL 3: FIVE-PLAYER WEAVE

The concept of a five-player weave is similar to that of a three-player weave but allows more involvement at one time and leads to additional drill variations that can be introduced later on.

- For this drill, the three-player weave still occurs as described before. The difference is that once a pass is made, the player will follow the pass and travel to the outside, around two players, instead of just the one.
- The basketball is always thrown to the inside player, rather than the outside player. Again, all five players will pass and cut, working together to travel down the basketball court. The drill can end merely with passes, or a layup at the end can be added, with a jump stop and bounce pass to the shooter.

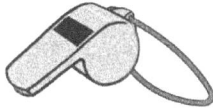

POINTS OF EMPHASIS

- Crisp pass, no lobs.
- Hit target.
- Lead teammate; do not break stride.
- Do not travel between catch and pass.
- Follow pass and run outside two players.

SKILL 4

PASSING IN ADVANTAGE SITUATIONS

Once the actual skill of passing begins to develop, it is important to teach angles and how to use other basketball skills, such as dribbling, to create better passing angles. These types of concepts can be learned within the context of advantage situations.

In general, from an offensive transition standpoint, if two players find themselves in a 2-on-1 advantage situation, the two players should immediately establish wide spacing, creating two lanes on the outside third of the floor.

- The player with the basketball should attack the basket on the dribble, until the defense commits to stop that player.
- If the defense never stops the basketball, the offensive player should shoot a layup.

- If the defensive player commits to stop the basketball, the player should make a bounce pass to the other player, who would then score the layup.
- In this case, attacking with the dribble and making the defender fully commit to the basketball is what creates the passing lane to the teammate.
- If a player does not attack, it will allow the defender to essentially defend both players and make any type of passing between teammates a challenge.
- Ideally, in a 2-on-1 advantage situation, a layup should be taken with one or less passes made. This is a tall order for players just learning this drill, but it is the ultimate goal.

DRILL 1: HALF COURT 2-ON-1

One way to introduce this drill is to have the players in a fairly controlled environment, starting with two offensive lines at half court and one defender under the basket.

- One side starts with the basketball, begins dribbling at the defender, and then executes a 2-on-1 situation.
- To begin, the defender may be a coach, again controlling the environment to ensure the players understand the drill and how the use of the dribble impacts the passing angles.
- Once the drill is learned, add a teammate as the defender.
- Make sure to switch sides of the floor with the basketball to ensure players are dribbling and passing with both hands.

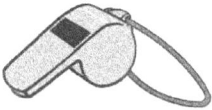 **POINTS OF EMPHASIS**

- Player with basketball attacks defense.
- Hit target when defender stops ball.
- Perform drill from both sides of the court.

DRILL 2: FULL COURT 2-ON-1

Starting similarly as the previous drill, here, move the two lines to the baseline, with one defender on the opposite side.

- Players with the basketball will dribble the length of the floor in one lane, the other teammate will run wide in the other lane, and together they will attack the defender and execute the 2-on-1 situation.
- Players who shoot the basketball (or turn it over) will become the defender with the next group of two players coming at them.
- Setting the drill up in this manner will only allow the players to complete the 2-on-1 at one end of the floor.

 **POINTS OF EMPHASIS**

- Create spacing; fill lanes.
- Player with basketball attacks defense.
- Score layup in one pass.
- Pass should not break stride of teammate.

DRILL 3: FULL COURT 2-ON-1 BLITZ

This drill allows for continuity by adding outlets to both sides of the floor.

- Players will execute a 2-on-1 advantage situation.
- The defensive player will make an outlet pass to the player waiting in the outlet line, then these two players will fill their lanes heading to the other end of the floor to execute a 2-on-1 advantage situation against the awaiting defender.
- This drill is a great way to get more players involved at the same time.

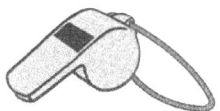

POINTS OF EMPHASIS

- Create spacing; fill lanes.
- Player with basketball attacks defense.
- Score layup in one pass.
- Pass should not break stride of teammate.
- Hit target.

DRILL 4: HALF COURT 3-ON-2

Generally speaking, from an offensive transition standpoint, in a 3-on-2 advantage situation, the three players should immediately space the floor, two wide and one in the middle lane.

- Start three players on offense at the half-court line and two as defenders under the basket in a tandem position. The middle line on offense starts with the basketball.
- Player spacing is an important element to allow for better passing angles.
- The three offensive players attack the basket and defenders to score.
- Typically, if the top defender stops the basketball, the first pass travels to one of the wings.
- The next pass is usually back to the top or to the opposite player for a layup, depending on how the defense reacts to the situation.
- Players will work toward making two or fewer passes to get a good shot attempt.
- Against a 3-on-2, a layup or a short jump shot is considered a good shot.
- If more than two passes are made, the defense will have time to recover and the offense loses the advantage.
- Again, this is a tall order for players just learning how to pass the basketball against a 3-on-2 advantage situation, but it is something to work toward. It is important to continue to reinforce the value of spacing for effective passing.
- Gain confidence in the half-court setting, and then move to a more realistic full-court environment.

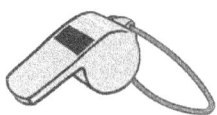

POINTS OF EMPHASIS

- Create spacing; fill lanes.
- Quality shot in two or fewer passes.
- Attack basket until defense stops ball.

DRILL 5: FULL COURT 3-ON-2 BLITZ

Similar to the 2-on-1 blitz, the 3-on-2 blitz is continuous with the two outlet lines on each side of the floor. The three offensive players will work to score against the two defenders.

- Once the play is over, the two defensive players will pass to the outlet player and progress up the floor, in respective lanes, to execute against the two defenders on the opposite end.
- The drill will continue in this manner.
- Once players begin to pick up the drill, challenge the offensive players to get a quality shot in two passes or fewer.
- Once a group is comfortable with that, coaches can put a shot clock on the players to help them simulate how quick they will need to execute this in a live-game situation.
- A twelve-second shot clock is appropriate to begin and should start from the time the basketball is secured by a defender.
- The shot clock can be decreased as the players improve.

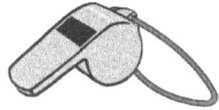 **POINTS OF EMPHASIS**

- Create spacing; fill lanes.
- Quality shot in two or fewer passes.
- Pass should not break stride of teammate; hit target leading to shot.
- Opportunity to incorporate pass fakes.

OFFENSIVE PRINCIPLES: RECEIVING

SKILL 1

CATCH AS A THREAT

Especially at this level, it is important to instill in players that they must always pose a legitimate offensive threat once they catch the basketball.

- Often, players catch the basketball and place it over the head, standing straight up. A good defender will jam an offensive player who does this, taking away most offensive options.
- The offensive player should always keep defensive players guessing and reactive. As soon as the basketball is received, encourage players to get the basketball into the shooting pocket, in triple-threat position, ready to make something happen.
- Reinforce this concept and create a positive habit with all offensive drills.

POINTS OF EMPHASIS

- On catch, immediately get basketball into shooting pocket.
- Catch to score.
- Triple-threat stance.
- Always look for offensive opportunities.
- Keep defense guessing.

SKILL 2

MEETING A PASS

When receiving the basketball, players should begin making a movement back toward the passer, especially when in the presence of a defender.

- Even the slightest movement back toward the basketball will not only save a potential turnover, but many times will draw a personal foul from an aggressive defender.
- Further, meeting a pass in the half court will many times help to create momentum, which can assist in squaring up to the basketball leading to a fluid and strong shot attempt. There are not many positives to catching the basketball flat-footed as an offensive player.
- Again, this concept can and should be reinforced in all drill work involving passing. It can be taught within the context of other drills, or a separate drill can be created to just work on meeting the pass.

POINTS OF EMPHASIS

- Make a movement back toward the passer while basketball is in the air.
- Catch with two hands.
- Triple-threat position.

DRILL 1: IMPERFECT PASS

Ideally, when receiving the basketball, the player will always use two hands to complete the catch. However, if there is an errant pass or long rebound, it will require the player receiving the basketball to go get it, sometimes only allowing the use of one hand.

- Players need to be trained how to secure the basketball and bring it back into the body gaining control.
- The idea is to "block, grab, chin."

- As the player leaves the position to go retrieve the basketball with one hand, the player will block the basketball, stopping the momentum. Then, grab the basketball and bring it into the other hand. At this point, immediately chin the basketball to secure it and gain control.
- Coaches should encourage players to grab the basketball with two hands, but when that is not possible, block, grab, chin.
- This drill is best introduced in passing lines, with the passer (or coach) making an errant pass, which forces the player to leave the positioning to go get it.
- Experiment with different locations, heights, and velocity of the basketball to challenge the player. Mix up where the pass is being received to make the player decide if one or two hands is needed to properly receive the basketball.
- Always encourage players to immediately chin the basketball or to get in a triple-threat position.

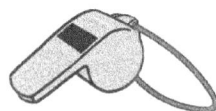 ## POINTS OF EMPHASIS

- Always try to go get basketball with two hands first.
- Block, grab, chin.
- Secure and control possession.

DEFENSIVE PRINCIPLES

SKILL 1

DENIAL POSITIONING AND FOOTWORK

DRILL 1: DENIAL POSITIONING AND CONCEPTS—NO MOVEMENT

In player-to-player defense, the whole premise of the defense begins with the player defending on the basketball. Any defensive player who is potentially one pass away from the basketball is in what is called a denial position. Essentially, the defender is denying the offensive player the opportunity to receive the basketball, through the correct positioning.

What does a denial position look like? For explanation purposes, the basketball is located at the top of the key while the other offensive player is on the right wing.

- Beginning with body position, a defender in denial will be in a defensive stance, with the backside of the body facing toward the basketball located at the top of the key.
- The right foot, in this case, would be high, near the three-point line, and the left foot would be low.
- The right arm is fully extended straight out to the side, with the thumb pointed downward and the palm facing the basketball.
- Positioning of the hand in the passing lane is important if a pass is actually made, in order to deflect the basketball and get the steal.
- In order to see both the basketball and the offensive player being denied, the defender's chin will rest on the right shoulder.

- The left arm will form an arm bar in order to make contact with the offensive player at the appropriate time.
- Lastly, it is good practice to begin the process of communication between teammates. In this case, the player should verbalize "deny" to the teammates on the floor.

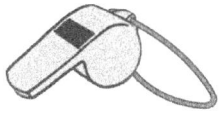

POINTS OF EMPHASIS

- Defensive stance, backside toward basketball.
- High-side arm fully extended.
- Thumb down, palm toward basketball.
- Chin on shoulder.
- Communicate "deny."

DRILL 2: DENYING V-CUT—PERIMETER

Building on the previous concepts introduced, defending a perimeter V-cut brings the denial to life. When adding offensive movement, it is important the denial defender's feet slide, same concept as with on-ball defense. The angle of the backside is different in that it is facing the offensive player with the basketball, rather than the hoop, but the mechanics of the slides are the exact same. It is also important to make contact with the offensive player, using the arm bar, the closer the offensive player is to the block.

- The player receiving the basketball this close to the basket is at much greater risk to score than catching the basketball at the three-point line, making the physical contact important at the block.
- As the offensive player cuts back up to the wing, the defensive player will release contact and move "up the line," creating an imaginary triangle with the path of the offensive and defensive players.
- The term "up the line" is referring to the imaginary line that is drawn between the two offensive players should a pass be made.
- To move "up the line" will require the defensive player to physically move up that line toward the offensive player with the basketball.
- This spacing is important for a few reasons. One reason is it makes it more difficult for an offensive player to make a backdoor cut by now being unable to get into the body of the defender and push off.
- It also makes the floor look smaller to the offensive player with the basketball, as there is less room to dribble penetrate if the defender takes some of that spacing away.
- Lastly, if the offensive player does decide to penetrate, the denial defender is already one to two steps closer to pinch the gap should the need arise.
- To begin introducing these concepts to the players, work on the footwork and positioning first, against a controlled offensive player.
- Make simple cuts and get the hang of it before going live with the drill. Reinforce contact when the offense cuts down to the block and increase space, or be up the line, when the offense returns to the wing position.
- Once players start to understand the basics, change the positioning to deny at the top of the key or at the baseline.
- Make sure players work both sides of the floor to be comfortable with both hands and feet up.
- At this level, do not worry too much with backdoor cuts against the denial; simply reinforce hand in the passing lane, not foot.

POINTS OF EMPHASIS

- Defensive stance, backside toward basketball.
- High-side arm fully extended.
- Thumb down, palm toward basketball.
- Chin on shoulder.
- Contact at block, up the line at the wing.
- Hand in passing lane, not foot.
- Communicate "deny."

SKILL 2

TRANSITIONING: ON-BALL DEFENSE TO DENIAL

In most every possession, a defensive player will play on the basketball, denial, and help side multiple times. Learning all of these skills is critical to any player's success. However, the ability to quickly and efficiently transition from each skill set may be just as important, if not more important due to the fluidity of the game. Thus, the transitions should be trained as well as the actual drills.

The important concept to introduce is to always jump to the basketball with the ultimate goal of being established in the proper position (on-ball, deny, or help) by the time the offensive player catches the basketball. This requires a bit of anticipation and a commitment to moving on the flight of the basketball.

DRILL 1: PASS LOW TO HIGH; ON-BALL WING TO DENY FROM TOP OF KEY

- Set up an offensive player and a defensive player on the wing with a coach at the top of the key.
- The offensive player has the basketball with the defender in proper on-ball positioning.
- As the offensive player passes to the coach, the defender will jump to the basketball and establish denial positioning.
- With a player-to-player defense that forces the ball handler toward the baseline, it is easier to transition from on-ball defense to denial on a pass from low to high because the feet are essentially already in position. All the player has to do is jump up the line on the flight of the basketball.
- Progress the drill to get additional players involved in more spots, all reacting to the position of the basketball and their player.

POINTS OF EMPHASIS

- Jump to the basketball on the flight of the basketball.
- Up the line.
- Proper denial stance on catch.

DRILL 2: PASS HIGH TO LOW; ON-BALL WING TO DENY FROM BASELINE

- This time set the offensive and defensive player up at the wing with the coach on the baseline.
- The offensive player will pass to the coach and on the flight of the pass the defender will move from on-ball defense to denial positioning.
- With a player-to-player defense that forces the ball handler toward the baseline, it is far more challenging to transition from on-ball defense to denial on a pass from high to low because of the positioning of the feet prior to the pass.
- If the on-ball defender does not immediately react and move to jump to the basketball, nearly completing a 180-degree turn, the offensive player will be able to face-cut the defender following the pass.
- The chance of a face cut illustrates the importance and urgent need to jump toward the basketball on the flight of the pass. This is an important habit to create from the beginning.

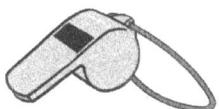

POINTS OF EMPHASIS

- Jump to the basketball on the flight of the basketball.
- Up the line.
- Proper denial stance on catch
- Be aware of face cuts.

DRILL 3: PASS LOW TO HIGH; DENY FROM BASELINE TO ON-BALL WING

- Position the coach on the baseline with the basketball and a defender in denial position guarding the offensive player who is on the wing.
- When the pass travels from low to high, transitioning from denial to on-ball defense is more challenging because of the principle to force the ball handler back toward the baseline.
- Again, on the flight of the basketball, the player will complete a near 180-degree turn, closing out on the top foot of the offensive player, pushing the player back toward the baseline, not allowing middle.
- It is important to establish a bit of spacing, depending on the offensive strengths, as the offensive player has a live dribble on the catch.

POINTS OF EMPHASIS

- Sprint to on-ball position on the flight of the basketball.
- Stay low in stance.
- Closeout to top foot, prepared for live ball handler.
- Push ball handler back to baseline.

DRILL 4: PASS HIGH TO LOW; DENY FROM WING TO ON-BALL BASELINE

- Position the coach on the wing with the basketball and a defender in denial position guarding the offensive player who is now on the baseline.

- When the pass travels from high to low, transitioning from denial to on-ball defense is much easier because of the positioning of the feet up the line.
- Pass the ball from the wing to the baseline player as the defender sprints from denial position to closeout on the ball handler.
- The defensive player will close the distance toward the offensive player, staying on the top foot and maintaining the appropriate space for a live ball handler.

 **POINTS OF EMPHASIS**

- Sprint to on-ball position on the flight of the basketball.
- Stay low in stance.
- Closeout to top foot, prepared for live ball handler.

FOUNDATIONAL LEVEL

OFFENSIVE PRINCIPLES: REBOUNDING

GENERAL OVERVIEW: *Most often, possession of the basketball comes as a result of securing a rebound after a missed shot attempt. Therefore, rebounding—whether offensive or defensive—is an important aspect of basketball to teach. This level will develop a player's ability to snatch the basketball with both hands, which was taught in the Introductory Level. In addition, players will begin learning what to do with the basketball once it is secured.*

SKILL 1

AFTER REBOUND, SCORE OR PASS

This drill teaches players what to do with the basketball once it is secured on an offensive rebound.

- Coaches should remind players on a frequent basis to rebound the basketball from the "ready position" taught in the Introductory Level. This position requires players to extend their hands and arms fully above the head. They must also bend their knees slightly to achieve the maximum height possible when jumping for a rebound.
- Instruct players to snatch the basketball with both hands at the peak of the jump, instead of allowing the basketball to come down to them.
- When a player snatches the basketball, the head and chin should be up, allowing the player to observe the scene.
- At this point, it is important for players to determine whether a shot is available. If no shot is available, the player should pass the basketball out from under the basket to a teammate on the perimeter.

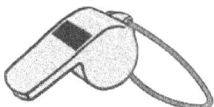

POINTS OF EMPHASIS

- Rebound from the proper ready position.
- Snatch basketball to the chin with both hands.
- Determine whether to shoot or pass.

SKILL 2

FREE-THROW REBOUNDING

When rebounding free throws, the offensive player should line up as far up the lane as possible in the box.

- When the basketball hits the rim, an offensive player should immediately step down the lane hard and quick, to try to beat the inside defender for the rebound.

- This makes it more difficult for the defensive rebounder to make contact and block out the offensive player.

POINTS OF EMPHASIS

- Create as much space as possible from the defensive rebounder.
- Be ready to step down the lane quickly with hands up.
- Eyes should be up at the rim watching for when the basketball hits the rim.

DEFENSIVE PRINCIPLES

GENERAL OVERVIEW: *In this level, the initial skills for defensive rebounding are taught, which include blocking out, securing the basketball from a missed shot, body positioning, and pivoting. After the rebound is the outlet pass, which starts the offensive transition.*

SKILL 1

BODY POSITIONING AND BLOCKING OUT

As the basketball is shot, players must locate their opponent first, achieve an inside position, and box out using a front or rear pivot to get into a position between their opponent and the basket while putting their rear in contact with the opponent. This is done to ensure that the offensive player is behind the defensive player and so that the defensive player can see the flight of the basketball when the shot is taken.

- The first movement is to find the offensive player.
- Step toward the offensive player as the shot is attempted.
- A front pivot allows the defensive rebounder to turn while watching the offensive player move toward the rebound.
- A rear pivot is used to move into the path of the offensive player without the same visual contact.
- Encourage defenders to use whichever method gets them in front of the offense, sealing the offensive player away from the basket.
- Once contact is established with an opposing player, the defensive rebounder wants to maintain that contact until releasing to jump for the rebound.

POINTS OF EMPHASIS

- Keep hands up.
- Keep eyes on the basketball as it is shot.
- Make contact with the offensive player.
- Secure the basketball.

SKILL 2

AFTER REBOUND, PIVOT AND OUTLET PASS

Immediately upon gaining possession of the basketball, the defensive rebounder should land wide with the legs and secure the basketball at chin height.

- Encourage players to get the rebound at the peak of the jump, with the hands and arms straight.
- Try to land on balance with both feet spread.
- The rebounder should bring the basketball quickly and forcefully to the chest, with the top of the basketball at chin height.
- The head should turn over the shoulder toward the best possible outlet area, and the elbows should be spread and wide.
- Protect the basketball by keeping it close to the body at chest height, with the elbows out and each hand on the side of the basketball.
- After the rebound is secured, the player must look away from the lane area, as this is where most of the players are located.
- Instruct players that a pivot should occur after the rebounder looks for and locates the outlet player.
- Pivot and pass to the perimeter player to start the offensive transition.

POINTS OF EMPHASIS

- Encourage proper rebound form with arms, head, and eyes.
- Look away from the lane for outlet.
- Make a pivot to pass to the outlet player.

SKILL 3

FREE-THROW REBOUNDING

For rebounding free throws on defense, the best rebounders should be placed in the positions closest to the basket, as this is where the rebounds generally go.

- Defenders should be in a balanced stance with the knees bent; the hands should be above the waist and their eyes on the rim in anticipation of the missed free throw.
- Hands and arms must be extended to go after the missed free throw.
- As the basketball hits the rim, defenders will step toward the opposite corner of the free-throw line (elbow) to block out the offensive rebounder next to them.
- A designated player should also block out the shooter.

 ## POINTS OF EMPHASIS

- Encourage proper rebound form with arms, head, and eyes.
- Assume the shot will be missed.
- Step toward opposite corner of the free-throw line.

FOUNDATIONAL LEVEL

OFFENSIVE PRINCIPLES: SCREENING

GENERAL OVERVIEW: *Screening is a fundamental skill that builds off of the ability to run and stop with body control taught in the Introductory Level. It is important that the young player at this level knows how to set a proper screen to get a teammate open for a pass and how to react to the teammate who uses the screen. This level also teaches the skill of how to use the screen based on the defender.*

SKILL 1

SETTING A SCREEN

The mechanics of setting a screen are developed at the Introductory Level, which is when running and stopping under control are taught.

- Basically, a screen is a jump stop with the knees slightly bent, feet wider than the shoulders, head and chin up, and hands and arms either crossed at the chest or at the hip area for protection.
- The knees cannot be out to the side but must be in a straight line from the hip to the feet.
- It is up to the teammate who is using the screen to come close enough so that the defender will run into the screen.

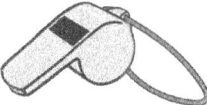

POINTS OF EMPHASIS

- Feet should be wider than the shoulders.
- Hands and arms should be inside the body.
- Keep knees in a direct line from the hip to the feet.

SKILL 2

USING THE SCREEN

Using the screen to get open may look easy but will take repetitions and an understanding of where the defender is located.

- To start with, the player using the screen must make a jab step in the direction opposite of how they want to use the screen.
- If the offensive player wants to go over the top of the screen, a step should be taken in the opposite direction first before cutting over the screen.
- When using the screen, the player should stay low. The shoulder should clip the hip of the screener. This will make it difficult for the defender to guard over the screen.

- Hands should come up as the player comes off the screen to give a good target and be in a ready position to catch and shoot the basketball.

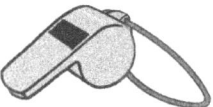

POINTS OF EMPHASIS

- Step opposite from the direction of the intended screen.
- Stay low.
- Hands in a ready position

SKILL 3

TYPES OF CUTS

The hard part of teaching screening is understanding what type of cut to make for the offensive player using the screen. This is determined by the defender. In this level, begin working on the types of cuts without a defender. Several types of cuts are introduced and then repeated so the offensive player becomes accustomed to the footwork for each cut.

- There are four cuts to teach using the screen:
    1. Back cut
    2. Curl cut
    3. Flare cut
    4. Straight cut
- The back cut may be used on a back screen, or if the offensive player refuses the screen. This cut is simply a hard cut to the basket.
- The curl cut is a tight cut around the screen.
- The flare cut is one in which the offensive player steps back from the screener, or when the offensive player will "flare" out to the sideline.
- The straight cut is used to get open at the wing, when the offensive player comes straight out to the wing to receive the pass.
- Regardless of the cut, players should stay low when using screens, with their shoulder at the screener's hip.
- As for the footwork for proper cuts, players should set the screen up by stepping high and going low, or stepping low and going high.
- Hands need to be up to be ready to catch the basketball when making the cut.

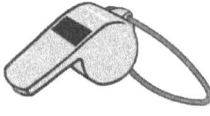

POINTS OF EMPHASIS

- Stay low.
- Proper footwork.
- Cutters keep hands ready.

SKILL 4

SCREENER REACTING TO THE CUTS

The screener's main job is to get set and let a teammate use the screen. Afterward, the screener will react to make an appropriate cut too.

- The screener must watch the teammate to determine which cut to make. When screening, instruct players to keep their feet wider than the shoulders and keep elbows inside the body.
- Once the offensive player cuts off the screen, the screener then reacts to the cut. Remind screeners to travel in the opposite direction of the cut.
- Many times, the player who is the most open to receive a pass is the screener, so hands must be ready to catch the basketball.
- If the offensive player makes a curl cut, the screener must pop out to create proper spacing.
- The screener will spin and roll to the basket on flare cuts or straight cuts.
- Coaches should drill the various cuts frequently to improve footwork.

POINTS OF EMPHASIS

- The screener must watch the teammate to determine the cut that is made.
- Screener will travel opposite the teammate.
- Screener should have hands ready to catch basketball.
- Emphasize proper footwork.

DEFENSIVE PRINCIPLES

GENERAL OVERVIEW: *This is an area that may be very new to players in the Foundational Level. It is imperative that the teaching be slow when going over defending the screens. At this level, awareness of screens is the most important aspect of defending the screen. The focus is on defending screens either by going over the top of the screen or switching after the screen.*

SKILL 1

GOING OVER THE TOP OF A SCREEN

First of all, it is important that players are in the proper help-side position on defense, so the screener has a much more difficult time setting a good screen.

- To go over the top of screens, instruct players that the top, or inside, foot needs to step over the screener. This will make it difficult for the offensive player to use the screen.
- As the inside foot goes over the top of the screen, the knees straighten to get over the screen.

- Make sure the inside arm is up to deflect any passes.
- Players may also use an outside arm bar to prevent the offensive player from pushing off into the defender.

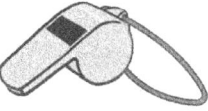

POINTS OF EMPHASIS

- Start in good help-side position.
- Inside foot goes over the top of the screen.
- Knees must straighten.
- Raise the inside arm to deflect the pass.

SKILL 2

SWITCHING

This is probably the easiest way to start teaching defending the off-ball screens.

- As the offensive player uses the screen, both defenders must talk on the screen with the player who first sees the necessity of a switch calling it loudly and clearly. The other player answers and completes the switch.
- It is important that both defenders have an awareness of the screen.
- As the offensive player uses the screen, the defender guarding the screener will call "switch" and take the cutter.
- The defender being screened will switch to guard the screener. Now defending the screener, the player should be positioned on the ball side of the screener to get into the passing lane.

POINTS OF EMPHASIS

- Communicate.
- Both defenders must have an awareness of the screen.
- Get into passing lanes.

FOUNDATIONAL LEVEL

OFFENSIVE PRINCIPLES: SHOOTING

GENERAL OVERVIEW: *Shooting is a necessary fundamental to learn in the game of basketball, as the object of the game is to score the basketball. This level will continue to emphasize the correct skills and mechanics necessary for a solid fundamental shot, which is important to developing players' shooting consistency.*

SKILL 1

ONE-HAND FORM SHOOTING

- Standing one step from the front of the rim with feet balanced, slight knee bend, and squared to the rim, the player will begin with one hand underneath the basketball. The palm should be facing upward and the basketball should be held at waist level.
- The guide hand, or "off hand," will be placed behind the back to allow the player to focus on the mechanics of the shooting hand.
- Once the player has the appropriate grip on the basketball (on the finger pads with a little light between the basketball and the thumb as described in Skill 2 of the Introductory Level page 60), move the basketball from the waist level to the shoulder level. This is a good step for the player to work on basketball control and the importance of using finger pads to do so.
- The elbow should be in a U shape, the wrist should be cocked backward, and the basketball should be positioned correctly in the hand. The elbow should be in line with the knee of the shooting hand. Pause briefly at this position to make any corrections before beginning the upward shooting motion.
- Following the pause and any corrections, the player will begin the upward motion, using the shooting arm and legs together for added strength. On the follow-through, the elbow should be slightly ahead of the ear. The middle finger should guide the follow-through and the hand should end with four fingers pointed toward the floor, as if players are grabbing a cookie out of a jar above their heads.
- The eyes should remain on the target, the rim, until the basketball hits the ground. Ideally, if the follow-through creates the correct backspin (and the basketball does not touch the rim), the basketball will spin back to the shooter off of the bounce without the shooter having to move to grab the basketball.
- Continue to reinforce proper mechanics, rather than makes and misses. As the player becomes comfortable with the skill, change locations on the floor along with the distance from which the player is shooting, careful not to extend too far.

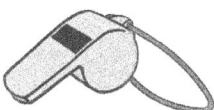 ### POINTS OF EMPHASIS

- Focus on details of mechanics from beginning to end.
- Encourage proper mechanics rather than makes and misses.
- Upper and lower body work together.

SKILL 2

TWO-HAND FORM SHOOTING

Once the above skill is completed, move the player back to the front of the rim one step from the rim.

DRILL 1: SHOOTING WITHOUT JUMPING

- With the same stance and mechanics listed above, have the player add the guide hand. This hand should be placed on the basketball creating a large, spread-out T with the thumbs of both hands.
- It is important to reinforce that the guide hand is intended to be a guide. The hand should stay with the basketball until just above the head. At this point, the guide hand will stop so the shooting hand completes the shooting motion.
- Beginning players have the tendency to push through the basketball with the guide hand, which is not the purpose of that hand. Continue to reinforce mechanics rather than makes and misses, as the consistency of a player's shot will develop through repetition of the proper technique.

POINTS OF EMPHASIS

- Reinforce correct shooting mechanics.
- Make sure the guide hand is a guide.
- Hold follow-through.

DRILL 2: SHOOTING WITH A JUMP

- Once the player is comfortable performing the skill, add a small jump to the exercise without increasing distance. This will help players get more familiar with how the upper and lower body work together throughout the shooting motion.
- The player should still remain on balance even with a jump. Ideally, the player will take off from and land in the same or slightly forward spot. Be sure to correct players if the momentum of the jump takes them to the side or backward. It is important to control momentum through movement and jumping.

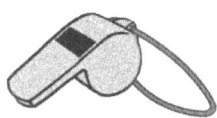

POINTS OF EMPHASIS

- Reinforce correct shooting mechanics.
- Make sure the guide hand is a guide.
- Hold follow-through.
- When adding jump, pay special attention to momentum.

SKILL 3

TWO-HAND SHOOTING FROM A SELF-PASS

Once the player becomes comfortable with the mechanics of the form shot, it is important to develop the footwork necessary to shoot a basketball after receiving it on a pass.

- Instruct players to begin in a triple-threat stance, about five feet away from the front of the rim. Players will pass the basketball to themselves by tossing the basketball directly in front of them, with the proper backspin so that it returns after the bounce.
- As the basketball is returning, the player will begin stepping toward the basketball with one foot, followed by the second, resulting in a one-two step. This concept is more commonly known as "ball in the air, feet in the air."
- If a player is right-handed, it is most natural to lead with the left foot, followed by the right. In this particular instance, the left foot would be considered the "inside foot."
- Players should receive the basketball with a bend in the knees. This is important for developing both strength and quickness as the player begins to extend the shooting range. In addition, the player should begin developing an understanding of timing for this type of footwork in order to avoid traveling, while maintaining momentum and quickness.
- It is important to begin this process with players passing to themselves, rather than receiving an actual pass from a teammate or coach. The basketball comes more slowly with this technique, allowing players to develop the correct footwork rather than rushing it. It gives players some control over the learning process and allows them to progress at their own pace.
- Once the player receives the basketball on the inside foot, the player will begin the shooting motion. Remind players to receive the basketball low, control the movement during the shooting process, and complete the shot as previously practiced.
- As the player begins to develop the proper footwork, have the player receive the basketball using the opposite footwork. At this level, it is important to begin getting players comfortable receiving the basketball using both feet as the lead.

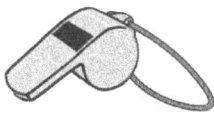 ## POINTS OF EMPHASIS

- Receive low.
- Ball in the air, feet in the air.
- Control movement.
- Continue to encourage and reinforce proper shooting mechanics.

SKILL 4

TWO-HAND SHOOTING FROM A HOP

Receiving the basketball on a hop tends to present many more issues for players than receiving on the inside foot, so be careful not to compromise proper mechanics just to teach this skill.

- Setting up and finishing this skill is very similar to the process just outlined. The only difference is that the player receives the basketball on a hop rather than on the inside foot.
- Instruct players to use the "ball in the air, feet in the air" technique. In this case however, players will move both feet at the same time instead of one and then the other.
- The timing is critical to avoid traveling, to increase the ability to get the feet set, and to help get the shot off quickly.
- Again, remind players to receive the basketball low, using a quick, low jump stop on the catch. It is important to pay close attention to the player's ability to control momentum during the movement, as it can be more challenging when receiving the basketball off of a hop.
- Once the basketball is received, the player will begin the shooting motion. Change location on the floor, distance from the hoop, and the angle at which the basketball is received as the player improves.

POINTS OF EMPHASIS

- Receive low.
- Ball in the air, feet in the air
- Control momentum during movement.
- Continue to encourage and reinforce proper shooting mechanics.

SKILL 5

FIVE-MINUTE WARM-UP SHOOTING ROUTINE

Many times, players will walk into a gym and immediately begin shooting from the three-point line. Although this may be a fun activity, it does not allow a player to warm up properly or work on shooting mechanics.

- A five-minute warm-up shooting routine players can do every time they walk into a gym may be as simple as performing skills from earlier in this level in succession. For example:
  - Drill: One-Hand Form Shooting; performed one to two steps from the rim
  - Drill: Two-Hand Form Shooting without Jumping; performed one to two steps from the rim
  - Drill: Two-Hand Form Shooting with a Jump; performed four to five steps from the rim
  - Drill: Two-Hand Shooting from a Self-Pass; performed six to seven steps from the rim initially, then work on increasing distance.
- Vary locations on the court along with varying distances as long as the player is able to maintain form, mechanics, and technique with the variations.
- Emphasize that this type of shooting routine should be used every time upon entering the gym to help warm up, as well as to create good habits.

POINTS OF EMPHASIS

- Reinforce all technical concepts.
- Encourage mechanics rather than makes and misses.

SKILL 6

LAYUPS

DRILL 1: LAYUPS FROM THE STRONG SIDE

- To begin learning the footwork and technique of a layup, it is best to begin without using a dribble.
- Start two steps from the basket, concentrating on the strong side first. For purposes of explanation, the right side will serve as the strong side.
- Have the player stand at a forty-five-degree angle on the right side of the basket, two steps away, holding the basketball at waist level. The player will then take one step with the right foot, then step and plant the left foot while driving the right knee upward.
- In an effort to help players remember which knee drives upward, you can provide the visual of a string being attached to the right knee and the right elbow. As the right elbow rises to shoot the layup, the string will pull the right knee upward with it.
- The right knee and right elbow will rise simultaneously, allowing the player to drive upward, jump toward the backboard, and shoot the basketball with the right hand.
- Remind players to follow through with the layup, just as they have done in the previous shooting skills.
- Players should aim to hit the square on the backboard. The momentum from the steps should lead players straight up or slightly ahead of where they took off. The momentum should be more upward, rather than straight outward toward the baseline.
- Once players get comfortable with the footwork, allow the player to move backward a step and add a dribble. Make sure they still end in a right-then-left stepping pattern, driving the right knee upward on the layup attempt.
- As a player improves, two dribbles can be added, etc.
- It is important to keep the player at a forty-five-degree angle to create the habit of shooting layups from this position. This is the ideal angle from which layups should be performed in a game, as it increases the likelihood of using the backboard and making the shot.

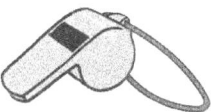 ## POINTS OF EMPHASIS

- Develop correct footwork and proper knee drive.
- Control momentum.
- Use the backboard properly.
- Develop comfort level using a dribble into footwork.

DRILL 2: LAYUPS FROM THE WEAK SIDE

- After the player gets comfortable on the strong side, begin layups from the weak side. Remind players to drive the opposite knee upward and use the opposite hand to shoot the basketball.
- Encourage players to use the weak hand, even if they are unable to make a basket. Having the ability to use both hands is critical to players' development.
- Work through the same process until the footwork and use of the weak side becomes more comfortable.

POINTS OF EMPHASIS

- Develop correct footwork and proper knee drive.
- Use both hands.
- Control momentum.
- Use the backboard properly.
- Develop comfort level using a dribble into footwork.

SKILL 7

SHOOTING FROM A PASS WHILE STATIONARY

This skill is similar to Skill 3, but the difference is that players will receive the basketball from a teammate or coach rather than from themselves. The biggest adjustment for the player will be developing timing with the footwork while receiving the basketball from another individual.

- Remind players to use the "ball in the air, feet in the air" technique.
- Players will square themselves to the basket, standing approximately six to ten feet away. The individual passing the basketball should do so from under the rim in order to keep the shooter squared to the basket.
- As the pass is made, the shooter will step with one foot at a time, beginning with the inside foot in the one-two step pattern. Then, the shooter will receive the basketball low and progress upward into the shot. The player will work on receiving with one foot first, then switch the lead foot.
- Once the one-two step pattern becomes comfortable, players may begin receiving the basketball on a hop.

POINTS OF EMPHASIS

- Ball in the air, feet in the air
- Receive low.
- Control momentum.
- Reinforce correct shooting mechanics over makes and misses.

SKILL 8

SHOOTING OFF A PASS—RECEIVING IN THE ONE-TWO STEP PATTERN

When first learning the footwork into a shot, it is best to create a natural angle that leads to an easy square-up. For example, having the player make a straight cut from the wing to the elbow and receiving the basketball from the opposite elbow will lead to a natural inside foot (one-two step) square-up.

- From the wing, the shooting player will begin cutting toward the elbow with the pass arriving at the same time as the shooter. The shooter will plant the inside foot and square up with the outside foot.
- Squaring up and catching the basketball low are both important in order to have leg strength behind the shot. Further, the player will need to change the momentum of the cut to use the momentum in the actual shot, elevating straight up or slightly forward from the take off point.
- At this level, getting comfortable with the different components is important and being able to get the body to work together throughout the shot, rather than working against itself.
- Once the player gets comfortable with this footwork, move the player to the other side of the court to use the opposite foot as the inside foot. As the player gains confidence in the footwork on both sides, adjust the angle from which the player receives the basketball, making some more challenging than others.

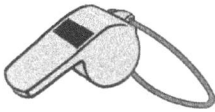 ## POINTS OF EMPHASIS

- Ball in the air, feet in the air.
- Timing of footwork.
- Square all the way to rim with shoulders.
- Catch low.
- Control and change momentum from cut to enhance shot.
- Reinforce proper mechanics with shot.

SKILL 9

SHOOTING OFF A PASS—RECEIVING ON A HOP

This skill is the same as detailed in Skill 8, except that the player will receive the basketball while both feet are in the air, catching it on a hop.

- It is important to concentrate on catching the basketball low to add strength to the shot. Remind players to control the momentum of the cut as well.
- The hop allows more freedom of movement for the player, but this is not always used positively. Sometimes, players fade to the side or backward. Ensure that any momentum from the cut itself goes straight upward or slightly forward on the shot.

- If learned properly, the hop can be used to get a shot off more quickly than by using a one-two step pattern. It is critical that the fundamentals are learned correctly in order to provide strength for the shot, especially as the player attempts to extend shooting range.

POINTS OF EMPHASIS

- Ball in the air, feet in the air.
- Timing of footwork.
- Square all the way to rim with shoulders.
- Catch low.
- Control and change momentum from cut to enhance shot.
- Reinforce proper mechanics with shot.
- Special emphasis on catching low and controlling momentum of cut.

SKILL 10

SHOOTING OFF OF THE DRIBBLE IN THE ONE-TWO STEP PATTERN

It is best to introduce this skill by using an easy angle on the basketball floor for the player to successfully square to the rim off of the dribble.

- Beginning with the player at the free-throw line, have the player take one dribble at a desirable angle in the direction of the shooting hand. For purposes of this explanation, the player will take one dribble to the right.
- As the dribble is taken, the player will plant the inside foot, in this case the left foot, followed by the outside foot, or right foot. It will be important that the player brings the outside foot all the way around the body to fully square to the rim.
- The player will want to go into the footwork low to add strength to the shot. Remind players to control the momentum of the cut as well.
- Again, the player should land where the shot started, or just slightly ahead of that spot.
- Instruct the player to receive the basketball from the floor directly into the shooting pocket while the footwork is being executed. Once the footwork is complete and the player is fully squared, the player will rise to complete a shot.
- Once the player becomes comfortable with the footwork on the strong side, change directions to the weak side. This side can be more challenging due to the dribble being on the opposite side of where the shot will originate.
- As the player takes a dribble to the left, the player will plant the inside foot, or right foot in this instance, followed by the outside foot, or the left foot.
- Squaring up to the rim properly and controlling momentum are very important.
- Remember that the player will need to get the basketball from the left side of the body to the right side in order to shoot the basketball.
- Many players will want to accomplish this by using a crossover dribble, but it would likely get stolen in the presence of a live defender. Therefore, instruct players to dribble with the left hand, which will require them to shift the basketball over to the right hand in midair without an additional dribble.

- If the player really pounds the basketball into the floor on the last dribble, it can help execute this shift more quickly.
- Once the basketball is in the shooting pocket and the player is squared, rise up and shoot a shot as described previously.
- As players improve, use more difficult shooting angles and incorporate additional dribbles.

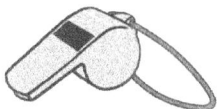 **POINTS OF EMPHASIS**

- Full square-up to the rim.
- Start low into the square-up.
- Control momentum for strength.
- Get the basketball from the floor to shooting pocket as quickly as possible.
- No extra dribbles.
- Reinforce proper shooting mechanics.

SKILL 11

FREE THROWS

There are many theories concerning the right way to shoot a free throw: jumping versus no jumping, long routine versus short routine, etc. The approach does not seem to be the most important; the consistency is.

- Players should develop a routine that is comfortable for them and that they are committed to completing during every single free-throw attempt. The consistency allows players to develop muscle memory so that they do not have to focus on technique or mechanics during a stressful game situation.
- The more consistency and successful repetition there is in the routine, the more confidence a player will have with the free-throw process.
- The routine should be short enough for the player to be able to catch the basketball from the official, complete the routine, and release the basketball all within ten seconds.
- The shot itself should contain the same mechanics and shooting fundamentals as outlined through the entire level, ending with a solid follow-through with the middle finger over the center of the rim.
- At this level, work on developing the preferred routine for each player's free throw. Then, repeat the routine to increase consistency.
- Also, work on a player's ability to execute the chosen routine at the free-throw line while others are watching, as this will be the case in a game. This will require a great deal of focus and concentration from the free-throw line, which is great to begin developing early on.

 ## POINTS OF EMPHASIS

- Develop routine.
- Execute the same routine with consistency, repetition.
- Encourage focus and concentration from free-throw li
- Encourage carryover from all shooting fundamentals and mechanics.
- Focus on technique rather than makes and misses.

FOUNDATIONAL LEVEL

TEAM DEFENSIVE CONCEPTS

GENERAL OVERVIEW: *Foundational Level team defensive concepts are introduced with the half-court team defense gradually progressing from 1-on-1 to 2-on-2, 3-on-3, 4-on-4, and finally 5-on-5 principles. Help-side defense is introduced along with rotations when the offense breaks down the defense. Defending the passing lanes, defending off-ball screens, and defensive transition are also introduced as part of the defensive concepts.*

SKILL 1

ON-BALL DEFENSE

- Stance wider than the shoulders, eyes on the waist of the offensive player, inside foot up, inside hand down, and head lower than the shoulders of the offensive player.
- The best drill for this on-ball defense is to start the offensive player with the ball on one baseline. The offensive player will zigzag on one-third of the court back and forth while dribbling to the opposite baseline. The defender will be in proper position while guarding the dribbler 1-on-1 full court.
- The alley drill starts at the wing position with the offensive player restricted to an "alley" to the basket using cones as boundaries. The defender stays in the proper stance and works to stop the offensive player from getting to the basket for the shot.
- Play 1-on-1 starting at any position on the half court and restricting the offensive player to one or two dribbles. The defender works on keeping between the offensive player and the basket. On the shot, the defender works on getting the hand up high, calling out shot and boxing out.
- The "cone drill" starts the players in two lines on the baseline with the player closest to the sideline with the ball.
- One cone is set in front of the offense's line and one in front of the defense's line; both cones are even and a few feet before half court.
- On command by the coach, the first offensive player dribbles out hard to the cone and dribbles around it, turning to attack the basket. The defensive player sprints up and around the other cone and gets in position to play defense on the dribbler.

 ### POINTS OF EMPHASIS

- Usually the player who stays the lowest wins the battle, so it is important that the defender's head is lower than the offensive player's shoulders.
- The inside foot is the foot closest to the rim line, which should be up in the staggered stance. This will force the offensive player to the sideline/baseline rather than the middle.

- As the dribbler works the defender down the court in zigzag fashion, the defender will drop-step with each change of direction of the dribbler.
- The defender must finish all the 1-on-1 drills by getting the hand up, calling out shot, and boxing out the offensive player.
- The defender must try to force the offensive player to use the weak hand in a 1-on-1 situation.
- The key to the defender's footwork is to move the foot first in the direction the offense will go to stop the dribbler.

SKILL 2

DENY THE BALL

- The goal of the deny position is to not allow offensive players to catch the ball in a position where they would like to catch.
- Proper denial position means the knees are bent and the chest is facing the offensive player. The inside hand is up and out with the thumb down and the palm of the hand open to the offensive player with the ball.
- The chin is turned to the basketball and is on the shoulder so the defender can see both the basketball and the offensive player who is working to get open for the pass.
- The top foot of the defender is higher or above the offensive player's foot in order to deny the pass directly to the receiver.
- The coach starts with the ball at the top of the key with the offensive and defensive player at the wing position. The offensive player will work to get open by making any type of offensive move—V-cut, L-cut, seal cut—while the defensive player works to deny the pass.
- Once/if the pass is complete, the offensive player will make a move to score going 1-on-1 against the defender who was in deny position.
- The drill progresses to 2-on-2 with the guard at the top being defended and the offensive player at the wing working to receive the ball against a defender.
- 3-on-3 allows both wing positions to be the potential receivers against a defender with the offensive player at the top trying to enter the pass to the teammate on either wing.

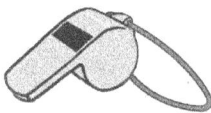 ## POINTS OF EMPHASIS

- It is important for the defensive player to keep a distance of about three or four feet from the offensive player who is working to receive the pass. The defender must not allow the offensive player to get into the defender's body and then make a move to get open.
- The deny position does not necessarily result in steals but will make offensive players work to receive the pass outside of their normal area.
- The arm and lead foot should be in the passing lane—which is the line between the ball and the offensive player.

- Even though the defender is in deny position, the defender must be aware of the potential to help stop the dribble from the offensive player at the top if the ball handler gets around the on-ball defender.
- 2-on-2 or 3-on-3 are excellent methods to implement the 1-on-1 defense and the deny defense together.

SKILL 3

HELP-SIDE DEFENSE

- Help-side defense is the first concept in putting the team defense together in order to create a defensive unit.
- The strong side is the side of the court that contains the basketball. The rim line is the divider for the strong side and the help side. The help side is the side of the court that does not contain the basketball.
- The help-side defense is predicated on the ball line, which is the path of the basketball from the offensive player on one side of the court to the offensive player on the opposite side of the court.
- The help-side defender should always be one step off the ball line in order to be able to see the basketball and the defender's player.
- A good introductory drill is to have a defender and offensive player on one side of the court with the coach on the opposite or ball side of the court. The defender is in proper stance and position on help side, one step off the ball line, pointing one hand to the ball and one hand to the offensive player.
- As the coach moves dribbling the ball from the baseline to the wing, the defender on the help side will adjust the help-side defense as the ball line moves. The offensive player on the help side stays in one spot while the coach dribbles to new positions.
- Next, the coach with the ball now stays in one spot while the offensive player on the help side moves up and down from the baseline to the wing with the defender adjusting the help-side position to keep one step off the ball line.
- Progress to 2-on-2 help side to strong side by the defenders. The ball starts on one side with the offensive player holding the ball in triple-threat position. The defender is in good on-ball position. The help-side defender is in position off of the ball line.
- The offensive player skips the ball to the opposite wing. The defenders now will move from ball side to help side and help side to ball side as the ball is passed back and forth.
- The drill progresses 2-on-2 with the offensive player dribbling baseline to wing and then making the skip pass with the defenders maintaining proper position and moving when the ball is in the air.
- Adding a top offensive player and two wings will make this drill a 3-on-3 drill. The offensive player at the top starts with the ball. The defenders now play deny defense on the wings and on-ball defense at the top and then moving to help-side and ball-side defense when the pass is completed at the wing position.

POINTS OF EMPHASIS

- The help-side defender needs to be in a defensive stance at all times and be ready to move quickly when the offensive player moves or when the ball moves.
- The ball line continually changes as the ball moves and the players move on the court and the defenders must be adjusting their position constantly.
- The rim line is an imaginary line that goes from rim to rim and is a focal point for the defender to be in good help-side position.
- A big emphasis is the position of the help-side defender depending on where the ball is located. If the ball is above the free-throw line extended, the help-side defender is one step off the rim line to the offensive player. If the ball is below the free-throw line extended, the defender's head is on the rim line.
- The key to being in great defensive position when moving from help side to ball side or ball side to help side is to move when the basketball is in the air on the pass. The defender then will be in great position when the pass is received by the offensive player.
- The ball-side defender must pivot on inside foot and turn to sprint to the rim line to be in good position when the ball is caught by the opposite wing.
- When playing 3-on-3, the defenders must move from deny position to help side as the ball is passed from wing to top to wing.

SKILL 4

ROTATION DEFENSE

- Rotation on defense occurs when the offense breaks down the defense by beating or getting by the on-ball defender with the use of the dribble.
- When the dribbler beats the on-ball defender, the help-side defenders must rotate to stop the dribbler from getting to the basket.
- The main rule for rotation is rotate over and down. This simply means to rotate the nearest next defender to the ball as the helper and then rotate the other defenders down to cover the helper. "Help the helper" is a term players must understand.
- The best way to teach the rotation starts with 2-on-2. The ball starts at the wing with an on-ball defender. The help-side defender is on the rim line in a position to guard the offensive player on the help side.
- As the offensive player dribbles toward the baseline, the help-side defender stays on the rim line and drops to adjust to the ball level.
- If the offensive player gets around the on-ball defender and goes baseline to the basket, the help-side defender must slide over to stop the dribbler preferably outside the lane on the ball side of the court.

- Progressing to 3-on-3 rotation, the help-side wing defender would slide over to stop the ball on the baseline while the top defender would slide down to cover the opposite wing offensive player and the pass across the lane using the over and down rotation concept.
- The 4-on-4 allows for the full rotation. The basketball is dribbled baseline from the wing, beating the defender. The opposite wing slides over to stop the dribbler outside the lane on ball side. This may end up in a trap situation or just a ball stop. The top guard on the help side slides down to cover the lane and pass across the lane. The ball-side wing defender then drops to the middle of the lane to prevent a middle lane pass.

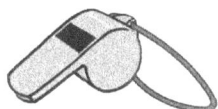 **POINTS OF EMPHASIS**

- The defenders must always be in a position to see the ball and see the offensive player they are guarding in order to make the proper rotation when the dribbler beats the on-ball defender.
- The help-side defender must be in position to rotate to the basketball and stop the offensive player outside the lane if the offensive player goes baseline past the on-ball defender.
- The defender on the ball should be shading the dribbler to go to the baseline so the rotation can stay constant with the over and down concept.
- On the 4-on-4 work, the defender at the wing who gets beat baseline now goes to the lane area to take away the middle pass.

SKILL 5

DEFENDING THE BALL SCREENS

- Defending off-ball screens involves communication and the ability of the defenders to react to the off-ball screen, which many times takes place on the help side of the court.
- Off-ball screen defenders need to stay in a stance and keep in proper help-side position.
- As the offensive player sets the screen off the ball, the defender who is guarding the screener steps back to create a "window" for the teammate being screened to use to slide behind the screen and continue guarding the offensive player.
- The defender guarding the player using the screen may also work to get over the top of the screen by getting a lead foot on the top of the screener, allowing for the defender to stay with the offensive player using the screen.
- The defenders need to stay wide in good basketball position with the arms out to help them adjust to the screener.
- The switch may also occur on the off-ball screen by the defenders if the defender who is guarding the screener calls out "screen" and then "switch" to indicate the oncoming screen and the decision to take the player using the screen.
- After the switch is made, the defender who is switching on the screener must be quick to get on the ball side of the screener to prevent the roll to the basket.

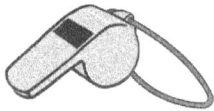

POINTS OF EMPHASIS

- If the defenders are in proper help-side position, it will be much harder for the offensive players to set the screen.
- The help-side defenders must always see the basketball and their player in order to get through the off-ball screen.
- By creating a "window," the defender guarding the player using the screen can easily avoid the screen.
- The key is to communicate by calling out "screen" if your offensive player is the one setting the screen.
- The switch is a good option to stop a strong shooter from getting the basketball, as the shooter will be defended by the screener's defender, who should jump in the passing lane.
- If the defender does not switch and goes over the top of the screen, the defender must chest up to the player using the screen and bring the rear end in to become as "thin" as possible in order to get over the screen.
- Keep in mind the screener may roll or pop to get open for a pass after the screen is set.
- The key for defending the off-ball screen is to communicate, stay in defensive position, and have an awareness of what can happen for the offensive player.

SKILL 6

DEFENSIVE TRANSITION

- Defensive transition is important to stop easy baskets by the offensive team pushing the ball up the court in a fast break situation.
- As the shot is taken, the designated offensive player—usually the point guard—should be the first player back to stop the initial fast break.
- The first defender back should not allow any offensive player to get behind the defense for an easy basket or a pass over the top.
- The second defender back should be in a position at the top of the key with the first defender in the lane.
- This may create a 3-on-2 situation, which would involve the back defender taking the first pass—usually to the wing—with the top defender dropping to the middle of the lane taking the pass away across the lane.
- The third player defending the transition should read the situation but most often will cover the free-throw line area, as this area is open when the top defender drops down to cover the lane pass.
- The fourth and fifth defenders will read which offensive players are open and will cover those areas, which are usually the weak-side area and the post area.
- The drill 3-on-2 with trailer is a good defensive transition drill for this level.
- Two teams are on opposite sidelines at half court.
- The drill starts with two defenders from one team in a tandem formation in the lane and three offensive players from the other team bringing the ball down the court to attack.

- The offense attacks the two defenders to score. As the offense dribbles down the court, the moment the basketball crosses the half-court line, a third player from the team on defense runs onto the floor from the sideline and touches the middle circle, then joins the defense, now creating a 3-on-3 scenario.
- Two players from the current offensive team also run to touch the half-court line and sprint to the opposite end and set up a tandem formation to prepare to defend the three players who are currently on defense and will be in transition.
- After a score or a turnover, the three defenders become offense and head down the court to face the next two defenders.
- The first offensive players go to the back of their team line.
- Each time the ball crosses at the half-court line, three players come in the action, one trailer defender to add to the two who are in the game plus two new defenders at the opposite basket.

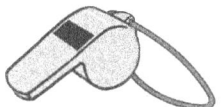

POINTS OF EMPHASIS

- The top defender in the tandem must try to stop the offensive player dribbling downcourt. This defender's main responsibility is to slow, stop, or push the dribbler to the side of the court and buy time to allow the defender running in to catch up and help stop the transition.
- The pass across the lane is a common action for the offensive team, so it is important the defense drops down to cover this pass, which may leave the free-throw line area open.
- The 3-on-2 trailer drill allows for both offensive and defensive work in a transition situation.
- Communication is the key to stopping a good transition team. Stop the ball first, which allows time for the other defenders to get back in defensive transition.
- A good defensive transition team must sprint to the lane area first and then scramble to find the offensive players to guard.

FOUNDATIONAL LEVEL

TEAM OFFENSIVE CONCEPTS

GENERAL OVERVIEW: *In this level, players are ready for more organized offensive tactics such as advantage opportunities in transition, lane responsibilities in the transition, half-court spacing, off-ball screening, attacking, and movement without the basketball. Motion concepts are now introduced with players playing all positions rather than being labeled as a post, point guard, or wing. Position skills are now being developed within the framework of the motion offense. Inbounding the basketball is now a vital part of the offense.*

SKILL 1

ADVANTAGE OPPORTUNITIES IN TRANSITION

- The transition is started either with an outlet pass from the rebounder to a teammate positioned downcourt or with a dribble by the rebounder.
- Once the basketball is advanced from the outlet pass, the player must center the basketball as quickly as possible at the midpoint between the two sidelines.
- As the transition begins, there should be one cutter on each side of the basketball filling the outside lanes of the court.
- The decision-making occurs by the player with the basketball in the middle of the court and must be drilled and executed in practice situations.
- One rule to guide decision-making in transition is to make only as many passes for the transition basket as there are defenders. For example, if a 2-on-1 situation occurs, a shot should be taken after one pass. In a 3-on-2 scenario, the shot should be taken after no more than two passes.
- The middle player with the basketball needs to look to advance the basketball to the cutters on the sideline as soon as possible. Then, the middle player fills the free-throw line elbow to possibly get the basketball back for a shot or a pass to the opposite cutter.
- As the basketball is advanced, the remaining two players will run to the low post and high post opposite the middle player.
- Drill the advantage opportunities starting at half court. Two offensive players start at half court with one defender in the lane. One of the offensive players will dribble the basketball at the defender and then make a decision as to either pass or shoot depending on the reaction of the defender.
- Start with three lines at half court with two defenders in a tandem position—one defender at the free-throw line area and the other one under the basket. As the basketball is passed to the cutter, the bottom defender will guard the first pass with the top defender dropping down under the basket to take away the pass from wing to wing. This leaves the passer open who filled the area of the free-throw line elbow.

 **POINTS OF EMPHASIS**

- The fast break is not started until the defensive team gains possession of the basketball to transition to offense. Players must not anticipate possession and start the transition early.

- The pass is the best option to start the transition, as this is a faster way to move the basketball downcourt.
- It is advantageous to have a cutter on one side be slightly ahead of the cutter on the opposite side of the court.
- The basketball should not be passed from sideline cutter to sideline cutter, as the defender should drop to stop this pass.
- The best pass to make from the sideline is to the middle player who passed the basketball and is now at the free-throw line area.
- When a 2-on-1 situation occurs, the best pass to make is the bounce pass when the defender stops the dribble.
- When the 3-on-2 situation occurs, the second pass should go to the middle player who is at the free-throw line elbow. There may be a third pass if the bottom defender rushes to close out on the middle player, leaving the opposite wing open.

SKILL 2

LANE RESPONSIBILITIES IN TRANSITION

- The responsibilities for running the lane in this level involve all five players in an organized transition. The lanes include two outside lanes, two inside lanes, and a middle lane.
- Start with two lines—one on the baseline and one at the wing on the same side as the baseline. The first player in the baseline line will face the basket and throw the basketball against the backboard, jump, and secure the rebound.
- The first player in the line at the wing is the outlet. This player calls "outlet" as the basketball is secured by the rebounder. Hands are up and back is parallel to the sideline.
- The rebounder will throw an overhead pass to the outlet player and then sprint to the outside lane for a layup at the opposite basket.
- The outlet player will dribble to the middle of the floor and then make the pass to the rebounder for a layup. The outlet player will dribble hard to the free-throw line elbow area to make the pass.
- The players will switch positions and return in the same method—the rebounder now is the outlet, and the outlet is now the rebounder.
- Progress the drill with three lines—two wing lines and one baseline line. The rebounder throws the basketball off the backboard and will pass to the outlet player on the near side. The rebounder follows the pass to fill the outside lane.
- The outlet player will dribble the basketball to the middle of the court and make a pass to the opposite wing who has filled the opposite outside lane for a layup. The rebounder will be in good position for another rebound and the dribbler will stop at the free-throw line for a possible pass back.
- Continue the drill adding another baseline line. The drill now is four players. The baseline player who does not rebound the basketball fills one of the inside lanes opposite the dribbler and will stop at the top of the key opposite the dribbler for a reversal pass.
- A fifth line may also be added. This player will run the rim line, which is the line going from rim to rim, looking for a pass from the middle player or the wing player.

POINTS OF EMPHASIS

- As the basketball is shot, all five players must be in rebounding position to gain possession of the basketball to start the transition.
- The outlet player must call "outlet" to let the rebounder know where to make the outlet pass.
- All players must rotate to each spot in the drill, which will make them familiar with all the transition lanes.
- Instead of an outlet pass, the rebounder may dribble the basketball away from the basket first and then make an outlet pass off the dribble.

SKILL 3

HALF-COURT SPACING

This was covered in the Introductory Level, but now half-court spacing is in relation to scoring in a half-court setting.

- Three players will set up with one at the top of the key and one at each wing at the free-throw line extended.
- The top player starts with the basketball and passes to one of the wing players, then makes a basket cut.
- The opposite wing makes a direct cut to the free-throw line and looks for the pass. If the cutter does not receive a pass, the cutter goes to the top of the key and replaces the player who made a basket cut to keep the proper spacing.
- The player making the basket cut goes opposite the basketball to the wing replacing the player who made the direct cut for the basketball.
- As the basketball gets passed from the wing to the top of the key, the wing who passed the basketball will execute a cut to get open for a possible pass back.
- The basketball gets passed from the top of the key to the other wing and a basket cut is made. The opposite wing now makes a direct cut to the basketball at the free-throw line area, popping out to the top of the key if no pass is made.
- This drill can expand to five players in the half court with two additional players now on the baseline. Fill the five positions by starting with the wing and baseline players exchanging position or the wings setting a screen for the baseline players.
- The player at the top of the key makes a basket cut after a pass to the wing. The opposite wing makes a direct cut to the free-throw line as the baseline player moves to fill the wing spot. The top cutter now goes to the baseline spot opposite the basketball.

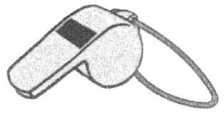
POINTS OF EMPHASIS

- The wing players must move to get open for a pass by executing a V-cut, L-cut, or seal cut.
- On basket cuts, the player should take a jab step in the opposite direction first to set up the defensive player.
- The wing making the direct cut to the free-throw line must have hands up, be ready to catch a pass from the wing, and on the catch pivot on the inside foot to square up to the basket in triple-threat position for a shot or a drive.
- Proper spacing after cuts is difficult at first. Putting tape on the floor with Xs may help players learn proper spacing and how to fill spots.
- As players move and cut, they should change speed and direction to make it harder to be guarded by defenders.

SKILL 4

ATTACKING AND MOVEMENT WITHOUT A BASKETBALL

At this level, attacking and movement without the basketball is extremely important for players to continue to develop court spacing and learn how to stay active away from the basketball.

DRILL 1: 4x4x4 EXCHANGE

- This is a fast-paced drill with teams of four lined up on the baseline side by side. Each team should have a different colored jersey to easily distinguish who is on each team. The coach is near the half-court circle and is the referee. The coach makes all calls and is the only referee for the drill. If another coach is available, place the extra coach on the baseline to make sure the next team comes on the court at the proper time.
- There are three main rules for the offensive team: 1. On every catch the player must square up to the basket; 2. after a pass the passer must move; 3. on a made basket the scorer must turn and point to the passer and yell, "Thank you."
- The offensive team works to score a basket within the framework of the rules and will stay on offense if they score. If the offensive team does not score or exits due to a rule violation, the defensive team goes to offense and a new team takes the court on defense. After a score or change of possession, the basketball is quickly passed to the coach out front and the coach will make the pass to the offensive team to start the new offensive possession.
- The drill works best with three or more teams involved. Keeping track of team wins and losses from day to day makes the drill very competitive. Change teams each day so players learn to work with new teammates.

POINTS OF EMPHASIS

- The team must come on the court in a very quick manner or the coach may tell them to go back to the end of the line.
- As referee, the coach may take points away for poor body language on a call or for exiting the court too slowly.
- If one of the rules is not done in a timely manner, the basket will not count and that team will be told to exit the court. Example: on a made basket, if the player is too slow to point and thank the passer, the basket will not count.
- Other rules may be added as the game is more familiar to players, such as limiting dribbles, requiring all players to touch the basketball before a shot can be taken, passing the basketball from strong to help side before a shot, or any other rule that the coach would like to use for help in the offense.
- If the basketball is caught and dribbled immediately, this is a violation of the squaring-up rule. Players must first catch and square up before putting the basketball on the floor.

SKILL 5

OFF-BALL SCREENING

- When teaching off-ball screening, it is best to start with 2-on-2 situations, with the screener going away from the basketball to set a screen.
- As the screen is being set, the player using the screen keeps eyes on the defender, which will dictate the movement.
- The 2-on-2 drill starts with the player making a pass to the coach. The player can start at the top of the key and pass to the coach at the wing.
- The passer then will set a screen for a teammate who is at the opposite wing. The player using the screen will take a V-cut in the opposite direction to set the defender up to run into the screen.
- This should be done at various positions on the court. Start the passer at the wing and the coach at the top of the key with the screen being set for a teammate at the block.
- The passer can also be in the post area and make the pass to the coach at the wing and set a screen across the lane for a teammate on the opposite block.
- This is easily expanded into a 3-on-3 drill, which is a great way to teach many basketball skills before moving onto 5-on-5. Instead of passing the basketball to a coach, the basketball is now passed to a teammate that is being defended.
- The 4x4x4 exchange drill mentioned previously is a great drill to teach off-ball screening. One of the rules for passers would be that after every pass they must go screen a teammate off the basketball.
- The 4x4x4 exchange drill may start with a down screen on each wing to the block area so the coach passes the basketball to the offense using an off-ball down screen.

POINTS OF EMPHASIS

- The screener always gets a good base with the feet wider than the shoulders and slight knee bend. The arms and elbows need to be inside the body to avoid illegal screens.
- The player using the screen should not watch the basketball but should keep eyes on the defender.
- The player using the screen must be able to execute a good V-cut and keep hands and fingers up as the screen is used to be in position to catch and shoot or make a quick move.
- The basketball action of using the screen must be one in which the player changes direction and changes speed, becoming harder to guard.

SKILL 6

MOTION CONCEPTS

- Motion concepts have already been touched on in several places and are the basis for most offenses.
- A simple motion offense can occur from a set with a point guard, two wings, and two baseline players, which is probably the most common motion set to start the offense.
- The offense may also start with two guards on top with two wings and a single baseline player in the post or on the baseline area.
- The smaller, quicker team will want to spread the court and create opportunities for drives to the basket. A five-out allows for good spacing that will be effective for drives to the basket because it keeps the middle of the court open.
- Court balance is necessary to allow the offense to make passes and cuts. The spacing described previously is always twelve to fifteen feet apart.
- Keeping the middle or lane area open is a very good offensive maneuver because it enables the cutters to cut through the lane to receive the basketball without much defensive traffic.
- When a player cuts to the basket and does not receive a pass, the player should continue through and fill an open spot on the side of the court with the fewest players. This is usually the opposite side from where the player came. Keep the middle open and the floor balanced.
- When a player makes a cut, the player who is the next player away from the cutting player should move in quickly to the vacated area.
- When replacing a player at the point, the new player should fill wide above the three-point line, creating a better passing angle. This is a great opportunity to reverse the basketball to the other side of the court and make a basket cut.

POINTS OF EMPHASIS

- Spacing the court can become an offense, as players have freedom to move but also have some structure.
- Proper spacing of twelve to fifteen feet between players will make it more difficult for the defenders to double-team and will allow better opportunities for screens and cuts.
- Offensive players should be spaced high at the top, wide on the wings, and at the midpoints between the basket and the corners on the baseline.
- Motion concepts are easier taught from a 3-on-3 situation before moving on to a 5-on-5 situation.
- Players must be aware that they should not stay in the post area, either the high post, mid post, or low post, for more than three seconds. A violation will occur after three seconds and the middle area will get congested if the player continues to go into the post area.
- Moving to a vacated spot is important when a player cuts from the top of the key because floor balance is needed for a rebound and defensive transition.
- The top of the key spot needs to be covered by different players. This occurs due to players moving to different spots on the floor in response to defensive movement.

PLAYER DEVELOPMENT CURRICULUM: LEVEL THREE

INTRODUCTORY LEVEL

FOUNDATIONAL LEVEL

ADVANCED LEVEL

PERFORMANCE LEVEL

ADVANCED LEVEL

OFFENSIVE PRINCIPLES: BALL HANDLING & DRIBBLING

GENERAL OVERVIEW: *At the Advanced Level, players will begin to refine and master the skills already learned and progress toward a high level of ball handling and dribbling. While most of the stationary ball-handling drills will not be replicated in a game situation, they allow players to develop a relationship with the basketball and motions become muscle memory, as the basketball has touched the hand in every possible way and angle during training. The stationary ball-handling skills are challenging and will push for mastery in familiarity with the basketball. The dribbling skills on the move will progress toward the application and efficiency of the skill in a game-like situation, in particular, performed under duress.*

SKILL 1

STATIONARY BALL HANDLING: ONE BASKETBALL

It is encouraged to continue working on speed, consistency, efficiency, and overall mastery for the previously introduced ball-handling skills while challenging players with new skills. Repetition is critical in learning how to become an effective ball handler.

DRILL 1: ONE BASKETBALL, ONE TENNIS BALL

Each player will have one basketball and one tennis ball, beginning in a balanced, defensive stance. Staying stationary, the player will work on a ball-handling skill, such as a crossover, while also working with a tennis ball simultaneously.

- Begin with the basketball in the right hand and the tennis ball in the left hand. The rhythm of the drill is easiest to learn as "toss, dribble, catch."
- With the tennis ball in the left hand, the player will toss it in the air to the right-hand side. Immediately after the toss, the player will perform a crossover dribble from the right hand to the left hand. With the vacant right hand, the player will catch the tennis ball, prior to it hitting the floor, with an overhand catch. The player will then continue the drill using the opposite hands.
- When players first learn this drill, they may use multiple dribbles between crossovers. Encourage players to eliminate as many dribbles as possible, eventually working to complete the drill without any extra dribbles. Once players are comfortable with crossover dribbles, challenge them to dribble between the legs in both directions and then behind the back.

 **POINTS OF EMPHASIS**

- Balanced, defensive stance.
- Keep eyes on tennis ball.
- Catch tennis ball overhand.
- Pound dribble.
- Work toward zero extra dribbles.

DRILL 2: SPIDER

The spider dribble is a skill that focuses on improving hand speed and control of the basketball. It begins with the player in a solid defensive stance.

- The pattern of the hands tapping the basketball is as follows: right hand tap in front, left hand tap in front, right hand tap in back, left hand tap in back.
- Ideally, the basketball will remain in the center of the legs, directly below the head, requiring players to sit their rear ends back and maintain a true defensive stance with the head up.
- Once the skill is learned, encourage the increase in hand speed, a low dribble, and head up.
- Coaches can progress players to take slow steps to move forward, backward, and sideways while completing the spider. This continues to teach players the importance of hand positioning on the basketball and to understand the role of motion, as slight as it is in this case.

POINTS OF EMPHASIS

- Solid, low defensive stance.
- Quick hands.
- Basketball maintaining the same location on the floor to gain efficiency.
- Head up.

DRILL 3: PHILADELPHIA

This skill involves coordination, movement, and timing with both hands and feet of the player, simultaneously. For description purposes, the basketball will begin in the right hand.

- The basketball will travel in the following pattern: crossover dribble from right hand to left hand, between the legs dribble from left hand to right hand, behind the back dribble from right hand to left hand, between the legs dribble from left hand to right hand.
- Once the basketball arrives back to the right hand, the pattern repeats. The pattern of the footwork is just as important.
- The right foot will move up and back during the dribble sequences as the ball moves from side to side via crossovers, between the legs and behind the back moves so the player stays in balance.
- Make sure the right foot steps forward to allow for the between the legs dribble each time.

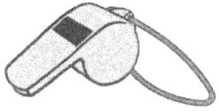

POINTS OF EMPHASIS

- Establish the proper timing first between hands and feet.
- Learn skill first, then gain speed.
- Head up.
- Efficient footwork.
- Sharp dribble lines for speed.

SKILL 2

STATIONARY BALL-HANDLING: TWO BASKETBALLS

Dribbling two basketballs simultaneously can be a fun, challenging way to continue progressing hand-eye coordination and confidence in a ball handler. Begin with a balanced, defensive stance, holding both basketballs. The player will begin dribbling both basketballs at the same time, preferably at waist level. Encourage players to pound the basketball evenly with both hands while keeping the head up.

After working on this skill, coaches can progress players to alternate hands, with one basketball hitting the ground, while the other is at waist level. Again, encourage pounding the basketballs evenly with the head up. Coaches can also have players alternate the height of the basketballs, making the dribbles lower at the ankle level.

Further, coaches can challenge players to dribble one basketball low at ankle level and the other basketball high at waist level. Being able to complete two different skills at the same time is challenging and continues to work on building a solid comfort level with the basketball in the hands.

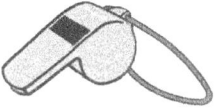

POINTS OF EMPHASIS

- Balanced, defensive stance; no bobbing.
- Pound basketball with finger pads.
- Head up.
- Control of the basketball.

DRILL 1: PENDULUM

Progressing from pendulum dribbles with one basketball, players can begin to move to two basketballs. Turning the hands over is important, while continuing to encourage head up.

- Beginning in the front, players will dribble both basketballs at the same time in the same direction, from knee to knee.
- Once this skill is learned, players can dribble the basketballs at and away from each other in front, with the middle of the body being the meeting point before moving the basketballs away from

each other. Control of the basketball, especially at the midpoint, is critical to assure the basketballs do not collide.
- Next, players can dribble the basketballs in the same direction at the same time along each side of the body in the pendulum motion.
- Finally, alternate the two-side pendulum dribbles so as one basketball travels up, the other travels backward along the side of the body.

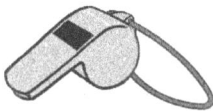

POINTS OF EMPHASIS

- Balanced, defensive stance.
- Pound basketball with finger pads.
- Head up.
- Turn hands over.
- Control skill, then progress for speed.

DRILL 2: FIGURE 8

There are several ways to challenge players using two basketballs in the figure-8 motion. Below are two examples.

PARTNER PASS

- Two players face one another, each holding a basketball, in a balanced, defensive stance.
- Players will each hold the basketball in the right hand and begin the figure-8 motion through the front door, without using a dribble.
- Once the basketball circles back to the right hand, after a full figure-8 shape, both players will pass the basketball from the right knee to the other player's left knee at the same time.
- The players will catch the pass and begin the pattern again, this time starting the figure 8 in the left hand and passing with the left hand to the player's right knee at the same time.
- This requires players to work together to complete the drill, while pushing one another to increase speed.

POINTS OF EMPHASIS

- Balanced, defensive stance.
- No dribbles as the basketball moves in the figure 8.
- Eyes on teammate.
- One-hand pass, straight line to teammate.

FOLLOW THE LEADER

- The player will again begin in a balanced, defensive stance dribbling both basketballs simultaneously. One ball is the leader and the second ball follows the leader's path.
- Beginning through the back door, dribble the first basketball through the legs, with the second basketball following.

- Once both basketballs have cleared one leg, move to the second leg, first with one basketball, following with the second basketball.
- Another variation of the figure 8 keeps one basketball completing the motion around each leg while the other basketball remains in front being dribbled up and down with one hand.
- Again, when first learning the skill it is easiest to begin dribbling through the back door, progressing to the front door.

POINTS OF EMPHASIS

- Balanced, defensive stance; no bobbing.
- Finger pad control.
- Head up.
- Control, then speed.

DRILL 3: BETWEEN THE LEGS

Both of these drills will begin with the player in a comfortable, balanced, shoulder-width stance, with a slight knee bend. It is easiest to begin by learning the skill one hand at a time before dribbling both basketballs at the same time.

ONE DRIBBLE

- With the basketball in the right hand, the player will cup the basketball and bounce the basketball between the legs, going through the back door, catching the basketball in front of the body with the same hand, in this case, the right hand.
- The basketball will stay in the right hand throughout the entire skill. Once the player feels comfortable with the right hand, move to the left hand only.
- The same dribble will be utilized, with the player only using one dribble to circle the basketball around the left leg.
- As players gain confidence using both hands, they can attempt the drill with two basketballs simultaneously, alternating the hand dribbling each time.
- Players can then progress to taking small steps forward and backward, traveling at a slow pace while performing the skill.

POINTS OF EMPHASIS

- Slight knee bend.
- Cup the basketball to bring backward (similar to behind the back dribble).
- Dribble basketball tight to body and directly between the legs.
- Head up.

TWO DRIBBLES

- For this skill, the player will use two dribbles to circle half of the body.
- Beginning with the basketball in the right hand, one dribble will occur next to the right foot, the other between the legs. The hand positioning on the basketball will help create efficient, quick dribbles.
- Again, it is easiest to teach the skill through the back door to begin. Once the right hand has picked up the skill, switch to the left hand.
- After both hands develop a solid comfort level, use both hands simultaneously, but in opposite directions. For example, if the right hand is dribbling the basketball next to the right foot, the left hand is dribbling the basketball between the legs.
- The coach can progress the player to walking forward and backward, after the player becomes comfortable with the stationary position.

POINTS OF EMPHASIS

- Slight knee bend.
- Hand positioning on the basketball depending on the angle of the next dribble.
- Control basketball tight to body.
- Pound basketball.
- Head up.

SKILL 3

DRIBBLING ON THE MOVE: ONE BASKETBALL

Being able to dribble the basketball on the move, in a game-like situation under duress, is critical by the time a player reaches this level. Players who excel at handling the basketball effectively are able to not only complete the skill, but understand why and when to use each dribble. Developing an understanding and awareness of the defender's tendencies, footwork, and ability will help to determine appropriate moves to use and when. When offensive players begin to understand what makes defenders uncomfortable, or what makes an offensive player difficult to defend, they are able to elevate each skill to a higher level. For example, if an offensive player attacks the feet of the defensive player with crossover footwork and body control, chances are the defensive player will shift their momentum in that direction. This will allow the offensive player to make a quick and effective crossover in the opposite direction. Further, if defenders cross their feet on every slide, a change-of-direction move at the exact time the feet cross will be highly effective. These little nuances of the game can transform an average ball handler to be a very good one. Continue developing all of the skills introduced in previous levels with a live defender, both in the full- and half-court setting.

DRILL 1: WARM-UP TEAM DRIBBLING

This particular skill is a good warm-up for a team, working on overall ball-handling skills, in addition to overall court awareness.

- Line half of the players up on the baseline facing a partner who is lined up on the half-court line. Every player has a basketball.

- The players will dribble toward each other in a straight line, meeting face-to-face at the halfway point
- Once players meet, they will perform a change-of-direction move to get past their partner and continue to move back and forth from the baseline to half court and back.
- Players will have to keep their head up in order not to collide with another teammate.
- Have players work on one particular dribbling move or allow players to be creative using several combinations.
- Once the skill is learned, coaches can adjust speed, have players use combination moves, insert coaches to swipe at the basketball as the players dribble by, etc. Be creative!

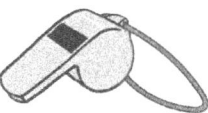

POINTS OF EMPHASIS

- Court awareness—head up.
- Stay low while making moves.
- Make several types of moves, including those which are less comfortable.

DRILL 2: IN-AND-OUT

The in-and-out dribble is a counter move for the crossover dribble. Teaching the in-and-out dribble in a progression seems to produce a more fluid overall move upon completion. Players will straddle a painted line on the court with their feet. The basketball is in right hand and always stays in the same hand.

- Dribble the basketball on the outside (right side) of the line twice, then inside (left side) of the line twice. See the basketball travel over the line.
- Progress to dribbling once on the outside, then once on the inside. See the basketball travel over the line.
- Dribble the basketball once on the outside, see the basketball travel over the line (take out dribble on the inside), dribble again on the outside. This is the in-and-out motion.
- Include the shoulder and head motion as the basketball travels over the line to fake the movement.
- Include a left jab step with shoulder and head motion as the basketball travels over the line.
- Players can then travel up the court, staying on the line, using the proper footwork and shoulder and head motion for in-and-out motion with basketball.
- Move up the court completing dribble without a defender.
- Move up the court completing dribble with a defender.

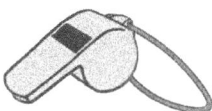

POINTS OF EMPHASIS

- All motions work together: basketball motion, footwork, shoulder and head.
- Basketball tight to body through move.
- Stay low during move; explode out.
- Efficient footwork coming out of move.
- Keep hand on top of the basketball.
- Basketball should travel over the line or the midline of body.

DRILL 3: COMBINATION MOVES

It is appropriate and necessary to begin working on developing a comfort level with dribbling moves used in combination. For example, if a player begins to attack a defensive player by using an in-and-out dribble and the defensive player anticipates the move and jumps to the strong side, denying the move, the offensive player can use a crossover move as a counter. Defensive players will begin to anticipate moves based on personnel or previous possessions; it is important that offensive players adjust appropriately. This can be accomplished through the use of dribbling moves in combination. Begin teaching this by dictating the moves to use in combination, such as in-and-out crossover, between-the-legs hesitation, or crossover behind the back. It is best to get to a point where players are being creative on their own, reacting to the defensive positioning. Set up full- or half-court scenarios and begin with moves without defense and then progress to add live defense.

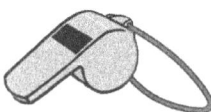 **POINTS OF EMPHASIS**

- React to defense.
- Be patient through moves.
- Head up.
- Low into moves; explode out.
- Basketball tight to body.

SKILL 4

DRIBBLING ON THE MOVE: TWO BASKETBALLS

Dribbling full court with two basketballs on the move is a way to continue challenging players and the overall comfort level of handling the basketball. The more players can progress to a level of comfort where the basketball becomes an extension of the hand, rather than a constant thought in the brain, the better players can react and play in live games. Handling two basketballs at the same time on the move will challenge players to reach this type of comfort level.

DRILL 1: SPEED DRIBBLE

- Sprinting from baseline to baseline, players will speed dribble while dribbling two basketballs simultaneously.
- Begin by having players dribble the two basketballs so they hit the floor at the same time.
- Encourage keeping the head up, even pounding of the basketballs, and speed with the run. Then progress to alternating the dribbles, with one basketball hitting the ground while the other is at waist level.
- Coaches can have players move forward, backward, execute jump stops, pivots, etc. Again, be creative!

POINTS OF EMPHASIS

- Waist-level dribble.
- Control, pound, finger pads with the basketball.
- Head up.
- Speed with control.

DRILL 2: CROSSOVER

- Performing a crossover while handling two basketballs at the same time should be done in a zigzag pattern, similar to performing the crossover with one basketball.
- The side that is working on the crossover should be dribbling closest to the body, to alleviate creating potential bad habits. For example, if moving toward the right, the player should cross over with the right hand, keeping the basketball close to the body.
- The basketball in the left hand performs a lighter version of a crossover, almost leaving the basketball in the middle of the body, on the outside of the other basketball.
- The player will change hands and begin moving in the left direction. The player will then crossover with the left hand, keeping that basketball closest to the body.

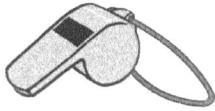

POINTS OF EMPHASIS

- Zigzag motion.
- Control and proper footwork, then speed.
- Crossover side keeps basketball closest to the body.
- Head up.

DRILL 3: BEHIND THE BACK AND BETWEEN THE LEGS

- To complete these two skills using two basketballs simultaneously, the player will move in a zigzag-type motion.
- If moving to the right, the actual skill will be completed by the right hand. For example, if moving to the right, the behind-the-back dribble is executed by the right hand.
- The basketball that is in the left hand will cross between the legs, under the right leg, allowing the player to switch hands and basketballs.
- The player would then proceed toward the left, completing the behind-the-back skill with the left hand.

POINTS OF EMPHASIS

- Zigzag motion.
- Control and proper footwork, then speed.
- Head up.

DRILL 3: DRIBBLING TO PASSING TO A STATIONARY TARGET

- Players will line up on one baseline, each holding two basketballs. A partner will be across from each player on the opposite baseline.
- The ball handlers will work their way toward the opposite baseline, executing two-ball dribbling moves.
- At the opposite free-throw line, the ball handlers will pass one basketball with one hand to the stationary target, while keeping the basketball in the other hand alive.
- Coaches can have players work on various moves down the court, leading to the pass, using both hands.

POINTS OF EMPHASIS

- Zigzag motion.
- Control and proper footwork, then speed.
- Proper passing; keep other basketball alive with the dribble.

DEFENSIVE PRINCIPLES

GENERAL OVERVIEW: *At the Advanced Level, it is appropriate and necessary to continue developing and mastering skills for a player to successfully and efficiently defend the basketball. On-ball defense is critical to learn for personal success, but also because of the importance of the role within a player-to-player team defensive scheme. Players at this level will begin to develop a greater understanding of team defense and how their role directly impacts the other four teammates on the floor. Further, great on-ball defenders begin to study and understand the strengths and weaknesses of the opponent, and constantly adjust and counter accordingly. Taking away an offensive opponent's greatest strength, or being able to dictate a certain direction or movement at a certain time, is a goal at this level. To move from being completely reactive to proactive on the basketball is ideal.*

SKILL 1

CLOSEOUTS: UNDERSTANDING TEAM DEFENSE AND PERSONNEL

Closeouts will begin to take on different forms based on team defense philosophies and individual players being defended.

TOP FOOT (TEAM DEFENSE)

Based on the team defensive philosophy that the middle of the floor is problematic, teams will focus on pushing offensive players and teams toward the baseline, not allowing middle penetration. To execute, the defender's feet must straddle or be fully ahead of the offensive player's top foot during the closeout. Closing out to an offensive player on the top foot makes middle penetration more challenging to the offensive player, influences baseline penetration (into the team's established help), and allows the defensive player to anticipate the first dribble of the ball handler toward the baseline. If the offensive player does attempt to penetrate middle, the defender's footwork slides along the same line toward half court, rather than drop-stepping to allow the middle action. This will likely cause some contact; it is important to take the offensive player on the chest, with both hands up.

Setting up breakdown drills or live play to create and establish this habit is best served from a wing or baseline position, in order to establish one side of the floor.

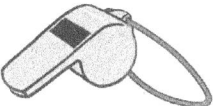

POINTS OF EMPHASIS

- Closeout technique from previous level.
- Footwork leading to body splitting or even closing out to the top foot of the offensive player.
- Force baseline; be careful not to open up with bottom foot, allowing direct drive to basket.
- If offensive player attempts middle penetration, take offensive player on chest and show hands.
- Progress from footwork and technique focus to live play.

SHORT VS. LONG (PERSONNEL)

Understanding offensive personnel can be advantageous to the defender if executed properly. From a closeout standpoint, it is critical to understand if the offensive player receiving the basketball is a shooting threat or if dribble penetration is preferred. If the offensive player is more of a distance shooter, a long closeout is necessary. A long closeout requires the defender to sprint the majority of the distance traveled because arriving on the catch, with a hand up to deter the shot, is critical. As an on-ball defender, you have won if you can chase a three-point shooter off the three-point line by making them use a dribble or pass the basketball. Conversely, if the offensive player prefers to penetrate, a short closeout is more effective. A short closeout is to sprint then close out just short of the offensive player, allowing more of a cushion to contain immediate penetration.

When setting up breakdown drills or live play to illustrate these concepts, put players in situations where they have to think quickly, make a decision, and react accordingly.

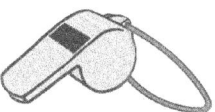

POINTS OF EMPHASIS

- Closeout technique from previous level.
- Long: Chase three-point shooter off three-point line.
- Short: Stop short, allowing cushion to contain.

SKILL 2

PLAYER CONTROL OPPORTUNITIES

There are opportunities to establish position for player control, or better known as taking a charge, all over the court, including while defending on the basketball.

TAKING AWAY MIDDLE PENETRATION

When closing out on the top foot, a great opportunity to take a charge exists if the offensive player chooses to penetrate middle. With the proper footwork, back toward sideline, beating the offensive player to the spot, and establishing position, the defender can draw a player control foul. The defender is creating the opportunity through the positioning on the closeout.

TAKING AWAY TENDENCY

Another great opportunity to take a charge on a ball handler is by taking away a commonly used move for that offensive player. For example, if a player continually uses a left-hand hesitation move in the open court, a high-level defender will make the adjustment, beat the offensive player to the left side, establish planted, solid positioning, absorb the contact, and take a charge.

POINTS OF EMPHASIS

- Beat offensive player to spot and establish planted positioning; no leaning.
- Position body to face offensive player square on.
- Arms low to make sure no pushing off.
- Absorb contact; no flopping.
- Head up on fall.

SKILL 3

FULL-COURT ZIGZAG FOR A PURPOSE

To progress from completing a skill to making it applicable and beneficial for a team, defenders will need a further understanding of the team philosophy and location on the basketball floor. As an on-ball defender, it is beneficial to turn the offensive player as often as possible in the backcourt. The defender can be more aggressive in the backcourt because there is ample time to recover. Once the offensive player crosses half court, push the basketball to one side of the floor or the other, depending on the team defensive philosophy. By establishing a side of the floor with the ball handler, it allows the other four teammates on the floor to anticipate positioning, namely, establishing players on the backside into a help-side position.

Using the previously mentioned zigzag skill, progress to having players complete the zigzag with a defensive purpose; turn the ball handler in the backcourt and establish a side in the frontcourt. This can also be accomplished through live play.

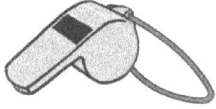

POINTS OF EMPHASIS

- On-ball techniques and concepts introduced previously.

- Backcourt: Turn offensive player as often as possible, create havoc, be more aggressive.
- Frontcourt: Establish one side of the floor; be more disciplined.

SKILL 4

ON-BALL DEFENSE: BASED ON PERSONNEL AND GAME SITUATION

Coaches will never be able to give a player every scenario possible. Players have to figure it out and make quick decisions. Below are some concepts to challenge players to increase basketball IQ while becoming a stronger on-ball defender.

STRONG SIDE VS. WEAK SIDE

Understanding an offensive player's weak hand and effectively pushing that direction can assist the entire team for that possession. It makes the individual player uncomfortable and potentially pushes the offense to a side of the floor not as familiar or prepared. Further, some teams are more effective offensively on a certain side of the floor; an on-ball defender can push the offensive player to the other side.

DISRUPTING OFFENSE

Disrupting a natural flow of an offense by dictating a direction on the ball handler can also make a big impact. For example, if a team runs a 1-4 high set and tends to experience success penetrating baseline, making help side difficult for teams, it would be beneficial to push the offensive player on the wing toward the middle (even though this goes against team defensive concepts) because this is where the help side is located.

IN FOUL TROUBLE

An on-ball defender who does not have any personal fouls will pressure the basketball differently than an on-ball defender with four fouls. If a player is not in foul trouble, the player can pressure more, be more aggressive with the hands, and turn the offensive player more. If the defensive player is in foul trouble, maintain more space, keep the hands visible, create better angles, and take fewer chances.

TIME AND SCORE SITUATIONS

Late in the game, it is important for players to understand the time and score situation. If the team is ahead late in the game, it would be beneficial to shadow the opponent in the backcourt to run time off of the clock, then play contain on-ball defense to avoid scrambling to help on penetration. If a team is down late in the game, it would be beneficial to pressure the basketball all over the court, making the offense make quick decisions and work.

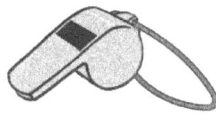

POINTS OF EMPHASIS

- Enable players to make decisions and think about the game of basketball.
- Teach through practice and game situations.

ADVANCED LEVEL
OFFENSIVE PRINCIPLES: FOOTWORK & BODY CONTROL

GENERAL OVERVIEW: *Footwork and body control now involve more game speed action with quick change of directions. This level builds on what was taught in the Introductory and Foundational Levels. This level will continue to emphasize the triple-threat position, from which all offensive moves should be made. From this ready position, the offensive player can perform any offensive skill—shooting, running, passing, dribbling, screening, pivoting, or jumping—in a very efficient manner because the player is ready to move quickly in any direction.*

SKILL 1

PIVOTING

This skill advances the footwork and body control of the pivot for the player.

- Coaches should continue to emphasize proper mechanics and technique of making a pivot turn. This includes ensuring that players maintain proper basketball positioning with the knees bent and hands above the waist, regardless of whether they are completing a front or reverse pivot.
- Players with the basketball may use a pivot to perform a crossover dribble, while players without the basketball may use pivots to make V-cuts in an attempt to get open for a pass.
- Remind players that pivots may be used when they are running or when they are stationary.
- Coaches should begin instructing players on when pivots may be valuable during a game. For example, pivots help players protect the basketball from defenders, make passes to teammates, and move effectively toward the basket.

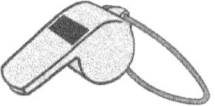 ### POINTS OF EMPHASIS

- Proper basketball position.
- Keep chin up.
- Pivot when running and when stationary.
- Use front and reverse pivots.

SKILL 2

BODY CONTROL WHEN CHANGING DIRECTION OR SPEED

- At this level, coaches should encourage the use of cuts to change direction quickly.

- A cut allows players to create space while still maintaining their balance. This is crucial when players are working to separate themselves from a defender in order to get open for passes or shots.
- To change direction using a cut, plant one foot on the court at the end of a slightly shortened stride. Then, push off of that foot to begin traveling in another direction. Make sure players' knees are slightly bent, and their heads stay over their feet.
- Instruct players to push off of the foot opposite the direction they wish to travel. For example, if players want to cut to the right, they should plant and push off of the left foot. In this scenario, the right foot and both shoulders should be turned to the right.

POINTS OF EMPHASIS

- Keep knees bent and the head over the feet.
- Push off the foot opposite the desired direction.
- Turn shoulders and foot in desired direction.
- Change speed when changing direction.

DEFENSIVE PRINCIPLES

GENERAL OVERVIEW: *At this level, the focus will be on defensive stance as well as body movement. It is important for defenders to be able to slide their feet when guarding opponents while remaining at an arm's-length distance. When opponents are attempting to drive or cut to the basket, the defender should move the leg nearest to the intended direction of travel first, then slide the other foot until the feet are close again. At the end of the movement, the feet should be shoulder width apart.*

SKILL 1

PROPER STANCE

Instructing the proper defensive stance should start at the Introductory Level with continued progression in the Foundational and Advanced Levels.

- Feet should be wider than the shoulders, hands above the waist, chin up with the head in a position that is above the knees and not leaning forward. This will give the defender the ability to move and pivot in all directions.
- When guarding an opponent with the basketball, the defensive player should maintain the defensive stance with one hand down to prevent the crossover dribble and the other hand up to deflect a pass attempt.
- The defender should keep both eyes on the ball handler's midsection.

USA Basketball

POINTS OF EMPHASIS

- The back should be straight with the chin up.
- Feet should be wider than the shoulders.
- One hand low and one hand high.
- Move the leg in the desired direction of travel first.

SKILL 2

360-DEGREE MOVEMENT

On defense, players should stay in basketball position, push off the top foot, slide in the direction the offensive player is moving, and remain an arm's-length distance from the offensive player.

- Many times, the defender needs to guide an offensive player who is dribbling around the basketball court based on the team defensive philosophy or strategy. In this case, the defender's foot positioning will change to try to dictate the offense.
- The player must position the foot closest to the rim ahead of the other foot and remain arm's length from the dribbler. The foot closest to the rim must be inside the dribbler's foot to force a baseline dribble.
- If it is necessary to change direction, defenders should use a drop-step pivot to do so.

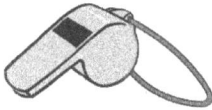

POINTS OF EMPHASIS

- Knees slightly bent with hands above the waist
- Push off the top foot to move in any of 360-degree movements.
- Top foot should be on the inside of the offensive player's foot to force baseline.
- Head must stay over the feet for great balance.

ADVANCED LEVEL
PASSING & RECEIVING
OFFENSIVE PRINCIPLES: PASSING

GENERAL OVERVIEW: *At the Advanced Level, passing and receiving continues to work toward mastery of each skill previously introduced, while transitioning the focus to game application. Further, beginning to gain an understanding of how best to incorporate other skills of the game, such as use of the dribble or pivot to obtain a better passing angle, will elevate the efficiency of the use of the pass.*

SKILL 1

STATIONARY PASSING

Two-ball partner passing is a great warm-up skill for players to continue developing accuracy and confidence in passing. Partners will line up across from one another, each with a basketball, completing a variety of passes.

DRILL 1: SIMULTANEOUS ONE-HAND CHEST AND BOUNCE PASS

- Simultaneously, both players will complete a right-hand chest pass.
- Both players will aim for the left hand of the opposite player to make sure the basketballs do not collide in flight. Accuracy with the placement of the basketball is critical.
- Work to develop a faster tempo once the skill is learned. Make sure to switch hands and also progress to the bounce pass as the players get comfortable with the skill.

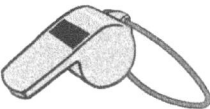 **POINTS OF EMPHASIS**

- Crisp passing.
- Accuracy of location to hit target.

DRILL 2: ALTERNATE TWO-HAND CHEST AND BOUNCE PASS

- Players will simultaneously pass back and forth, one player making a chest pass and the other a bounce pass.
- Designate which line is making each type of pass to start.
- Encourage players to concentrate on crisp passes and location accuracy. Coaches can have players switch pass types on the whistle to make the skill more challenging.

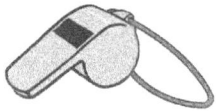 # POINTS OF EMPHASIS

- Crisp passing.
- Accuracy of location to hit target.
- Eyes up.

DRILL 3: ABOVE SHOULDER PASSING

- This skill will help develop ball control using one hand.
- Each player will hold one basketball in the right hand while the arms are both at ninety-degree angles above the shoulders.
- Keeping the basketball at, or just above, shoulder level, both players pass straight across to the partner's left hand, simultaneously.
- The pass should stay on one side only of the body and players will catch the basketball in the air and control it at shoulder level, trying not to drop the arms.
- It is important to deliver the basketball to the teammate at or above shoulder level or the one-hand catch will be quite challenging. Once players learn the skill, encourage them to make the pass on more of a straight line, as players tend to lob this type of pass to begin.

 # POINTS OF EMPHASIS

- Crisp passing.
- Accuracy of location to hit target.
- Gain speed as skill is learned.

SKILL 2

ENTRY PASSING OFF THE DRIBBLE AND AWAY FROM THE DEFENSE

These two skills are important details to learn within the confines of passing in a game situation.

PASSING OFF THE DRIBBLE

This skill is important to learn for all positions, not just the point guard. Players will find themselves in a situation where a teammate is open while the dribble is being used and will need to react immediately before the passing lane is gone. To begin learning this skill, players can pass to one another or use a wall. Have players dribble one time then immediately make a two-hand chest pass, working on a quick transition from dribble to pass. Work on both hands and vary passes to include bounce passes and one-hand passes with the guide hand. Once this is comfortable, put the player in motion, passing to both a stationary and moving target. Finally, although this type of pass should be used only in specialty situations, work on passing off the dribble with one hand without the guide hand. Many times, players find themselves in a position where they cannot get the guide hand to the basketball quickly enough, having to pass the basketball with one hand. With this type of pass, it is important the player adjusts the hand position to be directly behind the basketball to gain strength in the pass but also control of the basketball.

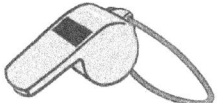

POINTS OF EMPHASIS

- Quick transition from dribble to pass.
- Head up.
- Accuracy hitting target.
- Crisp passes.
- Work on all types of passes off of dribble with two hands and one hand for special situations.

PASSING AWAY FROM THE DEFENSE

Placement of the pass away from the defense is a critical skill to learn. This is especially important when making entry passes, either to perimeter or post players. For a perimeter entry pass, the basketball should be placed in the teammate's outside hand, away from the body. If the basketball is delivered at the chest, the defender will likely be able to get a hand on the basketball. The same concept for post entry passes applies. The basketball should be delivered away from the defensive player, either high or low, depending on positioning and where the teammate gives a target to receive.

This concept can be worked on and reinforced in any drill that includes passing. It can be developed through specific drills, such as entry passing against live defense, or even within the confines of team-centered drills, such as 5-on-0 offensive review. Incorporate everywhere possible to create the habit.

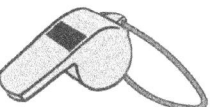

POINTS OF EMPHASIS

- Pass to outside hand of teammate.
- Hit target.
- Place basketball where defender cannot get a deflection.
- In every drill, think about where the defender is likely at and pass away from that spot.

PERIMETER ENTRY

Although there are many types of perimeter entries and passes, the most challenging can be the initial wing entry pass to begin an offense, as the defense can expect this type of pass at that time. If making a perimeter entry pass with access to a live dribble, it is best to use the dribble to take the on-ball defender one way, then quickly change directions, allowing for a passing lane to open. If making the pass from the top of the key to the wing, the player will want to break the plane of the free-throw lane closest to the wing to allow for a short enough pass for a successful completion. Using the two skills previously mentioned will be helpful, passing off the dribble and away from the defender. The most important concept, especially the higher talent level of defenders, is to create a passing lane by changing directions or creating the appropriate space at the right time with the use of the dribble to be able to deliver the pass. Further, timing with the teammate is imperative; one player must be in a position to pass while the other is in a position to receive, simultaneously.

POINTS OF EMPHASIS

- Create a passing lane at the right time.
- Pass off of the dribble with two hands if possible.
- Pass away from defender.
- Crisp passes.

POST ENTRY

Just as with perimeter entry passes, it is important to create the appropriate passing lane at the exact time the post player is ready to receive the basketball. When making a post entry pass, it is typically most useful to fake a pass to make a pass, creating the passing lane. The ball handler can use a quick pass fake high before making a bounce pass post entry or use a low fake to then make a pass in the air. One trick that can be helpful is to make passes by the on-ball defender's ear, as arms naturally raise outside of the body, leaving time for a pass by the ears to travel by before it is possible for arms to be there to deflect the pass. Further, once the passing lane is created, players should deliver the pass when the post player is on balance and ready to receive. The basketball should be placed away from the defender and in some cases lead directly to a score.

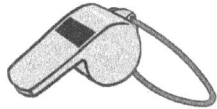

POINTS OF EMPHASIS

- Use ball fakes to create passing lanes.
- Use pivots and step-through to create passing lanes.
- Pass by the ear if delivering high.
- Deliver when post has a balanced seal.
- Pass away from defender; lead to score if possible.
- Crisp passes.
- Hit target.

SKILL 3

USE OF PIVOTS TO CREATE PASSING LANES

The use of pivots can many times be just as effective as use of a dribble or pass fake to create a passing lane. If a player finds they are in need of reversing the basketball, many times a front pivot will provide a controlled way to do that under duress. For explanation purposes, if the player is on the right side of the floor trying to reverse the basketball toward the middle, the player will rip the basketball from the right hip to the left hip, moving the basketball from one side to the other either over the head or below the knees. The left foot will be the pivot foot for the player to complete a front pivot, stepping through with the right foot. This will put the defender on the back of the offensive player, creating a passing lane back toward the middle, for the offensive player to pass with the left hand. One important emphasis: complete a front pivot rather than a reverse pivot as to not turn the back on the basketball floor in case a defensive player jumps in the passing lane.

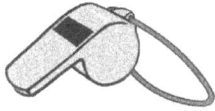

POINTS OF EMPHASIS

- Front pivot.
- Rip the basketball through high or low.
- Use body to create passing lane on step through.
- Pass with outside hand.
- Crisp passes.
- Hit target.

SKILL 3

ZONE PASSING

Passing against a zone can be highly effective in combination with movement, spacing, and use of screens. Quick and efficient passing against a zone can be challenging to defend. Below are a few concepts to consider.

EFFECTIVE PASS FAKES

Defenses are taught to move on the flight of the basketball, making pass fakes effective, especially against zone defenses that fly around on rotations. If used properly, a ball fake will shift the zone one way, allowing for an open passing lane or penetration the other way. On ball reversal, or any time a defender is rotating toward the basketball, a pass fake is effective to keep movement in a certain direction.

PENETRATE AND KICK

Being able to penetrate the gaps of a zone and kick the basketball to an open teammate as a result is a skill needed at this level. An opportune time to penetrate a gap is on ball reversal because the gaps tend to be larger, as the defense is rotating and not completely set. Further, penetrating a gap typically requires two defenders to stop, possibly creating an open opportunity for a teammate, whether on the perimeter or in the post.

GARDEN SPOT

Being able to pass to the garden spot against a zone will open up many sealing and three-point opportunities within a zone offense. If the basketball is either on the right block or the right short corner, the garden spot is the left wing. Typically, when a zone is flattened out or collapsed, the opposite wing is open for a quick skip pass, putting the zone in a tough position. This pass is best served overhead, using a front or a reverse pivot, depending if space is needed to create the passing lane to complete the pass.

UNDERSTANDING TEAM OFFENSE

Understanding and anticipating openings within the team offense will help the player make more advanced passes. For example, understanding when a post player is sealing and where the defender likely will be will help the delivery of the pass from a timing and location standpoint. Further, understanding where and when teammates are cutting will allow a passer to anticipate openings that can be exploited by the pass or dribble. Without this understanding, many players will put teammates in tough situations rather than situations to be able to catch and score. All four of these skills can be drilled in breakdown drills as well as encouraged within the confines of the team offense.

POINTS OF EMPHASIS

- Pass fake to shift the zone.
- Penetrate gaps and kick out to teammates.
- Find the garden spot on opposite wing.
- Anticipate cuts and seals to deliver better passes.

SKILL 5

UNDERSTANDING PERSONNEL AND HOW TO DELIVER PASSES TO TEAMMATES

When delivering a pass to a teammate, it is important to understand the personnel and how a pass will impact a teammate's ability to be effective on the catch.

POST VS. GUARD

Know your players! Understand who is receiving the pass and the offensive strengths of the player upon the catch. For example, it would not be the best situation to pass the basketball to a five-foot-five point guard under the basket with two six-foot-five players defending. Likewise, it can be challenging for a six-foot-five post player to catch the basketball in transition and put the basketball on the floor with two five-foot-five guards approaching. Deliver passes to teammates in a position to experience success upon the catch. For the two examples given, wait for the five-foot-five guard to pop out for a jumper and wait for the six-foot-five post player to seal at the rim. Waiting two extra seconds can get a teammate into a situation that is positive for them, rather than challenging. These concepts can be addressed in skill work (i.e. have a guard wave off a post in an outlet line and instead run the lane), but more than likely will be addressed in live-game action.

SHOOTER'S PASS

The type of pass a shooter receives matters. If the pass is delivered at the knees, or the shooter has to move sideways to catch the basketball, it will impact the mechanics of the shooter. In a perfect world, shooters love to receive the basketball in the shooting pocket, off of a crisp pass in the air, with the laces up. As a passer, strive to make all of these ideals occur every time the basketball is delivered. This can become especially important late in a game, especially when a shooter has to get the shot off quickly. A good pass can help a shooter get the shot off much more quickly.

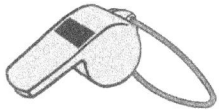

POINTS OF EMPHASIS

- Know your players.
- Deliver the basketball appropriate to position and situation.
- Lead teammates into position to be successful.
- Strive for perfect passes to shooters.

OFFENSIVE PRINCIPLES: RECEIVING

SKILL 1

GIVE UP POSITION TO GAIN POSSESSION

It is important to establish proper positioning to receive the basketball. It is also equally important to understand when one must give up the earned positioning in order to gain possession of the basketball. For example, a post player has established a seal for a high-low look, the teammate passes the basketball behind the player sealing. Is it more beneficial to maintain the seal, or give up the positioning and go grab the basketball? Of course, the post player should give up the positioning to go grab the basketball to maintain possession for the team. This is a fine line and players will need to work through the process of understanding when and when not to give up the positioning earned. The thing to remember is the basketball is the most important thing in the game to possess!

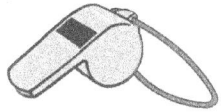

POINTS OF EMPHASIS

- Provide feedback to players in practice and games to get a better feel of decision making.
- The basketball is most important—pursue the basketball over positioning.

SKILL 2

IMPORTANCE OF TARGETS

Coaches constantly encourage players to communicate to one another vocally on the basketball court. When receiving the basketball, providing a hand target is a form of nonverbal communication which can make a difference between a score and a turnover. Both skills should be reinforced in breakdown work and in games. Below are two types of targets to consider.

PERIMETER TARGETS

Providing a target on the perimeter is important to communicate with the passer, so the passer knows where the cut is headed. For example, if a player is simply making a V-cut and would like to receive the basketball on the wing, while making the cut place the outside hand (open) directly out, essentially telling the passer to deliver the basketball to that hand. If that same player is being overplayed by the defender on the wing, making a backdoor cut a great option, the player will cut to the three-point line with a fist (closed) on the outside hand, signaling to the passer a backdoor cut is to follow. This simple nonverbal communication can lead to a wide-open layup, rather than a potential turnover. Lastly, if a perimeter player is making a cut and feels an opening for a shot, give the passer a target with both hands, signaling for the passer to deliver the basketball to the shooting pocket. In combination with this nonverbal cue, it is also good to verbally call for the basketball as well.

POST TARGETS

Providing a target while posting up is important not only for the passer to know where to deliver the basketball but also for the passer to know when the post player is on balance and ready to receive the basketball. If the post player is ready to receive the basketball without the need for an additional pass, provide an open hand where the basketball should be delivered. Depending on the placement of the defense, the delivery may need to be low or high, toward the middle, or toward the baseline. Make sure the positioning is established so the defender cannot get around the post player or get a hand on the pass. If the post has a player sealed on the top side, for example, with the basketball on the wing, do the work early and push the post player up the lane, while pointing to the top of the key and communicating "top" to the passer. Once the basketball is passed to the top, complete the appropriate seal, now using an open hand as the target for basketball placement. Do not be afraid as a post player to guide and direct where the basketball should go by pointing, using an open hand, and verbally communicating to teammates.

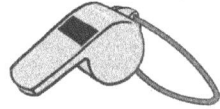

POINTS OF EMPHASIS

- Open-hand and closed-hand signals.
- Shooting pocket.
- High or low.
- Direct entry or reverse basketball for seal (open hand or pointing).
- Verbally call for basketball.

DEFENSIVE PRINCIPLES

GENERAL OVERVIEW: *The majority of the time spent playing defense off of the basketball far exceeds the time spent on the basketball, making denial defense imperative. At the Advanced Level, in addition to continuing to develop more efficient denial skills, progress toward game application while introducing how to defend cuts and transitioning in and out of denial defense to strengthen the collective team defense, ultimately interfering with the flow of the offensive team. Further, in addition to progressing through physical skills, encourage players to communicate throughout the defensive possession.*

SKILL 1

DEFENDING THE BACKDOOR CUT

Depending on the defensive player's strengths, the philosophy of the team defense, and the opposing team's offensive strengths, the following methods may be used to defend the backdoor cut and pass.

OPEN UP

If there is not a concern with the quickness of the offensive player, the ball handler penetrating, or if the preference is for players not to lose sight of the basketball momentarily, coaches should consider opening up as the method of defending the backdoor cut. As effective as this method is, the potential negative to be aware of is the defensive player will lose contact and sight of the offensive player being guarded while opening up. As the offensive player cuts backdoor, the defensive player will slide as far as possible toward the hoop without getting beat. Once the defender is beat backdoor, open up by completing a reverse pivot, seeing the basketball with hands up. Once recovered, assuming the defender remains one pass away from the basketball, return to a denial position, up the line toward the basketball.

FLIP HEAD

If there is a concern about the speed of the offensive player cutting, if the offensive team attempts many backdoor passes, or if the preference is for the defensive player to avoid changing positioning too much, coaches should consider flipping the head to defend the backdoor cut. A potential negative with this method is the defensive player will lose sight of the basketball momentarily, which could lead to the basketball passing the defender or could give the ball handler an opening to penetrate without timely help side from the defender denying. As the offensive player begins the cut backdoor, again, the defender should slide maintaining the proper positioning as long as possible without getting beat. Once the defender feels the offensive player has beat the defender, flip the head from one shoulder to the other, immediately switching the deny hand. Look for the basketball while maintaining contact with the offensive player. Once the defender has established positioning on the bottom side of the offensive player, flip the head and hand to establish proper denial positioning, assuming the basketball remains one pass away.

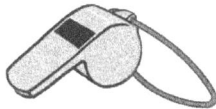 **POINTS OF EMPHASIS**

- Do not open up or flip head if not beaten backdoor. Attempt to maintain proper denial positioning.
- Open up/flip head urgently to look for basketball.
- Arm positioning.
- Once recovered to low side of offensive player, establish proper denial positioning.

SKILL 2

PERIMETER STEAL

Once players begin to learn and execute the correct denial positioning and angles, up the line toward the basketball, the ability to steal the basketball becomes more prevalent. There are many positives that can come with this, along with a possible tendency to get out of position going for a steal. For example, a defender guarding a wing player on the right wing will be in denial position with the right hand leading. The defender may see the pass being thrown from top to wing, causing the player to react if in reach of the pass. If the player maintains a disciplined position and reaches with the correct hand, in this case the right hand, even if the player does not steal the basketball, the defensive player will remain in position to become an immediate on-ball defender. However, if a player reaches with the incorrect hand, or left hand in this case, and the player does not secure the steal, the result is an out-of-position defender (back facing the offensive player) who will not be able to defend a live dribble. Behind the defender, the team will likely face a 5-on-4 situation until that defender can recover. Depending on the team defense strategies for that game or player, this could provide a significant disadvantage for the team. This is a subtle detail that can make a big difference in a game, allowing a denial defender to stay in the play should the basketball not get stolen.

POINTS OF EMPHASIS

- Disciplined in the stance (right hand starts forward, reach with right hand).
- Stay in the play.
- Reminder: If steal is not completed, offensive player is a live ball handler.
- Tip basketball with hand (if complete catch cannot occur), then go get it.

SKILL 3

BUMPING CUTTERS FROM DENIAL

One offensive maneuver that can be troublesome to defend without proper defensive technique is a cut to the basket, especially a face cut on the defensive player. Face cuts occur after a pass is made, as the defender moves from on-ball defense into denial. To prevent the offense from stepping in front of the defender while cutting to the basket, the defender must bump the cutter. Teaching the technique in a progression can be helpful for the player to pick up the skill.

To begin, have the defender play on-ball defense on a wing offensive player. If on the right wing, the right foot should be high, forcing to the right baseline. If the pass is made from the wing to the top of the key, the defender should immediately jump up the line to establish a denial position, with the right hand in the passing lane. Once this positioning is established, have the offensive player take one to two steps toward the pass, simulating an attempted face cut toward the basket. The defender in denial will maintain the same positioning as the denial with the back to the top offensive player, using the bottom arm, in this case the left, to bump the cutter with the arm bar on the offensive player's bottom side. If the player is bumped on the high side, it will open the offensive player up for a backdoor cut. Bumping on the low side will deter this cut and influence a high cut, rather than a backdoor. Once the defender bumps the cutter, the offensive player can retreat to the wing starting the skill over. To progress the skill, the defender will bump the cutter and then stay with the offensive player through the cut. If the cut ends up toward the basket, the player will flip the head, switching the hand used for denial, maintaining the proper denial positioning through the cut. If the cut ends up high, maintain the proper denial originally established, up the line toward the basketball. Once the skill is learned, play live defense against a live offensive player, with the offensive player trying to successfully complete a face cut. Progress the player to a pass from the wing to the baseline, followed by an attempted face cut. This is more challenging because of the on-ball positioning on the top foot of the offensive player. It is critical that the defensive player moves on the flight of the pass, so the denial position is established on the catch, making the bump realistic.

These skills can be learned through breakdown drills, in shell-type drills, and progress to live play. The key is jumping to the basketball and transitioning from on-ball defense to denial defense as quickly as possible. Once the skill is learned, progress players to learn how to bump a cutter from a help-side position. This can be more challenging, as many defenders tend to lose sight of the offensive player while in help side. If the basketball is on the left wing and the defender in help side is defending the offensive player on the right wing, the defender should be in a help-side position at midline. Once the offensive player attempts to make a cut, the right foot should immediately move to a high position, simulating a denial position. Again, the bump should occur with the low arm on the low hip of the offensive player. The same principles of the bump apply. Once the perimeter bump is learned, progress to bumping from the post position using the same principles.

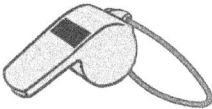

POINTS OF EMPHASIS

- Immediately jump toward basketball on flight of pass.
- Bump with bottom-side arm bar on hip of offensive player.
- Do not allow face cuts.
- After the bump, continue into proper defensive positioning.

SKILL 4

POST DENIAL

Denying the post can be more complicated than perimeter denial, depending on where the basketball is located and where it is headed. Below are several passing options and the resultant steps for proper denial. These skills should be drilled through breakdowns, 2-on-2, 3-on-3, 4-on-4 scenarios, and live play.

For purposes of explanation, the post play described will occur on the right block.

TOP OF KEY TO WING

With the basketball at the top of the key, post denial is similar to perimeter denial in that the post can take a step up the line toward the basketball, making the floor look smaller to the offensive team. The space also allows the defensive player to make future movements more freely than if tangled up with an offensive player attempting to establish positioning. Once the basketball moves to the right wing, on the flight of the basketball, the defender will immediately straddle the offensive player's top foot, establishing a denial position with the right foot and right arm high, deterring an immediate post entry pass. At this time, it is appropriate to establish contact in the post. As much as possible, it is best to deny with the offensive player in the block area and keep the offense in as low of a position as possible. If the defensive player is pushed out too far from the block by the offensive post, a denial position will not benefit the team defense, as the entry pass on a lob or a seal is likely to occur. In this situation, if the post defender is significantly pushed out, let go of positioning and play behind the offense, pushing the offensive player out toward the perimeter.

WING TO BASELINE/BASELINE TO WING—X-STEP

From a proper denial position with the basketball on the wing, many coaches prefer an X-step on the flight from wing to baseline. This strategy allows the post defender to see the basketball the entire time, while maintaining contact with the offensive player. Once the basketball is passed from wing to baseline, the defender will take the bottom foot, left in this situation, and step it out high and around the post offense and toward the sideline. The right foot then steps through and behind to establish a denial position on the low side of the offensive player. The motion of the post defender's steps would make an X, hence the name of the skill. Once the player picks up the skill, work on speed and efficiency along with providing different types of physicality looks from an offensive player. For a pass from baseline to wing, reverse the steps. This type of footwork can nicely coincide with the perimeter defenders opening up on a backdoor cut, if the goal is to keep principles and philosophy similar from position to position for the team defensive strategies.

WING TO BASELINE/BASELINE TO WING—BEAR HUG

From a proper denial position with the basketball on the wing, many coaches prefer a bear hug on the flight from wing to baseline. This strategy allows the defender to maintain contact with the offensive player the entire time, while allowing the defender a possibility of holding a low position for the offensive player. Once the basketball is passed from wing to baseline, the defender will maintain contact and face the offensive player through the entire movement. Ideally, the player will require two defensive slides with the right foot leading to get from high-side to low-side denial position, switching arms and flipping the head halfway through to find the basketball. Once the player picks up the skill, work on speed and efficiency along with providing different types of physicality looks from an offensive player. For a pass from baseline to wing, reverse the steps. This type of footwork can nicely coincide with the perimeter defender's flipping the head on a backdoor cut, if the goal is to keep principles and philosophy similar from position to position for the team defensive strategies.

BASELINE TO TOP OF KEY

With the basketball on the baseline, the post defender will be playing low-side denial defense. If the basketball is skipped to the top of the key, the defender will immediately move low side behind the offensive player to establish a denial position up the line toward the basketball. The reason for moving on the low side is to prevent any type of seal the offensive player would be able to establish if the movements were to be on the high side. In order to travel low side of the offensive player, the defender will take the high foot and X-step through toward the middle with the low foot following to become the high foot. Once the defender has successfully maneuvered around the offensive player, move up the line into proper denial positioning with the basketball located at the top of the key.

 # POINTS OF EMPHASIS

- Up the line if basketball is at top of key.
- Proper footwork.
- Be in position on the catch—urgent movements.
- Proper side based on location of basketball.
- Proper hand high, head on proper shoulder.
- Keep offensive player low—if pushed out, move to behind.

SKILL 5

TRANSITIONING: DENIAL/HELP SIDE

As with all defense, the importance of quick and efficient transitions from one position to the next is critical for team success on the defensive end. For explanation purposes, the defensive player will be defending the offensive player on the right wing.

FROM HELP SIDE TO DENIAL

With the basketball on the left wing, the post defender will be in a help-side position at midline. It is important to close the triangle while in help side so the distance to travel to the defender's player will be shorter. As the basketball is passed from the wing to the top of the key, the defender will throw the right arm and foot forward to create momentum in the direction up the line toward the basketball, rather than toward the offensive player. Up the line is a shorter distance, allowing the defender to be in position more quickly while also being in position to help on any dribble penetration. On the catch, the defender should be in proper denial position.

FROM DENIAL TO HELP SIDE

With the basketball at the top of the key, the post defender will be in proper denial defense. It is important to be up the line in order to arrive in proper help side more quickly. As the basketball is passed to the opposite wing, the defender will swing the right arm and foot, creating momentum toward the midline. Maintain a closed triangle position in help side in order to efficiently rotate to the next position required. The goal is to be in position on the catch.

Both of these transitions can be drilled through 2-on-2 breakdown, shell defense breakdowns, and reinforced through live 5-on-5 play.

POINTS OF EMPHASIS

- Efficient first steps; no negative steps.
- Throw arm and foot to create momentum.
- Stay low through movements.
- Transition to appropriate position location (up the line or closed triangle).

ADVANCED LEVEL

OFFENSIVE PRINCIPLES: REBOUNDING

GENERAL OVERVIEW: *Rebounding, both offensive and defensive, is a fundamental skill that correlates to increased offensive possessions. Possession of the basketball comes more often from missed shots than any other way. More than any other basic basketball skill, the success of offensive rebounding relies largely on players' desire and courage. It is important to teach and understand the angles of missed shots. The offensive rebounder must be careful of charging over the top of the defensive player and must be especially careful about keeping the hands at shoulder height. Using the body with the hands up is not observed or called to the extent that it is when the hands are down.*

SKILL 1

UNDERSTANDING ANGLES OF THE REBOUND

When preparing to rebound a basketball, the offensive player should be in the ready position with hands above the shoulder and knees slightly bent to achieve maximum height on the jump to go after the basketball. When rebounding shots from the side, offensive players should be aware the basketball is likely to rebound to the opposite side of the basket. Players should not watch the basketball in flight, but they should look for an opening on the opposite side so that they can position themselves for the rebound. Offensive rebounding for shots taken from the front will usually rebound straight out from the rim. The same tactics to get the offensive rebound from a side shot will be used to get the rebound from the front.

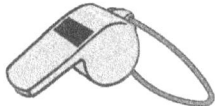 ### POINTS OF EMPHASIS

- Knees bent for maximum height on jump.
- Hands above the shoulders.
- Know where the shot was taken on the court.
- Move to the correct angle for a rebound.
- Work to time the jump as the basketball comes off the rim.

SKILL 2

MOVEMENT FOR OFFENSIVE REBOUNDS

Movement for offensive rebounds is a key to getting the basketball from missed shots. The offensive player can get into offensive rebound position by taking a V-cut toward the baseline in order to get inside position on the defender. The player can also use a pivot to make a spin move or a swim move to go around the defender for an offensive rebound. A step-through, or a crossover move, to the side of the defensive rebounder is another method to get around the defender for an offensive rebound. The key for any offensive rebounder is the ability to move as the shot is taken so the defender has a difficult time locating the offensive rebounder.

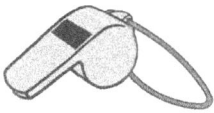

POINTS OF EMPHASIS

- Movement as the shot is taken is key to rebounding.
- Make a V-cut toward the baseline in order to get inside position on the defender.
- A swim move is made with the inside arm moving over the top of the defender to get inside position.
- When contact is made by the defender on the offensive player, a 360-degree pivot can be used to spin off and gain an advantage.

DEFENSIVE PRINCIPLES

GENERAL OVERVIEW: *As players get stronger, it is important for the defensive player to perform three main areas of defensive rebounding to aid them in boxing out the offensive player. First, get the players to assume every shot will be missed and aggressively rebound their area. Players need to understand that repeated efforts are extremely important to obtain possession. Second, get players to automatically bring their hands to shoulder height with the fingers pointed to the ceiling and palms facing the basket as soon as the shot is attempted. Third, get the defensive players to play the basketball rather than the opponent when the shot is attempted. The main concentration should be on getting the rebound rather than keeping the opponent from getting it. This is considered positive rebounding rather than negative rebounding.*

SKILL 1

FACE-TO-FACE DEFENSIVE REBOUNDING

There are times when the defense will play against a very skilled and aggressive offensive rebounder. The traditional boxout method may not work against this type of offensive rebounder. If this is the case, rather than being concerned with the defender getting the rebound, place emphasis on the offensive player not being able to get to the missed shot. A Dennis Rodman type of rebounder needs more than a boxout to keep from getting the offensive rebound. A face-to-face defensive boxout may be used on this type of rebounder. As the shot goes up, the defender will not pivot but will face the offensive player at all times during the flight of the basketball to keep the offensive player from getting the rebound. The defender does not watch the flight of the basketball, but only the offensive player being face-guarded to prevent this player from getting the basketball.

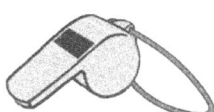

POINTS OF EMPHASIS

- The first movement is to see where the offensive player is on the court.
- Instead of making a pivot, face-guard the opponent as the shot occurs.
- Do not let the opponent get to the missed shot.
- Stay low in basketball position.

SKILL 2

HELP-SIDE BLOCKOUTS

Help-side blockouts are more difficult to execute. The defensive rebounder must have a greater awareness about where the shot is taken and the location of the opponent. From the help-side position, when the basketball is shot by the offense, the help-side defenders are typically positioned in the lane area. The first movement by the help-side defense is to attack opponents outside the lane area. If the shot is taken from the three-point line, the rebound will likely be long on the opposite side of where the shot was taken. This means help-side defenders must go outside the lane to make contact, using a pivot to keep the weak-side offensive players from getting the rebound.

POINTS OF EMPHASIS

- Be aware of player positioning when the shot goes up.
- Weak-side defenders in the lane must step outside of the lane to make contact with the offensive players.
- Know where the shot was taken to predict the rebound location of the missed shot.
- Stay in great basketball position when meeting offensive players to box them out.

SKILL 3

BLOCKING OUT IN ROTATION

There are situations in games where the defensive players must rotate to stop an offensive player from driving to the basket, such as to double-team a strong penetrator or to pick up a player who has beat the on-ball defender off the dribble. When this type of rotation occurs, the defenders must rotate to the basketball, which may cause the defenders to box out someone other than the player they were originally guarding. For example, if the basketball is driven to the baseline and beats the defender, the help-side wing must move over to stop the driver. In a normal defensive rotation, this would be a guard dropping into the lane area and covering the helper's player. By doing so, this guard could be blocking out a player stronger and bigger. In these mismatch situations, teach players to stay low on the blockout and work on perfect boxout positioning, which may draw an offensive foul such as an over-the-back violation. Players should still aggressively go after the basketball and try to keep the offense outside of the lane.

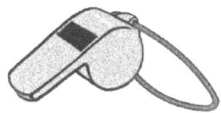

POINTS OF EMPHASIS

- Be aware of the player who needs to be blocked out as the defensive rotation takes place.
- Stay low to block out a bigger opponent in the rotation.
- Make contact outside the lane if possible.
- Be aggressive in going for the missed shot with the hands above the shoulders.

SKILL 4

DISADVANTAGE BLOCKING OUT

At the Advanced Level, disadvantage blockouts need to be addressed as this happens at times during the game. Disadvantage blockouts occur when there are more offensive players to box out than just the one player being guarded. This may happen due to scramble defense, defensive rotations, double-teams, or missed defensive assignments. At this level, it is crucial for players to know their opponents and understand who the best rebounders are as well as having a good grasp on the angles the shot may come off of the rim. If the defender is in a disadvantage situation, block out the offensive player closest to where the basketball may come off the rim on a miss. At the very least, make sure to block out one offensive player when at a disadvantage.

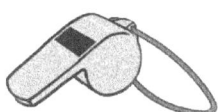

POINTS OF EMPHASIS

- Be aware of where the shot is taken.
- Box out the offensive player where the basketball will most likely be missed.
- Box out at least one of the offensive players.
- Stay low and go get the basketball off the miss after the boxout.

ADVANCED LEVEL

OFFENSIVE PRINCIPLES: SCREENING

GENERAL OVERVIEW: *Screening for the Advanced Level expands to setting screens on the basketball as well as off the basketball. The main purpose of the screen is to get a teammate open for a shot or at very least a pass. A screen also will make the defenders make a decision on how to defend the pick and roll and the off-ball screen. By creating indecision, the offensive players can take advantage of the defenders to score.*

SKILL 1

SETTING AND USING OFF-BALL SCREENS BASED ON THE DEFENSE

Setting and using screens is influenced by the defenders.

- The screener must be alert to where the defenders are located when seeking out the defender to screen.
- The screener should try to make contact with the defender as the screen is set, making it difficult for the defender to get over the screen. Too much room on the screen will allow the defender to get over the top.
- When using the screen, the offensive player needs to stay low with the shoulder clipping the hip of the screener.
- Before using the screen, the offensive player needs to set up the defender by taking a step in the opposite direction of the cut off of the screen.
- The screener should run to set the screen to make it difficult for the defender on the screener to switch or hedge.
- The offensive player using the screen should not watch the basketball but keep an eye on the defender, which will determine the cut to perform.
- When using the screen, the offensive player will curl-cut if the defender tries to go over the top of the screen. The screener will then step to the basketball.
- If the defender does not allow the curl cut, the offense will reject the screen and make a basket cut.
- The straight cut occurs when the screen is set for the offensive player to cut to the wing to receive a pass. This most often occurs as a down screen.
- A flare cut is used if the defender is on the ball side of the screen, which will allow the offensive player to flare back out and not use the screen.

 **POINTS OF EMPHASIS**

- The screener must seek out the defender to screen and make contact on the screen.
- Offensive player must not watch the basketball but watch the defender so the proper cut is made off the screen.
- Stay low coming off the screen, shoulder to hip.
- Hands ready to catch the pass off the screen.

SKILL 2

TECHNIQUES OF USING ON-BALL SCREENS

Screens on the basketball will take a much different look than off-ball screens for both the screener and the ball handler.

- The screener should run to set the screen on the basketball so the defender on the screener has a difficult time to hedge or double-team on the screen.
- Set a screen with the knees slightly bent, feet wider than the shoulders, elbows inside the body, and head and chin up.
- The screener needs to make contact with the defender guarding the basketball. This will allow the dribbler to run the on-ball defender into the screen with more ease and create indecision as to how to guard the screen and roll.
- The dribbler should stay low while dribbling off the screen with the shoulders clipping the hip of the screener. This will help the dribbler rise into a shot if open off the screen.
- The head and eyes should be looking at the basket in order to see any cutters open as well as the screener rolling to the basket.
- The dribbler will take two dribbles after using the screen. This allows the dribbler to create separation from the defender being screened.
- The dribbler will try to square the shoulders and turn to face the basket to be squared away for a shot or a pass to the screener.
- As soon as the dribbler clears the screener, the screener will pivot to open up to the dribbler and roll to the basket looking for a pass.
- Most of the time the bounce pass will be the choice for the dribbler to get the basketball to the screener.

 ## POINTS OF EMPHASIS

- Dribbler takes two dribbles past the screener for proper spacing.
- Head and shoulders must be turned to the basket.
- The dribbler should look to make a bounce pass to the screener on the roll.
- The dribbler must stay low, shoulder to hip.

SKILL 3

SPACING OF PLAYERS

The spacing of the players not involved in the screen is crucial to good team offense. The spacing creates open shots or drives to the basket.

- The most important concept about spacing is that the offensive players should be twelve to fifteen feet apart to alleviate double-teams and defensive help.
- As the dribbler comes off the screen, the next player closest to the dribbler must create space so that if the defender slides over to help on the drive, that player will be open for a shot.
- It is best to have one offensive player in each corner properly spaced from the basketball, again, to take away the possibilities of a double-team.
- The dribbler must know where the players are located on the court during the drive off the screen.
- Any players cutting through the middle of the court during the screen and roll action must clear out quickly for the screener on the roll to the basket.
- If the dribbler drives to the baseline, the offensive team must move to fill two specific spots for a possible pass: in the middle of the lane and the opposite baseline.
- Remind players that spacing is an offense.

POINTS OF EMPHASIS

- All players must be twelve to fifteen feet from the screener and dribbler.
- When a defender helps on the dribble penetration, the offense should get feet set to be ready to catch the basketball and shoot.
- On-ball screens will create help from defenders not guarding the basketball or the screener, so the offensive players must have an awareness of what the defense must do.
- Offensive players should be on each baseline to stretch the defense.

DEFENSIVE PRINCIPLES

GENERAL OVERVIEW: *Defending screens creates indecision for the defenders, as there are several ways to defend the screen depending on personnel. The burden of responsibility in defending the various types of screens is upon the defender guarding the screener. However, every defender must be aware of the possibility of oncoming screens and offensive positioning to identify scoring threats.*

SKILL 1

DEFENDING OFF-BALL SCREENS

The key term for defending off-ball screens is awareness. Defenders should always be aware of the possibility that they could be screened.

- The player guarding the screener must always clearly warn teammates of a potential screen.
- The defender who is in a vulnerable position to be screened should feel with one hand toward the direction from which a screener is most likely to come.
- Defenders must always be in help-side position so that the screen cannot be easily made on the defender.

- Defenders have the option to go under the screen. In this case, the defender on the screener must step back to create a window or gap for the defender being screened to go through.
- The defender may decide to follow, or chase, the offensive player around the screen. When this happens the defender on the screener must step up to take away the curl cut.
- A switch may take place between the two defenders—the one guarding the screener and the one guarding the player using the screen. Both players will need to communicate the switch with the first player who sees the necessity of the switch, calling it loudly and clearly.
- The defender guarding the screener may also jam up the screener so the defender on the offensive player can go under both the screener and the defender. The jam also prevents the screener from rolling to the basketball.

POINTS OF EMPHASIS

- If the defenders are in proper help-side defensive position, screens are much more difficult to execute.
- Communication is the key for both defenders. The defender on the screener must call out that a screen may occur.
- Be aware of the possibility that screens can occur at any time, especially when the offense goes away from the basketball.
- The defenders need to stay in a basketball position to be ready to move quickly and avoid the screen.

SKILL 2

DEFENDING ON-BALL SCREENS

When defending an on-ball screen, communication by the defender guarding the screener should let the teammate know of the screen approaching. The defender guarding the basketball then can have an awareness where the screen is coming from and can make adjustments to guard the basketball.

- A switch with the defenders is one method to defend the on-ball screen. The defender on the screener will call out "screen" and communicate the switch. The switch should take place as the dribbler comes off the screen so the dribbler cannot turn the corner to the basket. The defender who switches to the screener should try to get on the basketball side of the screener to defend a pass.
- The defender guarding the screener may also step back to create a gap or a window for the defender on the basketball to go through under the screener. The player on the dribbler will continue to defend the dribbler through the gap or window.
- The on-ball defender at times may need to get over the top to defend a dribbler who is a good shooter. The defender will get the lead foot on top of the screener and bring the rear in so the defender can slip by the screener to stay with the dribbler. The defender on the screener can help this by stepping up to jab at the dribbler.
- A trap may occur as the dribbler uses the screen by the two defenders. The defender on the screener will quickly jump up in front of the dribbler, and then form a trap with the dribbler's defender. Both defenders must get their hands up and move their feet to set a good, tight trap.

- One way to slow the dribbler or prevent a direct drive to the basket is to hedge. A hedge is when the screener's defender steps up hard in front of the dribbler, blocking the path to attack off the screen. This will not allow the dribbler to turn the corner to the basket. As the hedge occurs, the defender on the dribbler will fight through the screen to regain position on the dribbler. Once back in position, the hedge defender will then go back to cover the screener.
- The final method to guard the screen and roll is to jam up the screener by the defender. In this case, the defender on the dribbler goes under both the screener and the jamming defender to meet the dribbler after the screen has been used. The defender on the screener must keep hands high to discourage a shot by the dribbler from behind the screen.

 **POINTS OF EMPHASIS**

- The defender on the screener must communicate to teammates that a screen is coming.
- When a switch occurs, the defenders must stay with the offensive players until they have an opportunity to switch back to original players.
- On a hedge, the defender on the screener should jump out to block the dribbler and then slide back to the screener after the teammate catches up to the dribbler.
- The defenders not guarding the screener or the dribbler must be aware of the screen action and be in help position to create great team defense.
- The defenders must not have indecision as to how to cover the screener and the dribbler.

ADVANCED LEVEL

OFFENSIVE PRINCIPLES: SHOOTING

GENERAL OVERVIEW: *Advanced Level shooting involves shots off the dribble, off the pass, and through contact. This level will continue to emphasize the correct skills and mechanics necessary for a solid fundamental shot, which is important to developing players' shooting consistency.*

SKILL 1

LAYUPS: FINGER ROLL

Building off of the overhand layups outlined in the Foundational Level, the next progression is a finger roll, or underhand layup. This type of layup allows players to extend beyond or under a defensive player's reach. It also offers a quicker and softer release, which increases the potential for the basketball to spin off of the backboard more easily.

Different types of finishes help players be more creative in the lane.

- To begin learning the underhand layup, repeat the same mechanics and footwork of the overhand layup. The only difference is how the basketball comes off of the hand.
- The player will extend upward with the basketball in both hands, with the shooting hand underneath the basketball.
- As the player extends the arm, the basketball will roll off of the fingertips, with the palm of the hand remaining upward and the fingers extending toward the square on the backboard.
- Much like a follow-through for a jump shot, the basketball will last touch the middle finger on its way to the basket.
- The player will develop a feel for how the basketball comes off of the hand and what type of spin the backboard requires, depending on the angle of the layup being shot. Once the player gets comfortable with the strong side (shooting hand), move to the weak side.

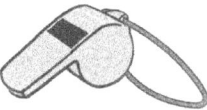 ### POINTS OF EMPHASIS

- Same footwork and mechanics as overhand layup.
- Extend shooting arm (do not short arm).
- Follow-through with palm facing upward.
- Learn needed spin on backboard based on angle of layup.

SKILL 2

LAYUPS: REVERSE LAYUP

A reverse layup is similar to the underhand layup. The difference is the angle of the approach from underneath the rim. Typically, this type of layup is used when a defender is coming from behind. The reverse layup allows the offensive player to cut the defensive player off and extend beyond the defense while using the rim as a means of protection.

- There are two ways to complete a reverse layup: one with the back facing the middle of the court, and the second with the back facing the baseline.
- The preferred method is with the back facing the middle of the court, as this allows the offensive player to protect the basketball with the body. Regardless, it is best to learn both methods to be able to apply either based on a game situation.
- The footwork of a reverse layup is the same, with two steps taken prior to the shot.
- Both the arm and the knee on the shooting side of the body will rise at the same time.
- The shot itself will most likely be shot underhand, with the proper spin placed on the basketball so that it spins back toward the rim once it hits the backboard. The spin is critical from this angle to be able to make the layup.
- If the player's back remains facing toward the middle of the floor, the player should use this positioning to protect the basketball and create space. This will help get the layup off by extending the arms outward and away from the body.
- If the back is facing the baseline, the principles remain the same; the difference is the spin on the basketball. In this instance, the player will need to put the appropriate spin on the basketball such that it bounces back toward the rim.

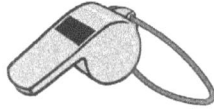

POINTS OF EMPHASIS

- Proper footwork and mechanics of a layup.
- Underhand layup.
- Develop understanding of appropriate spin direction.
- Extend arm fully.
- Use body when able for protection.

DRILL 1: LAYUPS—THREE-WAY MIKAN

The Mikan drill, named after Hall of Famer George Mikan, is a continuation drill that works on the footwork and different types of finishes under the basket. The drill involves continuous, alternating shots on each side of the rim. To define the drill duration, coaches may do one of the following:

- Put a time limit on the drill.
- Limit the number of shots players can take.
- Provide a target number of made shots for each player to reach.

The different types of finishes include:

- Overhand layup (tight, from shoulder)—back facing middle of court.

- Overhead layup (out wide, away from shoulder; similar to baby hook)—back facing middle of court.
- Underhand layup (out wide, away from shoulder)—back facing baseline.

The footwork remains the same with the knee and shooting hand rising simultaneously as the player alternates shots from the left and right side.

- As the player learns the continuous footwork, the key to increasing speed is to get the feet moving while the basketball is coming through the net.
- If the feet are already moving once the basketball is caught through the net, the next layup can be shot immediately.
- Also, it is important to keep the basketball high through the entire drill, never bringing it down. This helps to increase speed and to create a habit of keeping the basketball high on layups.
- The player can be challenged within the confines of this drill by increasing goals for number of made shots in a certain amount of time based on the player's ability and the type of finish. It is important that the player works to master all types of finishes, because any one of them may be needed during the course of a game.

 **POINTS OF EMPHASIS**

- Proper, quick, efficient footwork.
- Jump up, not out; control momentum and body.
- Move while basketball is in air for speed.
- Correct type of finish with proper spin.
- Extended arm.
- Finish off of backboard.

SKILL 3

LAYUPS: FINISHING WITH CONTACT

During the course of a game, the likelihood of shooting an uncontested layup decreases as the level of play increases. Therefore, it is imperative to learn how to finish layups while receiving contact from a defender.

- One of the safest and easiest ways to begin learning this is to have a coach hold a blocking pad to apply the contact. Be careful to apply the contact on the shoulders and body rather than the knee area or the head area.
- Many players are visual learners, making the use of lines painted on the basketball floor invaluable. With this thought in mind, begin teaching players how to use their body against contact by using the free-throw lane.
- Start the player at the elbow. Have the player take two dribbles down the lane line toward the rim.
- Once the player gets to the block, the player will change direction and move directly toward the rim instead of toward the baseline. This will create a ninety-degree angle.
- At the moment the player changes directions, the player will plant the outside foot and push off of that foot toward the rim, allowing the direction change off of two feet.
- The shoulders should stay parallel to the baseline, allowing the player to lead with the shoulder so the body is protecting the basketball from the defender.

- The leading shoulder will absorb the contact, which leaves the basketball on the outside shoulder and creates space to execute the overhand layup.
- During a game, if a defender takes the shooter's inside hand away, ideally the shooting player will still be able to finish the layup using the outside hand. This is how many players are able to finish the layup while being fouled, sending them to the free-throw line.
- Develop the ability to finish on both sides of the court while absorbing contact.
- Mix up the timing of when the player experiences the contact and from which angle, again, being careful to stay away from the head and knee areas. Also challenge the player to finish from different angles using different types of finishes.
- Ideally, a player will develop a love for contact and an ability to finish regardless of whether foul calls are made.
- It is important for the player to finish through, but not anticipate the contact. Being able to maintain momentum, body control, and proper footwork will help a player develop in this area.

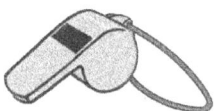

POINTS OF EMPHASIS

- A coach should hold the pad for safety.
- Use body to absorb contact; keep basketball away from defender.
- Finish on outside of body; extend arm.
- Take off of two feet; change direction to absorb contact.
- Don't anticipate contact; be able to finish if not hit.
- Embrace contact.

SKILL 4

SHOOTING OFF THE DRIBBLE: HOP

The hop can be more challenging for players than a one-two step pattern due to the difficulty in controlling momentum. However, if learned and implemented properly, the footwork can allow a player to get a shot off more quickly by using the hop.

- For ease of learning, begin with players at the top of the key. Players will take one dribble toward the elbow of the shooting hand and end on a subtle two-foot hop, landing square to the rim.
- From this squared, low position, the player will rise up tall into the shot as outlined throughout previous levels.
- It is critical that the player remains low through the hop and is ready to rise directly up immediately so there is not any wasted motion to decrease strength.
- It is also important to control the momentum of the movement, landing at or just in front of where the player took off for the shot.
- The player should not fade to either side or fade backward. This will take strength and accuracy away from the shooter.
- Once the player is comfortable with the footwork dribbling toward the shooting hand, introduce the weak hand. Again, the player will need to get the basketball from the weak hand to the shooting hand without a crossover dribble.
- A hard, powerful dribble right before the basketball is picked up will help transfer the basketball from the weak hand to the shooting hand, quickly through the air close to the body. This transfer

may need to be practiced before adding the footwork, and then put the remaining concepts together.
- To continue challenging the player, have the player penetrate from more difficult angles, requiring a concentrated square up to the rim. Vary distances and number of dribbles used. Be creative in developing this skill once the player becomes comfortable.

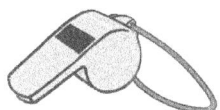

POINTS OF EMPHASIS

- Square to rim.
- Control momentum.
- Get basketball from dribble to shooting hand quickly and efficiently.
- Land hop positioned low and ready to rise.
- Reinforce proper shooting mechanics from start to finish.

SKILL 5

SHOOTING OFF THE DRIBBLE: ONE-TWO STEP PATTERN (HALF COURT VS. OPEN FLOOR)

Once the skills are developed for shooting a jump shot off of the inside foot or one-two step pattern, it is important to understand the difference between using this skill in the open floor, like in transition, as opposed to in the half court when players are being heavily pressured by the defense. How the skill is used in these situations varies greatly, and thus should be practiced differently.

OPEN COURT

- When in an open-court situation, the player will most likely be utilizing a speed dribble, or sprinting the wing to receive a pass in transition, for example. The speed with which the player will be approaching the jump shot off the dribble is fast in this environment.
- When in this situation, the player will need to corral the energy moving forward and transition it to an upward motion to elevate into the jump shot. This momentum change is drastic and should be drilled at full speed to simulate game speed.
- The placement of the basketball does not necessarily have to be as precise since the player is in the open court, but it certainly should be under control and moved quickly from the dribble to the shooting hand. Be quick with the feet, but not quick with the shot. Encourage players to finish tall.

POINTS OF EMPHASIS

- Practice at full, game-like speed.
- Control speed and momentum of movement.
- Quick with feet, not with shot.

- Finish tall.
- Reinforce proper shooting mechanics from start to finish.

HALF COURT

- When being pressured in the half court, the one-two step into a jump shot is a very different approach. The important concept is that offensive players will need to force defensive players onto their heels, allowing for an opening to take a jump shot with an immediate stop and pullup.
- The offensive player will force this type of reaction from a defensive player with a strong, quick, convincing dribble (or two) at the rim, getting the defensive player to react to this urgent penetration with a retreat, drop step, or slide.
- Once this has occurred, the offensive player has the advantage if the rest of the jump shot is completed correctly. In addition to this urgent dribble, the offensive player will want to be in a lower position than in the open court, almost placing the inside shoulder into the belly of the defensive player. (Please note this is for visual purposes only; players should not shoulder defenders.)
- At this point in time, with the natural inside foot (one-two step pattern) footwork and a quick rise, the offensive player will be able to get the jump shot off before the defensive player can recover.
- The footwork has to be natural and quick. The basketball will need to transfer from the outside of the body on the dribble quickly and efficiently to the shooting pocket and immediately rise up into the shot, finishing tall.
- Work on different angles and number of dribbles against various types of defenders to help the player develop an understanding of how to use the dribble when being pressured to create an opening for a jump shot.

POINTS OF EMPHASIS

- Urgent dribble to rim; make it believable.
- Low, forceful body movements on penetration.
- Force defender to retreat.
- Natural, efficient inside foot (quick feet, not quick shot).
- Protect basketball on outside of body.
- Get basketball from dribble to shooting hand quickly and efficiently.
- Rise up tall.
- Control momentum.
- Reinforce proper shooting mechanics from start to finish.

SKILL 6

PERIMETER: THREE-POINT SHOOTING

In addition to developing an attacking game off the dribble as a perimeter player, it is important to begin working on extending consistency from the three-point line in order to create a well-rounded offensive threat that is challenging to defend. As the player begins working on extending range, it is important not to jeopardize proper shooting mechanics just to shoot farther back. With the use of the legs in conjunction with the upper body, it is possible to extend range without altering mechanics, especially at this level.

- The important concept when moving farther back to shoot is using the legs more in the shot. If there were a video taken of the player shooting from both the free-throw line and from behind the three-point line, the only difference that should be seen is that the legs will be utilized more from behind the three-point line.
- Because of the importance of the legs, it is critical to receive the basketball low and ready to rise into the shot immediately. Being squared up and having the entire body working together to provide the needed strength for a three-point shot is critical.
- It is best to begin learning the skill of the three-point shot by remaining stationary. Begin to develop the skill without having to deal with momentum and movement.
- Once this becomes comfortable from all areas on the floor, begin working on catching the basketball off of a pass, while moving into the three-point shot.
- It is best to begin with a one-two step before moving to a hop, due to ease of controlling the movement.
- Progress players to shooting three-point shots off of the dribble, beginning with a one-two step, then moving to a hop.
- It is also worth noting that a true three-point shooter should also work on consistency and range beyond the actual three-point line painted on the floor. Extend the range beyond so that if the player catches the basketball one step off of the three-point line in a game, there is no thought or a need to take one dribble to get the shot off.
- Extending beyond the three-point line will allow for more flexibility in a fluid game situation.
- Lastly, as a player improves with all of the above concepts, it is also important as a coach to have the player practice shooting under duress. Use of a broom to contest and distract the shooter can help create a sense of extraordinary focus. Do not block the shot but use the broom to create a more challenging look than what the player will see in a game.
- Continue to challenge the player to make more shots each time. Be creative with how these challenges are placed on the player. Vary distance, how the pass is received, types of cuts, and angles.

POINTS OF EMPHASIS

- Do not jeopardize proper shooting mechanics for distance.
- Increase use of legs.
- Begin stationary, then off a pass, then off a dribble.
- Extend consistency in range beyond three-point line.
- Contest shots as players improve.

SKILL 7

PERIMETER: SHOOTING OFF OF SCREENS

Anytime players are using screens, they should be thinking and preparing for a scoring opportunity upon receipt of the basketball. The player should set the defender up and use the screen as discussed in the Screening section.

- At the point of the screen, the player should note where the defender is in order to understand the proper cut and footwork needed to execute a shot. Once the cut is determined, the preparation leading up to the shot is critical for a shooter.
- An explosive cut out of the screen is important, but so is the angle with which it is executed. This allows for the spacing to execute a shot.
- As the player is approaching the basketball, step into the path of the potential defender, cutting the defender off. Use a one-two step pattern, or inside foot, to create space and momentum toward the rim in order to shoot a strong, balanced shot.
- In addition to taking the proper angle and using efficient footwork, it is critical to communicate with the passer verbally and physically. Players may use a hand target to indicate where they desire to receive the basketball.
- With talented defenders, this can mean the difference between getting a shot off or not. As the basketball is delivered, efficient and quick footwork will be important to lead directly into the jump shot.
- It is important to have players practice this at full speed. Remind them to pay attention to details, especially how the screen is being used, which cut to use based on the defender's position, the communication made with the passer, and the proper footwork leading into the shot off of the pass.

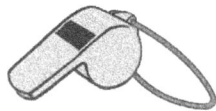

POINTS OF EMPHASIS

- At point of screen, read cut that should be made based on defense.
- Communicate with passer.
- Prepare on approach with target and proper angle and footwork.
- Rise immediately into jump shot.
- Reinforce all shooting mechanics previously outlined.
- Game-speed cuts, approach, and shot.

DRILL 1: PERIMETER—SHOOTING OFF OF FLARE SCREENS

The footwork and approach off of a flare screen is much different than the cuts outlined above.

- As the shooter approaches the screener, the defender jumps the screen or slides underneath in anticipation of a straight cut. The shooter will immediately change directions, in many cases moving directly backward or at a slightly different angle.
- Typically, at this point, the momentum of the shooter is heading in the complete opposite direction of the basket, making this type of cut and shot one of the most difficult for a player to be consistent with.
- The player needs to understand on a flare that the momentum is headed in the opposite direction, making the catch and the footwork imperative.
- As the basketball is received, players will need to gather their feet underneath them, stopping the backward fading motion, and redirecting the momentum toward the rim.
- It is easiest to learn by using a one-two step to maintain a low position as the basketball is received. In this case, it can take longer to execute a shot using a one-two step because of the awkward angle of a flare. This makes a hop a good option, but again, the importance of directing the momentum positively toward the rim needs to be developed.
- Develop this at game speed and from various angles and directions on the floor.

POINTS OF EMPHASIS

- At point of screen, read cut that should be made based on defender.
- Communicate with passer.
- Provide target for passer to hit.
- Redirect momentum toward rim to gain strength to complete shot.
- Learn one-two step and hop; catch low in order to gather properly.
- Reinforce proper shooting mechanics from beginning to end.

SKILL 8

POST PLAYERS: SHOOTING OFF A PASS

It is important for a post player to develop a dual threat offensively to make the player more challenging to defend. Common outside shots that post players get in game situations include those from the high post and from the short corner, especially against zone defenses. It is valuable for a post player to learn several different types of footwork on the square up.

ONE-TWO STEP/INSIDE FOOT

- Just as with perimeter play, posts can utilize the inside foot or one-two step footwork to square up, allowing all of the strength and momentum of the shot to naturally head toward the rim.
- A post player would execute the inside footwork the same as outlined in previous sections.
- If there are other areas of the floor from which the player will receive the basketball on a regular basis, have the player work in those areas as well.
- Remind players to use the "ball in the air, feet in the air" technique to square and rise up to take the shot.
- It is important for the post players to square this way, even if they do not end up taking the shot. Maintaining this proper positioning makes the defense respect the possibility of a shot attempt, thus opening up other areas of the offense. Anytime the basketball is caught, the player should be a threat.

REVERSE PIVOT

- The use of a reverse pivot (outside foot is pivot foot) on the perimeter can be useful for a post player because it allows enough space to be created to get a jump shot off prior to the defender reacting. This can be especially effective if the post catches and keeps the basketball high while reverse pivoting.
- If this occurs, as soon as the front foot touches the floor and the body is squared, the shot can be taken. These steps can be completed quickly, allowing for a jump shot to be taken prior to a defender reacting in many cases.

- It is important to control the momentum of a reverse pivot, as the natural movement would send a player backward. The player will need to gather and redirect momentum straight up or just slightly ahead of where the player initially takes off.
- Game-speed repetition in practice will help the player gain confidence in this skill.

HOP

- It is less likely that a post player will use a hop on the perimeter, but it is still best to work on all types of footwork to increase the number of options a player will have during a game.
- As the basketball is in the air, the post will take a quick hop, catch the basketball squared, and be ready for the immediate shot. Again, controlling momentum from the cut is important to make sure strength is put into the shot.
- Have the post player cut from various angles and speeds, simulating team offensive strategies. Also, ensure that the player catches the basketball using the various types of footwork to complete the jump shot.
- Challenge the player to understand when to use each type of footwork, while developing consistency in finishing shots.
- Further, challenge the post player to finish jump shots under duress and with distractions.

POINTS OF EMPHASIS

- Do work early; "ball in air, feet in air."
- Understand why to use each type of footwork.
- Catch ready to shoot.
- Control momentum to put all energy into shot.
- Reinforce proper shooting mechanics from start to finish.

SKILL 9

POST PLAYERS: MOVE PROGRESSION (DIFFERENT TYPES OF FINISHES)

Post players should learn to love and embrace contact on the low block. It is hard work to gain positioning in order to receive the basketball in the post.

- Instruct post players to position themselves low, but above the block. Once the basketball is received, a post should be able to score based on the positioning of the defender.
- On the catch, the post player should quickly work through the three Cs: Catch, Chin, Check.
    - Catch: Catch the basketball with two hands.
    - Chin: Secure the basketball by bringing it to the chin.
    - Check: Check where the defender is located to identify which move to use.
- The following is a progression of moves and countermoves to have post players work through on the low block. It requires the player to develop different types of footwork using both feet. Players are also challenged to finish with both hands using several different types of finishes at the rim.
- As players improve, they should be able to read the defense to make the appropriate moves and countermoves.

Drop-step baseline, front-pivot-middle progression:

1. DROP STEP Defense on high side, point bottom foot to rim, seal defense on rear, jump up strong with both hands to glass.
2. TURN-AROUND JUMP SHOT/HALF HOOK Defense on high side or behind, fake the drop-step baseline, pivot away from defense, finish high.
3. UP AND UNDER Same steps as (B) but then add shot fake middle, defense jumps, use body to seal and step through, protect basketball on outside of body, finish off the glass.
4. MIDDLE DRIVE Defense on low side, pivot middle, shot fake, drive across lane, protect basketball with body.
5. MIDDLE DRIVE SPIN BACK Same steps as (D). If defense cuts off middle drive spin back, whip base leg for seal with live dribble, finish high off the glass.

Drop-step middle, front-pivot-baseline progression:

- Repeat same progression as before but switch direction of pivot and steps.

Reverse-pivot middle, middle-foot-pivot-foot progression:

1. JUMP SHOT Defense on low side or behind, create space with reverse pivot, basketball high, square shoulders, finish high.
2. DRIVE MIDDLE, FINISH OPPOSITE-SIDE LAYUP Same steps as (A), then shot fake defense, one dribble to middle, protect basketball with body, finish off the glass.
3. DRIVE MIDDLE, SPIN BACK Same steps as (B). When defense jumps the middle drive, whip leg to seal, keep basketball close to body, finish high off the glass.
4. DRIVE MIDDLE, FAKE SPIN, JUMP SHOT MIDDLE Same steps as (C). Defense jumps on the spin, turn back to middle, finish high with jump shot.
5. DRIVE MIDDLE, SPIN/JUMP SHOT, UP AND UNDER Same steps as (D), defense jumps at the shot middle, step through up and under, keep pivot foot down, protect basketball, finish high.

Reverse-pivot baseline, baseline-foot-pivot-foot progression:

- Repeat same progression as before but switch direction of pivot and steps.

As the player begins to develop the footwork and an understanding of when to use the moves, along with gaining confidence in finishing, begin to focus on the details. Keep the basketball high through the move, use clean and efficient footwork, seal and use the body, finish soft off of the glass or with touch on the jump shot. Any missed shots should be followed up with a made one. All movements should be at game speed with a high amount of repetition. Begin to add contact and contest shots as the player improves. Lastly, add a live defender to work on reading the defense, making moves, and finishing against a live body.

# POINTS OF EMPHASIS

- Three Cs: Catch, Chin, Check.
- Catch with low center of gravity.
- Read defense to make move and countermoves.
- Proper footwork without traveling.
- Secure basketball throughout all moves; keep high.
- Finish high.

SKILL 10

PRESSURE FREE THROWS

In addition to proper shooting mechanics and a consistent routine, it is important to begin developing a higher level of focus and concentration from the free-throw line to prepare players for pressure situations.

DRILL 1: FREE-THROW GOLF

Players may use this game to create individual challenges against themselves, or they may choose to compete against others.

- A player will shoot eighteen shots, just as a game of golf consists of eighteen holes. The objective of the game is to score the fewest points, preferably under par. Here, "par" is zero.
- Each shot will count in the following manner:
    - Missed free throw = +1
    - Made free throw (not clean, touches rim) = 0
    - Made free throw (swish, does not touch rim) = –1
- If a player makes all eighteen free throws and the basketball never touches the rim, the player has achieved the best score, –18. If a player misses every free throw, the score is +18.
- Remind players to make the game competitive, regardless of whether they are "golfing" alone or with teammates.
- The scoring of the game helps put pressure on the shooter, which requires a different level of focus and concentration.
- Coaches can be creative in making the game more challenging or simulate more game-like scenarios. For example, players could sprint the length of the floor in between free throws to improve conditioning and develop an ability to shoot free throws while tired.
- Coaches could also have players compete in one game of golf that continues throughout an entire practice. Shooting one or two free throws between drills requires stamina and the ability to constantly regain composure, focus, and concentration for a longer period of time.

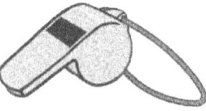 **POINTS OF EMPHASIS**

- Create pressure situations.
- Reinforce focus and concentration.
- Assist with any shooting mechanics issues.

ADVANCED LEVEL

TEAM DEFENSIVE CONCEPTS

GENERAL OVERVIEW: *At this level, the half-court defense adds situations such as on-ball screens, post and perimeter defense, run and jump situations, trapping defenses, zone defenses, time and score situations involving team defense, press defenses, defending inbound plays, and transition defense with scramble situations.*

SKILL 1

ON-BALL SCREENS

- On-ball screens create indecision for the defenders. In order to defend on-ball screens, the defenders must stay in a stance, communicate with each other, and have an awareness of where the screen is being set.
- The defender on the dribbler at times will need to get over the top of the screen if guarding a very good shooter.
- As the screen is being set, the defender guarding the screener must call out "screen left" or "screen right" as the screener approaches the on-ball defender to announce where the screen will be set.
- The defender on the screener will hedge on the screen, which simply is stepping up and squarely facing the dribbler momentarily.
- The hedge makes the dribbler go wide off the screen and flattens out the dribbler so the defender guarding the dribbler can get over the screen to stay with the dribbler.
- The switch on the ball screen may also be an option when the dribbler uses the screen. As the dribbler uses the screen, the defender who is guarding the screen will call out "switch" and will guard the dribbler.
- The defender on the dribbler will switch to guard the screener as the dribbler uses the screen.
- The defender on the dribbler can also go underneath the screen. To make this happen, the defender on the screener will step back to allow the defender on the dribbler to go behind the screen and stay with the dribbler. This creates a "window" for the defender to go through to stay with the dribbler.

 ## POINTS OF EMPHASIS

- The hedge defender must be aggressive but be able to get back to defending the screener and being aware of the slip by the screener.
- When switching the screen, the defender who switches to guard the screener must get in front of the player to stop the pass on a roll to the basket.
- Using the switching defense works best if the defenders are of the same size and quickness.
- When creating a window for the defender on the dribbler, the defender on the screener must take one step back to allow the dribble defender to go under the screen.

SKILL 2

POST DEFENSE

- Post defense will include playing defense on any offensive player who is in a position with the back to the basket, usually in the block area but can be at the high post.
- Post defense can vary depending on where the ball is located. Defending the post on the ball side is important to stop the ball from easily entering the post area.
- If the ball is above the free-throw line, the post defender takes a position in the lane area on the side of the offensive post player with the chest contacting the shoulder of the offensive post.
- The outside hand is high with the palm open to the ball so passes into the post are discouraged.
- The off arm is an arm bar that is placed on the offensive post player so as to create a space between the defender and the offensive post player.
- When the ball is passed or dribbled below the free-throw line, the defender must keep contact with the offensive post player and move around front to stop the pass.
- As the ball is passed or dribbled to the baseline, the defender now quickly moves the feet to go from the high-side defensive stance to the low-side defensive stance, "hugging" the offensive post player and keeping the arm high.
- Another method to guard the post as the ball is moving from top to wing to baseline is by the step-through. This allows the defender to keep an eye on the ball at all times rather than turn the back to the ball while "hugging" the post player.
- By using the approach of the step-through, the defender will swing the back foot in front of the offensive post player to a total fronting position as the ball is dribbled or passed to the baseline.
- The defender then uses the pivot foot to drop to the baseline side of the offensive post player so as to make an X pattern, which allows for keeping sight on the ball.

 **POINTS OF EMPHASIS**

- The arm bar of the defender is placed on the offensive post player at about shoulder level.
- The defender is in a position to deny the pass to the offensive post player by having an arm in the passing lane.
- By "hugging" the offensive post player, the defender can get from side to side when the ball goes from wing to baseline.
- By playing defense on the side of the offensive post player, the defender must be aware to not give up the angle for the pass and easy basket.
- If the ball does enter the post, the defender must be quick to get between the post player and the basket so an easy drop step does not lead to a basket.
- The rebounding angle is more difficult when the defender is playing the offensive post player in a deny position and a shot is taken. The defender must be quick to get in front of the post player to get a rebound.

SKILL 3

PERIMETER DEFENSE

- Perimeter defense occurs when guarding an offensive player facing the basket any place on the floor.
- The most important part of perimeter defense is the correct stance: feet wider than the shoulders, arm's length from the offensive player, eyes on the midsection of the offensive player, and the hands and arms above the waist.
- As the offensive player moves with the ball, the defender must move the foot and leg first in the direction the offensive player is headed to stop the dribble.
- The movement of the defender is a big step in the direction of the dribbler with a hard push with the opposite foot.
- A drill to work on this is the sideline drill. Line players up on the sideline with one foot on the sideline. On command by the coach, the players will step first with the inside foot wide and push with the sideline foot.
- The players will continue in this manner to the opposite sideline, making sure the big step is taken in the direction of the opposite sideline.
- The players will progress to sliding then turning to sprint to the opposite sideline when they reach the lane line.
- A further progression will take place by the players sliding to the lane line then turning to sprint to the next lane line and ending up sliding to the sideline.
- The zigzag full-court drill is a good one to defend the on-ball dribbler. The offensive player starts on the baseline and will use one-third of the full court to zigzag dribble to the opposite baseline.
- The defender will be in a good stance and stay in front of the dribbler using slides and drop steps to contain. The offense starts at half speed in order for the defender to have proper footwork.
- The cone drill works on game-like 1-on-1 situations. Start players in two lines on the baseline with the player closest to the sideline with the ball.
- One cone is set in front of the offense's line and one in front of the defense's line; both cones are even and a few feet before half court.
- On command by the coach, the first offensive player dribbles out hard to the cone and dribbles around it, turning to attack the basket. The defensive player sprints up and around the other cone and gets in position to play defense on the dribbler, working to stop the dribbler from scoring.
- Coaches may adjust cones to give the offense or defense an advantage by reducing the distance of one cone to the basket.

POINTS OF EMPHASIS

- The head of the defender should be lower than the shoulders of the offensive player.
- If the offensive player dribbles the ball to the left, the defender must move the right foot first in a big step to stay between the ball and the basket.
- The movement of the first one or two steps of the defender will determine the probability of staying in good position and stopping the dribbler from getting to the basket.

- The feet of the defender should not cross or come closer than shoulder width apart unless the dribbler gets ahead of the defender, in which case the defender must turn and run to catch up with the dribbler.
- The drop step occurs any time the dribbler changes direction with the ball. The defender must drop the top foot at a 45-degree angle in order to contain the dribbler and keep the dribbler in front. Too much of a drop step, for instance a 180-degree drop, will allow the dribbler to go by the defender.
- During the cone drill, the dribbler stays on half of the court and cannot cross the rim line. A good rule is to limit the dribbles to two or three once around the cone.

SKILL 4

RUN AND JUMP DEFENSE

- Run and jump defense, or run and switch, is usually performed in a full-court defensive setting and includes a surprise element for the offensive players.
- This involves switching defenders as the ball is dribbled up the court. The defender guarding a player who is in close proximity to the dribbler will leave the player and run to guard the dribbler.
- The defender that is guarding the dribbler will leave the dribbler and sprint to the offensive player who is left open by the defender running to guard the dribbler.
- The element of surprise will dictate the success of the run and jump—if the run and jump can come when the dribbler's head is down or if the dribbler is out of control, the defense has an opportunity for success.
- The best method to teach the run and jump is to have both defenders at the free-throw line and two offensive players working to advance the ball.
- As one of the offensive players dribbles to the middle of the court, the help defender runs to cover the dribbler while the original defender guarding the dribbler jumps to cover the open offensive player.

 # POINTS OF EMPHASIS

- The run comes when the help defender runs to the dribbler and the jump refers to the defender on the dribbler switching to guard the open offensive player.
- The defender that runs to the dribbler will need to sprint and get hands up on the approach to discourage a high pass.
- The defender running to the dribbler must call out "switch"; this initiates the run and jump defense.

SKILL 5

TRAPPING DEFENSES

- Trapping defenses are used to cause disruption to the offensive team and take advantage of a poor passing offensive team.
- Good trapping defenders will keep the hands up so the offensive player has a difficult time throwing the ball over the trap.
- Trapping defenses occur when the ball is forced up the sideline or when the offensive player with the ball stops the dribble in the corners.
- The two defenders who make the trap form the L trap with one defender with shoulders perpendicular to the sideline and the other defender has shoulders parallel to the sideline.
- The feet form the letter L, therefore the name L trap. The defenders must not let the offensive player step between the defenders to make a pass or continue dribbling.
- To teach the trapping defenses, start with an offensive player with the basketball on the baseline who dribbles toward a defender on the sideline. The defender guarding the ball will make a trap with the defender on the sideline.
- The offensive player will pivot and pass the basketball to an offensive teammate who is a step behind the offensive player with the ball and on the ball side of the rim line.
- The player with the basketball now dribbles to the opposite sideline while the two trapping defenders turn and sprint to trap the new offensive player at the other sideline.
- The original player with the ball will be the new receiver for the offensive player in the trap by staying a step behind the ball and on the ball side of the rim line. This continues for four traps the length of the floor.

POINTS OF EMPHASIS

- The defenders trapping will probably not steal the ball when trapping the offensive players, but the steal or turnover will occur when the ball is passed out of the trap.
- Most traps are made in a full-court pressing defense set up by a made basket or dead-ball situation.
- The offensive player without the ball in the trap drill must stay a step behind the ball so that the pass can be made out of the trap. The offensive player must also stay on the ball side of the rim line, which is the imaginary line from rim to rim.
- The traps should occur on a dribbler out of control or when dribblers turn their back to the defender coming to trap.

SKILL 6

ZONE DEFENSES

- Zone defenses are when defenders guard an area and subsequently any players in that area as opposed to guarding a specific player. Zone defenses have many different looks.
- A 2-3 zone defense has two defenders at the free-throw line and three defenders closer to the baseline.
- A 1-3-1 zone defense sets up with a defender at the top of the key, three defenders stretched across the free-throw line and wing areas, and one defender in the lane.
- A 1-2-2 zone positions one defender at the top of the key, two defenders at the free-throw line corners or wings, and two defenders at the block areas of the free-throw lane.
- A 3-2 zone defense has three defenders across the free-throw line wing areas and two defenders at the block of the free-throw lane.
- Each of these zone defenses can be very effective in defending a team with a strength at that area. For example, if the offensive team is big, a 2-3 zone may be most effective to defend the bigger offensive players inside the lane and make the offensive team shoot from the perimeter.
- If the offensive team is a good perimeter shooting team, a 1-3-1 or a 3-2 zone may be the best to defend the shooters.
- A key point to any zone defense is that when the offensive team has the ball on the baseline, all zones, no matter what type of zone the defensive team started in, will look like a 2-3 zone. There will be a baseline defender guarding the ball, a player in the post area, and a player on the help side with a guard defender at the ball-side free-throw line corner and the other guard defender at the opposite free-throw line corner.

POINTS OF EMPHASIS

- A zone defense must be well coached in player-to-player principles so the defenders understand guarding a player who is in the area of the zone.
- The zone defense can cover up weaknesses in a team such as lack of height or quickness to cover the opponent.
- All five defenders must move when the ball is in the air so they are in good defensive rotation with the zone as the ball is received.
- Zone defenses lend to trapping defenses as the offensive players try to attack the gaps in the zone.
- Communication is key to playing good zone defense, as the offense may have two players in the same area of the zone defense with one defender.
- The defenders in the zone defense should keep their hands and arms high and wide to distort the passing lanes.

SKILL 7

TIME AND SCORE SITUATIONS

- Defenders must always be aware of the score and remaining time in the game so adjustments can be made.
- If the offensive team is leading late in the game, the defensive team should know if they have fouls to give before the offensive team gets into a bonus situation.
- The defensive team needs to be aware of the offensive player who should be fouled late in the game—the player with the worst percentage from the free-throw line.
- If the defensive team is ahead late in the game by three points, the defenders should know if a foul should be made against the offensive team to put them at the free-throw line, thereby taking away the three-point shot.
- On inbounds plays with the clock less than one second, the defensive team needs to be aware if the shot must be tipped by the offensive team or can be a catch-and-shoot play.
- Switching defenses between zone and player-to-player depends on the score and time.
- The defensive team may use the press if behind to potentially steal the ball or make the offensive team take quicker shots.

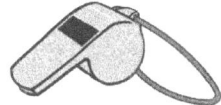

POINTS OF EMPHASIS

- Communication is very important so all players understand the situation and the options available.
- The defenders must be ready to scramble on defense due to trapping the offensive players.
- All defenders must maintain awareness of the game time and score, as this influences team strategy.

SKILL 8

PRESS DEFENSES

- Pressing defenses must fit the personnel of the defensive team as well as the basic philosophy of the team.
- The trapping skills will be very valuable when using the press defenses, as the trap is a vital part of the press.
- Pressing defenses may occur at full or three-quarter court with different areas of pressure for the traps.
- The press defense may take the form of a player-to-player pressing defense or a zone-pressing defense.
- The player-to-player pressing defense requires the defenders to guard an offensive player in a full or three-quarter court set with the opportunity to run and jump, switch, or trap.

- One full-court zone defense is the 1-2-1-1 with a bigger player guarding the inbounder, two guards starting at the free-throw line area, the point guard in the middle, and the center in the back of the press.
- The initial trap is made when the ball is thrown to the corner. The inbound defender and the closest guard form the trap with the opposite guard coming to ball-side lane elbow and reading the next pass.
- The point guard playing the middle of the press then takes the passing lane straight up the sideline and the center comes up to the center line to defend the offensive player in the middle.
- The 2-2-1 is a more passive press, with the two guards at the free-throw line, two forwards at the center line, and the center back at the top of the key.
- The offensive team is encouraged to try to bring the ball up the sideline where a trap may occur. All defenders will shift so the middle is covered, the sideline pass is covered, and the basket is protected.
- The 1-2-2 press can be either a full or three-quarter court press with the defender on top of the key, two players at the center line, and two players at the free-throw line area in the back.
- The 1-3-1 press usually starts at three-quarter court with three players across the midline to take away the middle offensive area.

POINTS OF EMPHASIS

- Any press defense is a gambling defense and requires continued effort and patience if it is to pay dividends.
- The press defense can speed up the game and take the offensive team out of their normal style of play, and cause frustration.
- The press defense should force the offensive player with the ball to the sideline or to the corner in order to trap or run and jump.
- A press does not necessarily need to create a turnover, but makes the offensive team work to get the ball up the court.
- The key to the player-to-player press defense is the ability to put pressure on the offensive player with the ball.
- A good rule for the press is the farther the ball is from the player you are guarding, the farther the defender can be from the offensive player.
- Try to permit only lob or bounce passes forward. Passes back toward your offensive basket will not hurt the defensive team, but the crisp passes forward cause the press defense trouble.
- Use tight player-to-player principles if the player in the defender's zone has the ball and floating player-to-player principles depending upon how far from the ball the offense is in the other areas.
- As soon as the ball passes a defender's individual line of defense, that defender must turn and sprint toward the defensive basket and pick up the most dangerous open player. The strong-side players may have a chance to tip the ball from behind or trap while the weak-side players may have a chance to intercept the pass.

SKILL 9

DEFENDING INBOUND PLAYS

- Defending inbound plays starts with recognizing and being aware of where the best offensive players are located in the inbound set.
- The defense of the inbound plays can be either a zone defense or a player-to-player defense or a combination of the two, such as the triangle zone with two defenders guarding a player.
- The paint area—area in the lane—should be well defended to avoid giving up an easy basket.
- If the defenders are in a player-to-player set, the screens must be communicated and either switched or the defender must get over the screen to stop an easy basket.
- A zone defense is common against the inbound play to stop easy shots around the basket and also to cover the perimeter shot.
- The defense can have a player guarding the inbounder to add pressure to getting the ball inbounds.
- The defenders must set up the defense quickly and be ready to guard as soon as the ball is handed to the inbound passer by the official.

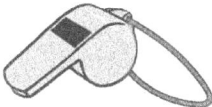

POINTS OF EMPHASIS

- The defenders must know where the best shooters are located in the inbounds set.
- If playing a player-to-player defense, the defenders must communicate and be aware of the roller in the offense after setting the screen.
- The zone defense usually takes the form of a 2-3 zone with the three players across the baseline.

SKILL 10

TRANSITION DEFENSE WITH SCRAMBLE SITUATIONS

- Transition defense involves sprinting back to cover the offensive basket as quickly as possible and matching up with the offensive players in a zone or player-to-player defense.
- The first defensive player back, usually the point guard, will work to stop the ball first and then sprint back to the lane area. This player will guard the first pass to the wing leaving the lane area.
- The second defender back will go to the top of the three-point line and then cover the basket when the offensive pass is made to the wing.
- The real scramble situation for transition occurs when the ball is stopped and the remaining defenders are sprinting back to the offensive end.
- Once the ball is stopped, the defenders then cover the ball-side post and weak-side wing areas.
- The "Laker Drill" is a very good drill for transition and scramble situations.
- Put players in three lines at each baseline. The drill starts with 4-on-4 play on one half court.
- The offense and defense play 4-on-4 until a basket is made, the defense forces a turnover, or the defense gets a rebound.
- The defensive player who secures the rebound, made basket, or forces a turnover now becomes the new offense and is joined by three new teammates from the line under the basket.

- The offensive team from the initial possession becomes defense and both teams transition 4-on-4 to the other basket.
- The drill continues play up and down and coaches can add time or score limits.

 POINTS OF EMPHASIS

- Communication in the form of talking and pointing is needed for great defensive transition.
- The ball must be stopped first in transition or at least slowed down in order to allow time to get more defensive help.
- The key is to sprint the court and be able to recognize where the open offensive players are located.
- Tipping the ball from behind by the defenders as they sprint back on defense is an option.
- The Laker Drill defensive transition uses communication, sprinting to get back, stopping the ball, and then scrambling to cover the offensive players.

ADVANCED LEVEL

TEAM OFFENSIVE CONCEPTS

GENERAL OVERVIEW: *Progressing from previous levels, many of the concepts in this level will be based on team play and making good decisions in the framework of team play. Players must be put in many situations that cause them to make quick and accurate decisions on the floor in order for players to improve.*

SKILL 1

PRIMARY AND SECONDARY TRANSITION

- In this level, the secondary transition is as important as the primary transition. The better the defensive team, the harder it is to get a primary transition basket, so the offensive transition depends more on the secondary break.
- The fast break follows the same basic pattern regardless of how the possession occurred—by defensive rebound, made basket, interception, jump ball, or backcourt out of bounds.
- There must be different options to advance the basketball quickly up the court, as continuation of any one method could soon completely be blocked by a good defensive team.
- Players must be drilled thoroughly so they will react quickly when possession is gained.
- Fast break opportunities are almost always made in the backcourt by quick reaction immediately upon gaining possession of the basketball.
- Drilling the secondary as well as the primary break should start with a five-player break against no defenders to make sure the players know how to fill the lanes.
- There should always be outside lanes filled along with the middle lane where the basketball should be passed or dribbled. A trailer, usually a post player, runs the rim line as quickly as possible. The player who takes the basketball out of bounds stays a step or two behind the player with the basketball for a reversal of the basketball.
- Possible finishes for the fast break include layup by the cutter on either side, jump shot off the glass by a cutter, jump shot by middle player after the cutter passes the basketball to the middle player at the free-throw line elbow, middle player shot or layup off the dribble, trailer for jump shot, or pass to post for shot on the primary break or from the cutter.
- Drill the fast break opportunities from 5-on-0 to a 5-on-5 scenario so the players know positions.

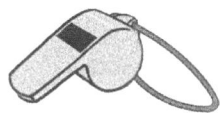 ### POINTS OF EMPHASIS

- As soon as possession is gained, players must instinctively be able to fill the lanes with the basketball getting to the middle of the court.
- If the players hesitate to think about what to do, they have not been drilled enough and opportunities may be lost.
- Encourage the post player to run in a straight line from rim to rim, which can result in a quick primary break basket.

- Cuts should be made in sharp angles when cutting to the basket and not arcs.
- Constantly emphasize keeping the head and eyes up and getting the basketball down the floor to the player in the most advantageous position as quickly as possible.
- The player with the basketball should look to pass the basketball quickly and safely to a teammate down the floor or drive it hard on the dribble if there is no one open.

SKILL 2

UNDERSTANDING ADVANTAGE/DISADVANTAGE

- This is a continuation of the fast break situations where the players need to recognize if there is an advantage for their team or a disadvantage.
- The best drill to recognize advantage opportunities is the continuous 3-on-2 drill.
- Two teams line up on sidelines. The drill starts with three players in the backcourt with the basketball in the middle. Two defenders are in the frontcourt waiting for the basketball to be advanced in a 3-on-2 situation.
- As the basketball crosses the half-court line, a third defender runs in to touch the half-court circle. This will then make the situation a 3-on-3 game if the offense does not score before the third defender gets into the action.
- At the same time the third defender runs to touch the circle, two players from the offensive team sideline run to touch the circle and go to the opposite end to be the two defenders.
- The original three offensive players will go to the end of their sideline line after a shot or turnover. The three defenders will now go on offense and attack the two awaiting defenders on the opposite end in a fast break situation. Every time the basketball crosses the half-court line, the third defender runs to touch the circle to make the drill 3-on-3.
- The offensive team may advance the basketball across half court by the dribble or with a pass to the outside lane player, which puts pressure on the two defenders.
- If there is not a 3-on-2 advantage, the offense must now perform offensive skills such as screening, cutting, and moving in a 3-on-3 situation to try and score.

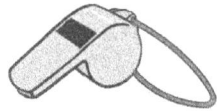

POINTS OF EMPHASIS

- As the basketball crosses half court, the players should be filling the lanes to make it difficult for the defenders to guard all three offensive players.
- The basketball needs to get to the middle of the court either by the dribble or with a pass as soon as possible.
- Keep score so there is a winner for the drill. Play to a certain number of points or time.
- The defensive team does not need to take the basketball out of bounds after a made basket. Grab the basketball out of the net and start the fast break.

- On a turnover, the drill continues with the defenders now becoming offense against new defenders at the other end.
- The first option is a layup or a jump shot from the outside cutters. The secondary option is ball reversal against the three defensive players.

SKILL 3

HALF-COURT SPACING AND MOTION

Half-court spacing in this level is taught in relation to a team offense.

- Player movements are not predetermined but depend on spacing and how and where the defenders are located.
- Look to screen the passer's player, as this will always give your team a backscreen, which is basic for the motion offense.
- Work with a partner—one player has the basketball and the other four will pair up and set screens.
- Never run by or bypass a player when screening, but rather set a screen for the nearest teammate and continue screening.
- Run to screen but walk to set up the screen. Cutters should be late rather than early using the screen.
- On down screens, the screener's back should face the basketball. On backscreens, the screener's back should face the basket.
- After a pass, the following options are available by the passer: basket cut, screen, fill a vacant spot, or wait to use a screen which sets up the backscreen.
- After setting the screen, the following options are available: continue to screen to the baseline when starting at the point position, rescreen, which is a backscreen to a down screen, slip the screen, step back to the basketball, or fill a space on the court.
- After receiving a screen, the following options are available: accept the screen or reject the screen with a back cut or a flare cut.
- The 4x4x4 exchange drill previously described in the Foundational Level (page 141) is one of the best to teach the motion game and half-court spacing.
- Breakdown drills include 2-on-0 with the player starting the drill by passing the basketball to the coach and then setting a screen for a teammate who has the options described above.
- Progress to 2-on-2 so the players now can read the defender and perform the proper cuts after passing to the coach.
- From 2-on-2, progress to 3-on-3 with the pass being made to a teammate being defended.

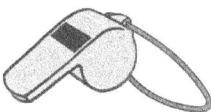 **POINTS OF EMPHASIS**

- When using the screen, watch the defender and not the basketball.
- After setting a screen, the screener will react and go opposite the teammate so if the player makes a curl cut around the screen, the screener steps out.

- Usually the screener is the player who will be open for a pass so the screener must step toward the basketball after the screen.
- Change of speed and direction will help the cutter get open for a pass.
- The player using the screen should be low, shoulder clipping the hip of screener, which will make it much more difficult for the defender to get between the screen and cutter.
- A slip screen occurs when the screener attempts the screen but at the last second cuts to the rim, which happens when the defender hedges or a double-team occurs.
- Spacing must occur after a screen away from the basketball, so always be aware of filling a spot on the floor, if needed.

SKILL 4

SPECIFIC SETS BASED ON PERSONNEL OR ADVANTAGE OPPORTUNITIES BASED ON OPPONENT

- When two teams match up, many times there is an advantage for one team based on size, speed, or experience, and the team should take advantage of these opportunities either on defense or offense.
- Keep in mind that one team may have an advantage on offense while also having a disadvantage on defense.
- If the offensive team has a mismatch based on size, this should be taken advantage of in the post area by passing the basketball into the post, where size can make a difference.
- When a team switches the screens, this may cause a bigger and slower defender guarding a smaller and quicker offensive player. The offensive player should immediately try to get to the basket around the slower defender.
- A quicker and smaller team may try to double-team the bigger post players when they receive the basketball. If this occurs, the passer should cut through to the opposite side of the court and get good spacing for a reverse pass.
- An advantage will occur if the defensive team hedges hard on the ball screens. The offensive team must reverse the basketball quickly to a player who looks for the screener rolling. Since the screener's defender stepped out to hedge, the screener should be open at the basket.
- The best method to take advantage of two big post players is placing one on each block and performing a cross-screen when the basketball is passed to the wing. The post screener must open up to the basketball after the screen is set.
- The smaller, quicker lineup should set fewer screens and make more basket cuts against the slower, bigger defenders.
- Spread the court with proper spacing for a smaller, quicker offensive team attacking a bigger, slower team.

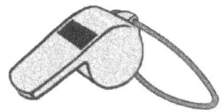

POINTS OF EMPHASIS

- If a size advantage is evident, run the offensive player to the post and swing the basketball to the player in the post.
- Spacing is important when a defensive team traps the post player. The players properly spaced will be open for a shot when the basketball gets passed quickly.
- Players must recognize size, speed, and quickness differences and take advantage of these differences in game situations by making sure there is always proper spacing.
- Quick ball reversal will eliminate defensive double-teams and hedges on the ball screens.
- Offensive players should make hard, direct cuts to the basket and not cut in an arc.

SKILL 5

ZONE CONCEPTS

There are some basic zone concepts that any specific zone offense should implement. These concepts may be taught against any of the zone defenses, whether an odd front or an even front zone defense.

- All zones look alike when the basketball goes to the baseline. The defense will take the look of the 2-3 zone defense no matter what the zone started out as when the basketball was at the top of the key. There must be a defender guarding the basketball on the baseline, a defender in the post, a defender on the help side, and two defenders at the top.
- The zone offensive team must use a dribble in the gaps of the zone to cause some indecision with the defense as to who will cover the dribbler.
- Screen the zone to pin defenders and cause the zone to scramble. The screen can either be set high or low.
- Advance the basketball quickly to create an advantage for the offense in a 2-on-1 or a 3-on-2 situation.
- The dribbler must make a great effort to get the basketball to the paint—lane area—to open up the perimeter.
- The stack formation can be two players at the free-throw line, on either side of the lane lines, or at the block area.
- There are four vulnerable areas against any zone defense: the gap areas between two zone defenders, the box area on the free-throw line blocks, the twelve-foot short-corner area on the baselines, and the rebound areas, which are both blocks and the area in front of the free-throw line.
- Offensive rebounding will increase due to the defenders not screening out players as easily.

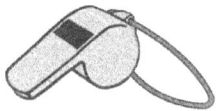

POINTS OF EMPHASIS

- The position of the players must be in the gaps of the zone. This is easily viewed by using cones or chairs as the zone defenders.
- Either the basketball must move or players must move on offense to attack a zone defense regardless of the type of zone used.
- The basketball must cross the rim line, the imaginary line which divides the court sideways running from rim to rim, to get an advantage on offense.
- When advancing the basketball against a zone, the primary break leading to a layup will probably not be available. The offense must look for the secondary break ending in jump shots from the wing.
- Skip passes from one wing to the other wing or wing to baseline are effective to get a shot against a zone.
- The best method to reverse the basketball is through the low, mid, or high post areas. The post turns opposite and passes the basketball to the opposite wing.
- Players should move to the gaps as the basketball is being passed so they can set their feet for shooting as they receive the basketball.

SKILL 6

FREE-THROW SITUATIONS

There are some free-throw situations that players should be aware of from the offensive standpoint.

- The offensive players should line up in their designated area on the free-throw line as far away from the defender as possible. By doing this, it will make it harder to get a good blockout by the defender.
- The best offensive rebounder should line up on the right-hand side of the lane as you look at the basket, as studies have shown that the majority of misses will be to this side.
- The offensive rebounders should step hard and quick to the opposite block when the basketball touches the rim to avoid the double-team blockout squeeze by the defenders.
- The offensive player on one side may roll baseline on contact by the defender in order to get a rebound.
- If the offensive rebounder cannot grasp the basketball with both hands, the player should tip the basketball to the free-throw line area, where the player who shot the free throw will be located.
- The offensive rebounders may try to cross the lane as the basketball hits the rim, which will make them more difficult to block out by the defenders.

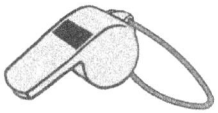

POINTS OF EMPHASIS

- The offensive rebounder should try to keep the elbow and forearm on top of the defender's elbow and forearm when in position on the free-throw lane.
- Keeping the hands above the shoulders prevents the arms from being pinned down.
- The free-throw shooter should stay at the free-throw line area after the basketball hits the rim to get any long rebounds or tip rebounds by teammates.
- The offensive rebounders should move as soon as the basketball hits the rim to be harder to block out.

SKILL 7

PRESS-BREAK CONCEPTS

At this level, teams must prepare for defensive pressure in the full court and develop the necessary skills to break the pressing defense.

- Try to keep the floor spread without getting bunched up and use give-and-go passes to advance up the floor.
- A good dribbler should be given some room to work, especially against a player-to-player press.
- There should be very little dribbling against a zone press. Look the situation over before putting the basketball on the floor and try to get a quick pass forward.
- Put the center or another taller player at the center circle and then break back to form an outlet in the middle of the floor.
- There should always be three players in position to catch the basketball against a press: one player in the middle, one player a step behind the basketball, and one player on the strong side at the half line. This gives the player with the basketball three passing options.
- When the basketball gets to the middle of the floor or is reversed to the player behind the basketball, the next pass should be to the opposite side of the floor.
- If playing against a passive press such as a 2-2-1 three-quarter court press, stretch the defense by having your best shooter on the baseline at your offensive end.
- Against good pressure on the inbound pass, start with two players in a stack formation at the free-throw line area. Players will break in opposite directions to get the pass from the inbounder.
- Screens may also be set to get the basketball inbounded. One player starts at each free-throw line elbow with the screener on ball side setting the screen for the other player. The screener will roll back to the basketball for the pass after the teammate has made a cut to the basketball off the screen.

POINTS OF EMPHASIS

- After a made basket, the inbounder may run the baseline, which provides some relief against a good trapping press.
- Inbound the basketball as quickly as possible to attack the press before it has a chance to set up.
- Keep the basketball out of the corners when facing a trapping zone press, as this is the area the press is most effective.
- When receiving the basketball in the middle of the floor, look opposite or down the court to attack the press.
- Once the offense has an advantage such as a 3-on-2 situation, the offense must try to score.
- A good dribbler must read the defense and not pick the basketball up in trapping areas, but should be able to back the basketball up to relieve the pressure.
- Rebounding areas are more vulnerable against a press, so offensive players should attack the glass on a missed shot.

SKILL 8

INBOUNDS CONCEPTS FROM UNDER THE BASKET AND SIDELINE

- The player taking the basketball out of bounds should take some time getting to the basketball to allow the other four players to hurry to the positions that they should take according to the play that has been called.
- As the players get to their positions, the play starts on a signal by the player with the basketball.
- The signal may be given orally, calling out a name or number, by slapping the basketball, or by raising the basketball above the head to initiate the movement for the play.
- The player inbounding the basketball must stand about three feet back from the boundary line and must keep perfect balance without leaning.
- Generally, the best shooter is the first option. The shooter may come off a screen or two. The second look is for the screener rolling back to the basketball.
- Plays should be run for both player-to-player and zone defense; some plays work against both.
- A box set is a good formation to run plays from out of bounds either from the baseline or from the sideline.
- A specific set must be drilled to use from any out of bounds position against a defense late in the game that will pressure the defensive players. A four-person stack is good against this type of pressure.
- Be aware that many times the inbounder stepping onto the playing court is the player who will be open for a shot.

POINTS OF EMPHASIS

- Make sure to practice the inbounds plays from both sides of the court.
- The player selected to handle the basketball for the inbounds must be most alert and have a lot of poise.
- The number-one priority for inbounding the basketball is to get the basketball inbounds and then look to score.
- The player taking the basketball out of bounds may not move from that spot or a traveling call will occur. The player may only move after a made basket.
- Out-of-bounds plays against a zone defense should have an overload on the ball side—three players in the zone area of two defenders.
- The players should know the timeout situation and if needed must call timeout before a violation occurs.
- It is better to take a five-second count than to throw the basketball inbounds and have it intercepted. At least with the five-second count, the team has a chance to set its defense up instead of the interception leading to an easy basket.

SKILL 9

JUMP BALL SITUATIONS

- Jump ball situations may be infrequent in games, to start the game and in any overtime periods, but jump ball situations can give your team an extra possession. Jump balls are a team affair and all five players must be alert. The player jumping the basketball must time the jump with the basketball. The player must neither jump too soon nor be caught waiting.
- The jumper must go straight up and extend the tipping arm to its full length.
- The basketball must not be slapped or batted but tipped with a flick of the wrist and the fingers.
- If you anticipate that the opponent may have the advantage to win the tip, try to cover every player except the one in front or to the side of the opponent's player jumping the basketball. The tip will then be encouraged to go to the open player, and you can coach players to time their movement to step in front of the open player and steal the tip.

POINTS OF EMPHASIS

- Different players jumping the basketball have different stances. Each should do what feels most comfortable and ensures the maximum height on the jump.
- Crowd the opposing player jumping the basketball as much as possible if the opponent has the advantage to win the tip.

- Prevent from being crowded if it appears that the control will be your team's or about even.
- Players jumping the basketball should land in good balance with the hands up and be ready to move into the play offensively and defensively.
- Do not foul the opponent on the jump, but be sure to protect the area each player is occupying.

SKILL 10

TIME AND SCORE SITUATIONS

- All players must be alert to the time and the score throughout the game, which will allow for a good play during the final seconds.
- There are two varying strategies when ahead by three in the closing seconds of a game. The first is to make a nonshooting foul, which will allow the player to shoot one or two free throws if in the bonus. Teams could also not foul and make the other team hit a guarded three-point shot to, at best, tie the game.
- The dribbler may use as many dribbles as there are seconds on the clock—four seconds to go means four dribbles and a shot.
- The advantage for the offensive team if behind in the closing seconds of the game is that the defensive team will not want to foul. This allows the offensive team to be the more aggressive team when trying to score.
- Try to run the best three-point shooter off a staggered double screen to get a late three-point shot.
- If the offense sets a ball screen, the player who set the screen should step back after setting the screen, as this player may be open for a shot.
- Extend the game by fouling, but try to foul the most ineffective free-throw shooter. Do not allow the best free-throw shooter to receive the pass.

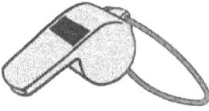 ## POINTS OF EMPHASIS

- Shoot the basketball with a few seconds to go so there may be a chance for an offensive rebound and put back.
- In the closing seconds, all five offensive players should crash the boards for an offensive rebound if the team is behind.
- When attacking the basket in the closing seconds, the goal is to get the basketball to the lane and take a balanced shot.
- A timeout may be called after the offensive team has made a basket. This will help to set up the defense.

SKILL 11

TEAM REBOUNDING

- Offensive team rebounding may involve some special situations for the offensive rebounding team to gain an advantage.
- One of the best methods to gain an advantage for an offensive team is to assign areas for each offensive player—one post player to the area in front of the rim, one player to the block area on one side, another to the block area on the other side of the rim, one guard to the free-throw line area, and the other guard to sprint back in defensive transition.
- By assigning specific areas, this makes the offensive players move immediately to that area on the shot and be much more difficult to screen off.
- The offensive player can do several moves to gain a better opportunity to get the rebound—a crossover swim move, a spin move, or an inside-out move.
- Players must know where the basketball is likely to come off the rim if the shot is missed. The basketball usually goes opposite of the shooter off the rim on a miss.
- Players should also be aware of the distance of the shot. The longer shot will become a longer rebound.

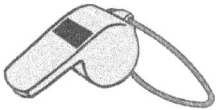 **POINTS OF EMPHASIS**

- A crossover swim move is one in which the offensive player will step across the defender and try to get the elbow above the elbow of the defender.
- A spin move is a full pivot upon contact by the defender to make it difficult to be screened out.
- The inside-out move is a hard step to the baseline and a move in front of the defender who is trying to screen out. This is a V-cut for the offensive player toward the baseline.
- The hands must go above the shoulders as the offensive player is moving to get the offensive rebound.
- If the offensive player cannot grab the rebound with both hands, the basketball can be tipped to the free-throw line area where the guards can get the long rebound.

SKILL 12

TRAPPING CONCEPTS

- Handling a trap situation requires offensive skills that are found throughout this level.
- Whenever a dribbler is aware of two defenders coming to trap, the player must keep the dribble alive and not pick the basketball up.
- As the defenders come at the dribbler, the basketball must be on the back hip away from the defenders and the other forearm up to protect the basketball.

- The dribbler can take several dribbles straight back with the basketball on the back hip and forearm up to release the defensive pressure in order for the dribbler to make a pass.
- As the defenders approach the offensive player to double-team, the dribbler may recognize the opportunity to split the double-team with the dribble, which will cause a scramble situation for the defense.
- The offensive player must not put the basketball above the head as the double-team approaches. This allows for an easy trap by the defense.
- As the dribbler comes off a ball-screen, the player must know where the screener will relocate so the basketball can be passed to the screener.
- The double-team may come before the offensive player has had a chance to dribble the basketball, such as on a full-court press. When this occurs, the offensive player must have awareness of all teammates and try to pass the basketball before the double-team is made.
- The offensive team should look to make the extra pass once the basketball is passed out of the double-team to get an easy score against the scramble defense.

POINTS OF EMPHASIS

- As the player keeps the basketball alive with the dribble, the chin must be up and the eyes search to find open teammates.
- The dribbler must stay low when continuing to dribble—the head must be lower than the defender's shoulders.
- After picking up the dribble, the offensive player must pass the basketball quickly to an open teammate rather than hold the basketball.
- The on-ball screener must see the possible double-team approaching as the dribbler comes off the screen and then roll to the open area and call for the basketball verbally and with hands up.
- When a double-team comes before the offensive player dribbles, the offensive player must protect the basketball and make a quick pass to a teammate.
- A key to breaking the double-team by the offensive team is to try to score quickly after passing the basketball out of the double-team.

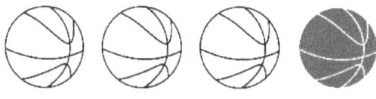

PLAYER DEVELOPMENT CURRICULUM: LEVEL FOUR

INTRODUCTORY LEVEL

FOUNDATIONAL LEVEL

ADVANCED LEVEL

PERFORMANCE LEVEL

PERFORMANCE LEVEL

OFFENSIVE PRINCIPLES: BALL HANDLING & DRIBBLING

GENERAL OVERVIEW: *At the Performance Level, players will continue to work on mastery of ball handling and dribbling, especially while performing the skills against intense pressure from defenses. Application to challenging, high-level game situations without thought or hesitation is the desired goal. Further, being able to create better angles for teammates, to split double-teams, to remove unnecessary use of the dribble, and to combine all offensive skills to better the overall team offensive schemes is a sign of mastering this skill.*

Although there are level-specific drills in this section, to continue to challenge and engage players, the Performance Level moves further away from mastering a specific drill. Instead, the mastery idea takes form through application in stressful game situations: understanding the situation, making a solid, quick decision, and reacting at a high, efficient level consistently. Teaching at this level may revolve more around game environments than drill work, although a healthy combination is always recommended.

SKILL 1

STATIONARY BALL HANDLING: ONE BASKETBALL

DRILL 1: ONE BASKETBALL, ONE TENNIS BALL

Once players are able to eliminate unnecessary dribbles from the skills presented in the previous levels, coaches can progress players to completing double moves.

- Instead of one crossover, the player will complete a double crossover. The pattern of "toss, dribble, catch" remains the same.
- The difference is the same hand that tosses the tennis ball, in this case the left hand, will also catch it, still in an overhand position. This allows for the basketball to be dribbled from the right hand to the left hand, finishing back in the right hand following the double crossover.
- Again, players will complete double dribbles using crossovers, between-the-legs, and behind-the-back moves.
- Once players develop this skill, have players add in slow, controlled movement forward and backward.

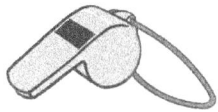 **POINTS OF EMPHASIS**

- Balanced, defensive stance.
- Keep eyes on tennis ball.
- Catch tennis ball overhand with the same hand that tosses it.
- Pound dribbles.
- Work toward zero extra dribbles.

DRILL 2: HAND SPEED

Developing hand speed is advantageous for many areas of basketball, offensively and defensively. One way to improve hand speed can be through ball handling.

- Players can partner up with one another or line up with a coach. One player has the basketball, standing in a balanced, defensive stance, facing the partner.
- While working on a specific skill, such as a crossover, the partner without the basketball will put up one hand, indicating to the ball handler to quickly tap that partner's hand, while continuing the ball handling skill.
- Coaches can designate which hand the ball handler must use to reach out and tap with, varying from the same side hand, the opposite side hand, or always right or left hand throughout the drill. Partners can also alter the height of the hand to tap and the pattern of hands to tap. Keep the ball handler guessing while completing skills, truly working on reacting with quick hand speed.

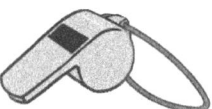

POINTS OF EMPHASIS

- Maintain solid stance; no bobbing.
- Head up.
- Pound dribble and keep alive while tapping.
- Quick hand speed and tap with appropriate hand.

SKILL 2

STATIONARY BALL HANDLING: TWO BASKETBALLS

DRILL 1: FIGURE 8—THROUGH DOOR AT SAME TIME

This skill is challenging in that there is a small margin for error in order to complete successfully.

- Beginning in a solid, defensive stance, the player will dribble both basketballs through the back door at the same time to complete the figure 8.
- This will require the player to be precise with the basketballs, especially at the center of the legs and just outside the legs in order to complete the skill.
- Progress to the front door at the same time as the skill is learned.

POINTS OF EMPHASIS

- Balanced, defensive stance; no bobbing.
- Finger pad control.
- Head up.
- Control first then add speed.

DRILL 2: FIGURE 8—FRONT DOOR/BACK DOOR

- In the same stance, the player will have one basketball entering through the back door, while the other is entered through the front door, simultaneously.
- Essentially, one basketball is traveling clockwise, while the other is traveling counterclockwise. Switch directions once the skill is learned.

POINTS OF EMPHASIS

- Balanced, defensive stance; no bobbing.
- Finger pad control.
- Head up.
- Control first then add speed.

SKILL 2

DRIBBLING ON THE MOVE: POSITION-APPROPRIATE SCORING; DRIBBLE MOVES OUT OF TEAM OFFENSE

At this level, application to a game scenario is what separates players and teams. It is beneficial for a player's overall game to learn every move possible because all situations cannot be predicted when it comes to such a dynamic game. However, there is also great value in understanding the situations one will find themselves in within the scope of the team's offense and how to best take advantage of those possessions. For example, if a team runs a set that vacates one side of the floor for a split second prior to another player cutting to that area, it is imperative to not only understand that split second of opportunity, but also to identify where the defense is coming from and which type of move would be most effective. When working on moves to score, put players in positions they will likely find themselves in during the game. Elevate their understanding and comprehension within the skill work to increase their awareness of everyone on the floor. Encourage players to execute moves at game intensity and speed. Break down the offense to involve only two or three positions and have all players catch the basketball at some point during the breakdown work from the spots to make the appropriate move to score.

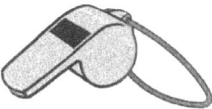 ## POINTS OF EMPHASIS

- Make moves applicable to game situations based on the offense.
- Game intensity and speed.
- Read defense within offense.
- Use multidimensional learning and teaching with drills in practice and application in games.
- Hand speed and tap with appropriate hand.

SKILL 3

DRIBBLING ON THE MOVE: RELIEVING PRESSURE

There is an art to relieving heavy, defensive pressure with the use of the dribble. It is a necessary skill to learn in order to avoid five-second calls and make entry passes or tough angle passes within the confines of the offense. The best players know exactly how to relieve pressure at the right time, setting themselves and teammates up to complete plays.

AVOID FIVE-SECOND CALLS

In addition to late-game situations, players can find themselves in a situation where they are supposed to reverse the basketball, but the teammate is not open. While dribbling, the official is counting if the ball handler is being closely guarded. This is a situation where an attacking dribble is needed to relieve pressure and reset the five-second count. This can be accomplished by taking a hard dribble or two toward the basket, simulating a legitimate drive, then pulling back abruptly, causing the momentum of the defender to travel backward while the offensive player separates and creates space. In addition to resetting the count, this can be an effective way to keep the defensive player off guard.

USE OF DRIBBLE TO CREATE PASSING LANE

As players progress through the game of basketball, offensively it becomes more difficult to make a simple entry pass to the wing. Defensive players get bigger, stronger, and faster as the game is played at higher levels, making the entry pass more challenging and dependent upon timing. An experienced ball handler will take the defender to one side of the floor and then change directions quickly, creating space in the opposite direction, in order to deliver the wing entry pass in stride with the teammate. This is fairly common and a good place to work on the use of the dribble. To take it to a higher level, think about the difficult pass that has to be made for a back door layup, for example. If the offensive player does not use a dribble to create separation from the defender, the pass remains difficult. When the dribble is used, most of the time toward the offensive player cutting, space is created and the pass can be completed with a much higher rate of success. Understanding the offense and anticipating two or three cuts ahead of actual occurrence will allow for this type of high-level ball handling.

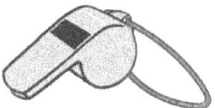 **POINTS OF EMPHASIS**

- Understand and exploit the momentum of defenders.
- Understand the offense and where the next pass is likely to occur.
- Create space at correct time and angle.
- Use dribble with a purpose.

SKILL 4

DRIBBLING ON THE MOVE: SPLITTING THE DOUBLE-TEAM AND SLICING THE FLOOR

SPLITTING THE DOUBLE-TEAM

Splitting the double-team with the use of the dribble can be tricky and should be used in the correct situation. As an observant and reactive offensive player, the right moment will present itself when the two defenders double-teaming are not quite in sync, as they work together to seal the middle of the trap, or are late arriving at the trap. A creative ball handler will get one of the two defenders going in one direction, usually with a jab or shoulder movement, then be able to perform a crossover through the trap and accelerate out of it. Common uses are in the backcourt against teams that press and in on-ball screen situations against teams that hard hedge defensively. Coaches can recreate these situations in training through breakdown skills or live-game situations.

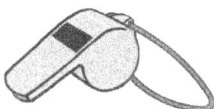

POINTS OF EMPHASIS

- Read when opportunities are open.
- Use momentum against one defender.
- Quick, low dribble at middle of trap.
- Explode out of the trap.

SLICING THE FLOOR: ADVANTAGE SITUATIONS AND SECONDARY TRANSITION

Slicing the floor is an action by the offense where the ball handler dribbles from one half of the court to the other, changing or slicing the attack from one side to the other. This skill is useful to create advantage situations and also on the secondary transition.

ADVANTAGE SITUATIONS

The dribble can be used to create an advantage situation that might not otherwise be there. For example, if a player has the basketball running the right lane, with one defender and one teammate in the same right lane ahead of the basketball, there is an opportunity for the ball handler to slice the floor, creating a 2-on-1 advantage situation. If the ball handler does not slice the floor, the lone defensive player can defend the two offensive players at once, taking away any type of advantage for the offense. Slicing the floor with the use of the dribble will create the advantage situation, forcing the defender to make a decision and leading to a viable scoring opportunity. It also creates a great passing lane back against the grain, which can be challenging to defend.

SECONDARY TRANSITION

Passing the basketball is always faster than using a dribble. However, dribbling the basketball can create situations that are challenging to defend as well, if used properly. In secondary transition, slicing the floor as a ball handler from one side of the floor to the other can be difficult to defend. For example, if the post player who is running to the rim has a defender on the ball side, slicing the floor quickly with a dribble may allow the post player to seal the defender on the back, creating a great angle for a layup. Also, slicing the floor on the dribble may create a 2-on-1 on the backside, many times creating a three-point opportunity for a teammate by penetrating and kicking. Slicing the floor with the dribble should be done with a purpose, to take advantage of the opponent's transition defense.

POINTS OF EMPHASIS

- Use for a purpose; create an advantage or better angle.
- Complete quickly or lose the opportunity.
- Be aware of players coming from behind in the transition.

SKILL 5

DRIBBLING ON THE MOVE: TWO BASKETBALLS

DRILL 1: FULL-COURT COMBINATION MOVES

- Progress players from stationary moves with two basketballs to performing change of direction moves with two basketballs while dribbling up the floor at game speed.
- Players will move up the floor in a zigzag pattern with two basketballs and execute a change of direction move with both hands on each basketball as they cut back and forth.
- The change of direction move can either be the same with both hands, for instance both basketballs crossing over simultaneously, or the moves can be different. For example, when moving to the right, the change of direction for the basketball being dribbled in the right hand can be a between-the-legs move from right hand to left hand while the basketball that was being dribbled in the left hand makes a behind-the-back move from left hand to right hand.
- Have players begin moving up the court without defense and then add in defenders to increase pressure.
- Allow players to be creative as they move up the basketball floor, reading the defense to make the appropriate move. Encourage players to pound the basketball and use both hands to make all moves while changing speed and direction.

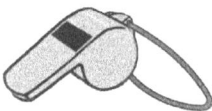

POINTS OF EMPHASIS

- Pound basketball.
- Stay low into move; explode out of move.
- Head up.
- Use both hands equally.

DRILL 2: DRIBBLE MOVES AND PASSING TO A MOVING TARGET

This is a challenging drill that incorporates many facets of offensive skills into one drill. Be creative in setting up various scenarios around the court to enhance team offense or specific player improvement.

- The drill will involve two individuals, one with two basketballs standing just behind half court and the other player standing on the block.

- The player with the two basketballs will prepare to make an entry pass by dribbling in the opposite direction of the teammate on the block, making a move to change directions before heading back toward the player on the block.
- The player on the block will step under the rim in preparation of a V-cut or an L-cut.
- Working on timing together, the player with the basketballs will break the free-throw line plane on the same side as the cut prior to making the entry pass. The player making the cut will hold the cut until the ball handler is in a position to be able to make the entry.
- Using the outside hand, the ball handler will make an entry pass to the outside hand of the cutter, ideally at the free-throw line extended three-point line or the wing. Keeping the second basketball alive, the player will then make a move at the top of the key to score at the rim or a pull-up jump shot.
- The player who caught the basketball on the wing will also make a move off of the dribble to score.
- Coaches can challenge players to make different moves when handling the two basketballs and vary scoring moves with one basketball. Further, coaches can challenge players to make different types of entry passes and cuts to get open, such as V-cuts, L-cuts, or post entries. Add in live defenders to progress players to make correct reads based on how the defenders play.

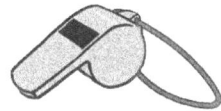

POINTS OF EMPHASIS

- Pound basketballs.
- Stay low going into moves; explode coming out for change of pace.
- Pass to outside hand of cutter.
- Keep second basketball alive while making the entry pass.
- Vary moves with two basketballs and one basketball after the entry pass.

DEFENSIVE PRINCIPLES

GENERAL OVERVIEW: *At the Performance Level, it is imperative to strive for mastery while training with the goal of applying the mastery in live-game situations. Players will need to understand scouting reports and execute them as designed. Further, players will need to have the ability to make adjustments on the fly through own personal basketball IQ, but also through instruction from a coach during live play and in timeout situations. Players who can take instruction and implement it immediately can have a huge impact on the outcome of the game.*

In addition to mastering previously introduced on-ball defensive skills, below are a few additional skills to impart. There are many drills that can be set up to reinforce these concepts, but the true indicator is application in live play.

SKILL 1

CHANGING FEET

Being able to change the angle of the feet to force an offensive player in a particular direction while midplay is a high-level and necessary skill to learn. This is most commonly seen while defending an on-ball screen. For example, on the closeout, the defender will close out to the top foot based on team principles. If a ball screen is set from the middle of the floor, depending on how the team is defending ball screens, the on-ball defender will likely need to switch the angle of the feet to force the offensive player to use the on-ball screen heading toward the middle of the floor. This midplay adjustment will allow teammates to position correctly based on the game plan.

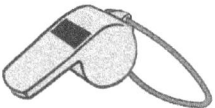

POINTS OF EMPHASIS

- Communicate to the on-ball defender who will switch positioning of feet.
- Maintain spacing or belly up on offensive player while switching feet, based on game plan.
- After direction is dictated, make urgent movements to return to ball handler.
- Once recovered to ball handler, return to team defensive principles.

SKILL 2

PERSONAL STRENGTHS/WEAKNESSES VS. OPPONENT STRENGTHS/WEAKNESSES

Understanding personal strengths and weaknesses defensively can be just as important, if not more important, than understanding an opponent's offensive strengths and weaknesses. Can a player who is slower on lateral slides defend a lightning-quick penetrator? Yes, but only if the defender understands personal skill sets and limitations and uses angles and teammates to defend the offensive player, rather than relying on pure speed. Coaches should work with players to understand strengths and weaknesses and how to counterbalance those with opponent's offensive skill sets, personnel, and tendencies. Players ideally should develop defensive skills and concepts to defend all types of offensive players, counterbalancing personal strengths and weaknesses.

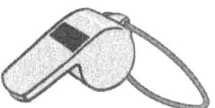

POINTS OF EMPHASIS

- Make sure players understand personal strengths and weaknesses.
- Make sure players understand how to use their skill set to offset offensive strength.
- Players should defend all types of offensive players in preparation.

SKILL 3

DISCIPLINE

Staying disciplined on the defensive end is imperative for a solid team defensive scheme, and this starts with the defender on the basketball. On-ball defenders who are not disciplined in their stance and positioning at this level will get beaten by good teams, which will create a disadvantage for the entire team. For example, when an offensive player shoots the basketball, it is important for the defender to contest the shot with the outside hand (same side as shooter), while staying on the floor. Defenders who are undisciplined and jump in the air to contest often foul the shooter or are blown by as a result of a shot fake. Further, on-ball defenders who constantly reach at the ball handler will be exposed by a good team, resulting in a foul or being beat off the dribble. Consequently, this puts the defensive team at a disadvantage, many times playing 4-on-5. At this level, steals typically occur on the backside of defenses from the help side, not on the basketball. Stay disciplined, influence the basketball in a certain direction, and allow the team defense to take shape.

 **POINTS OF EMPHASIS**

- Disciplined positioning of feet, body, and hands.
- Do not leave feet to contest the shot.
- Contest with outside hand to alleviate foul calls across the offensive player's body.

SKILL 4

IN-GAME ADJUSTMENTS

Basketball can become a chess match at the Performance Level, between two teams on both ends of the court. Defensively, a team may begin the game pushing the offensive player to the baseline with an extended help-side system to cover penetration. This may work for a few possessions before the offensive team makes an adjustment to counter the defense. At this point in time, a coach will make an adjustment midgame to push the ball handler in a different direction, or be more conservative in help side, as an example. This adjustment will require players to quickly change the mindset with which they entered the game. Players and teams who can successfully make these types of adjustments will impact the outcome of the game. Players should also be able to make in-game adjustments without the coach having to provide all of the answers. For example, if an on-ball defender gets scored on by an offensive player catching and shooting a three-pointer on ball reversal, the defensive player should adjust the help-side distance and execute a long closeout to chase the offensive player off of the three-point line. Players should understand how they are scored on and make appropriate adjustments. Many times, coaches cannot get instruction out to players, especially when the defense is on the other end of the floor. This is where the player needs to be able to make an in-game adjustment to influence the game. Empower your players to make adjustments!

POINTS OF EMPHASIS

- Clarity of priority for team defense scheme.
- Empower players to make decisions.
- Provide precise instruction in timeouts for adjustments.
- Understand player's comprehension and instruct accordingly.

PERFORMANCE LEVEL

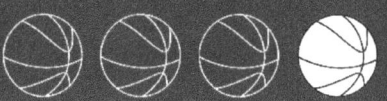

OFFENSIVE PRINCIPLES: FOOTWORK & BODY CONTROL

GENERAL OVERVIEW: *Footwork and body control now involve more game-speed action with quick changes of directions. Remember that players can be at different levels for different skills and that skill development is a constant, ongoing process. This is particularly true for footwork and body control, which play a key role in so many aspects of the game. Even at the Performance Level, this skill must continue to be emphasized frequently.*

SKILL 1

PIVOTING

This skill advances the footwork and body control of the pivot for the player. A pivot takes place when one foot is lifted off the floor while the other foot remains planted and is used to turn the body. When players receive the basketball, they can use either a front or a reverse pivot to protect the basketball from the defense, to pass to a teammate, or to make a move to the basket. A pivot can be made while on the run, with or without the basketball, such as when performing a crossover dribble or a V-cut. A pivot can also be made when a player is stationary, such as when a player uses it to gain an advantage. In this level, we now use the pivot in team offensive work such as 2-on-2, 3-on-3, and 4-on-4. The pivot now involves use at the different positions—post play, after receiving the basketball at the wing, and at the guard position.

 ### POINTS OF EMPHASIS

- Pivot on one foot using a front pivot, which is turning the body forward 180 degrees on the pivot.
- Pivot on one foot using a reverse pivot, which is turning the body backward 180 degrees on the pivot.
- When attacking after a pivot is made, stay low and push off to go to the basket.
- Keep the basketball close to the body and keep the body between the basketball and the defender.
- Keep low with the feet spread, knees bent, and rear end down, but keep the chin, head, and eyes up.
- Shifting the head forward or sideways while making the stop is likely to result in lost balance.

SKILL 2

CHANGING DIRECTION/SPEED AND BODY CONTROL

Offensive players use cuts to change direction quickly while staying in balance in order to create space between them and the defender to get open for passes or shots. Change of pace and change of direction with and without the basketball are two of the best assets a player can have but must be performed with quickness. Making changes in angles rather than arcs is very important to improving one's individual game. The length of the step may vary based on the player and the game situation, but generally short, choppy steps are better to attain quickness. At this level, the change of direction is now emphasized with quickness and speed.

POINTS OF EMPHASIS

- Change directions in angles and not arcs.
- Push off the foot in the opposite direction you want to go.
- Turn shoulders and feet in the direction you want to go.
- Head should stay over the feet.
- Short, choppy steps will help increase quickness.
- A change of pace should be taught with a hesitation move; use a head fake up and a quick pushoff with the back foot.

DEFENSIVE PRINCIPLES

GENERAL OVERVIEW: *In this level, the defense will be working on stance along with movement. Defenders must be able to slide their feet and maintain an arm's-length distance from an opponent who is attempting to drive or cut to the basket. The player should move the leg nearest the intended direction about two feet to that side and then slide the other foot until the feet are once again shoulder width apart.*

SKILL 1

PROPER STANCE

The proper defensive stance should be introduced at the Introductory Level with continued progression in the Foundational, Advanced, and Performance Levels. Feet should be wider than the shoulders, hands above the waist, and chin up with the head in a position that is above the knees and not leaning forward. This will give the defender the ability to move in all directions and make pivots. When guarding an opponent with the basketball, the defensive player should maintain the defensive stance with one hand down to help prevent against the crossover dribble and the other hand up in the passing lane to deflect a pass attempt.

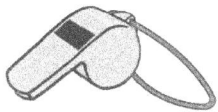

POINTS OF EMPHASIS

- The defender's weight should be evenly distributed on both feet with the feet a little wider than the shoulders.
- Legs should not cross, except when trying to catch up, and instead slide and glide with the feet.
- Keep head at the same height without permitting it either to bob up and down or to get forward or backward of the midpoint between the two feet.
- The distance from the offensive player is judged according to how far the player is from the basketball and the basket.

SKILL 2

360-DEGREE MOVEMENTS

The footwork involved with movement on defense requires low, basketball position, pushing off the top foot, sliding in the direction of the offensive player, and staying arm's distance from the offensive player. Many times, the defender must turn the offensive player, such as when the offensive player is working to dribble the basketball up the court. In this case, the defender's foot positioning will change. The player must position the foot closest to the rim line, which is the imaginary center line running from rim to rim, ahead of the other foot and keep an arm's length from the dribbler. The foot closest to the rim line must be outside the dribbler's foot to force a baseline dribble. Proper defensive positioning off the basketball also requires movement. Using peripheral vision, defenders must keep their player and the basketball within sight at all times. To help defensive movements, keep one hand pointing toward the basketball and the other hand pointing toward the assigned player whenever the offense has the basketball.

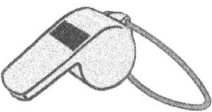

POINTS OF EMPHASIS

- Knees slightly bent with hands above the waist.
- Use drop-step pivot footwork to change directions.
- Push off the top foot to move in any of 360-degree movements.
- Keep moving and anticipating. Never get caught standing still or standing straight up.
- Keep the head level when moving; no bobbing.

PERFORMANCE LEVEL

OFFENSIVE PRINCIPLES: PASSING & RECEIVING

GENERAL OVERVIEW: *At the Performance Level, passing and receiving focus on skill mastery within game application. Understanding your personnel, team tendencies, and opponent's tendencies will allow for a higher level of decision-making, improving and allowing for precise passing.*

SKILL 1

PASSING OUT OF THE DOUBLE-TEAM

Developing an understanding of how to pass out of a double-team can be challenging, as there are many variables to consider. The timing and location of defenders on the floor, where offensive players are spaced, and the time and score of the game all play into passing strategies. A few examples are discussed below, by position.

PERIMETER

Double-teams most commonly come in the backcourt or in a half-court trap or run-and-jump situation for perimeter players. Consequently, many times the double-team is coming from behind the offensive player. For purposes of explanation, in this scenario the trap is occurring on the sideline with the individual forcing the trap coming from the middle of the floor.

- A few things to consider while passing out of a double-team are timing of the trap, one's location on the floor, and the location of the other offensive players.
- If the individual forcing the trap is late, passing off of the dribble immediately out of the double-team to an open player, in the middle of the floor, can be most effective. With proper spacing and timing, there will likely be no need for a ball fake but rather a quick pass-off of the dribble, splitting the double-team.
- By drawing two defenders, offensive players can create an advantage situation, if spacing is correct, with quick movement of the basketball out of the trap.
- Another effective move to create a passing angle out of a double-team, in particular from the middle of the floor, is to ball-fake sideline or back toward the middle. With a convincing ball fake, the defender will likely jump in the air to attempt to block the pass, creating an opportunity to pivot in between the two defenders and open a passing lane to a teammate.
- A quick pivot through the double-team with a crisp pass is necessary in order to take advantage of a small window of opportunity.
- Another effective move to pass out of a double-team is the use of a pivot around one of the defenders. If the double-team is coming from the middle, with momentum heading toward the sideline, it can be highly effective to use a front pivot, stepping completely around the defender, and use the body to protect the basketball while making a one-hand chest pass back to the offensive player. This type of pivot allows the offensive player to place the body between the basketball and the defender, creating a passing lane back to the teammate. A front pivot is preferred to maintain vision of the rotating defenders. If a reverse pivot is used, a defender can rotate to steal the pass without being seen.
- Patience and poise are always necessary components while passing out of a double-team.

POINTS OF EMPHASIS

- Be aware of where and when the double-team is coming.
- Keep vision of defenders and teammates—make pass early.
- Drawing two defenders will create an advantage to attack out of the double-team if the pass is completed properly.
- Use appropriate ball fakes and pivots to create passing lanes and protect basketball.
- Complete crisp pass out of double-team.
- Patience and poise.

POST

At this level, double-teams will occur in various ways: on the catch, once a dribble is made, from the middle of the floor, from the top of the floor, out of player-to-player or zone defense, etc. To determine where the double-team is coming from initially, the fundamental principles to utilize are the 3 Cs: Catch, Chin, and Check.

- Feel where the post defender is located; this will indicate which direction the double-team may be coming from or, at the very least, which direction to make a post move toward.
- For purposes of this explanation, the double-team is coming from the top of the key, with the ball-side denial defenders staying home.
- In this scenario, the individual creating the double-team typically has some space to cover if the entry pass into the post is not anticipated, making a quick move toward the direction of the double-team potentially effective.
- If the defender does anticipate the pass and arrives on time, then it is imperative to protect the basketball while surveying the court to see the rotating defenders on the floor.
- In many cases, the use of a reverse pivot can buy time as well as create space to make an effective pass out of the double-team. It is important to remember in many cases, the opposite wing (garden spot) is open after all of the rotations.
- If the double-team is coming from the top, a quick pass to the top before the rotation is set could also be effective. Vision of the defenders rotating is critical.
- Use of a pivot, ball fake, or in some rare cases a dribble can help create space to complete an appropriate overhead pass out of the double-team, allowing the offensive team to attack on the backside of the defense.
- Just as with perimeter play, patience and poise are necessary components to completing effective passes out of any double-team.

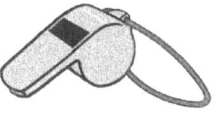

POINTS OF EMPHASIS

- Three Cs: Catch, Chin, Check.
- Be aware of where the double-team is coming from and if the defender is arriving on time or late.
- Vision of the defenders rotating.
- Use pivot, ball fake, or rare dribble to create space to complete overhead pass to attack on backside.
- Patience and poise.

SKILL 2

ATTACK DEFENSE BASED ON TEAM AND PERSONNEL TENDENCIES

Having a comprehensive understanding of how both an individual defender and a team tend to play on the defensive end can help an offensive player and team execute the offense using different types of passes to score. For example, if a team plays an overaggressive defensive style, denying every catch, an offensive team may clear a side out to set up a backdoor cut. Knowing this as a passer will allow the player to establish the appropriate angle to make a bounce pass off of the defender's back side, arriving at the appropriate time. Without creating this angle at the right time and selling the entry pass to allow for an open backdoor cut, the pass will likely be unsuccessful at this level.

- In addition to understanding team tendencies, a great passer will understand individual defensive tendencies to create opportunities on the offensive end.
- For example, if the post defender is in a low-side denial position when the basketball is located on the ball-side corner and is not continually adjusting defensive position on the basket side when the ball is reversed, then a high-low seal and pass would make sense.
- In this scenario, the player at the top of the key should recognize the high-low opportunity prior to it occurring in addition to the baseline player recognizing the basketball needs to be reversed for the seal. The high-low pass must be a quick, efficient, and appropriate pass into the post player sealing the defender on the backside.
- If either player does not recognize the opportunity, the passing lane will likely close quicker than a pass can be made.
- Another great example of recognizing tendencies is if a defender routinely neglects to position in help side, which would allow for a post lob or back-door cut. These are opportunities that should be recognized on the floor, in live play, and used for an offensive advantage.

Establish these situations in practice to help players develop strong decision-making skills based on how defenders are positioned. Continue to enforce the concepts during games, when appropriate, and reinforce them in post-game reflections or film sessions. The goal is for players to recognize advantage situations, make passes on time during offensive possessions, and execute strategies accordingly.

# POINTS OF EMPHASIS

- Observe defenses and defender's tendencies during live game play and attack accordingly.
- Create passing angles to take advantage of defenders out of position.
- Recognize where the basketball needs to be passed in order to take advantage of how defenders are positioned.

SKILL 3

NO-LOOK PASS

Many coaches prefer for players to have vision of where their passes are being made, but at this level, it can be appropriate to master the art of a no-look pass. A no-look pass requires complete awareness of the basketball court, including an understanding of speed and location of the teammate being passed to, in order to successfully complete. Many times, an ideal situation for a no-look pass comes in an advantage situation, such as in transition. By looking in one direction and getting the defender to think, freeze, or even move in that direction, a passing lane in the opposite direction opens up. A believable no-look pass can lead directly to a layup if performed properly in the advantage situation.

The actual no-look pass will require the offensive player to make it appear they are really passing to a specific player. Eyes will be on the false target, body language and momentum also traveling toward that direction. Once the player opposite becomes open, seen out of the peripheral, a crisp pass across the body will be made to the newly open teammate. Just as with all passing, lead the teammate to the open spot, completing a crisp pass that leads directly to the shot.

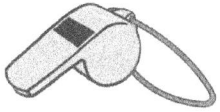

POINTS OF EMPHASIS

- Complete floor awareness.
- Sell the defender in one direction with eyes, body, and momentum.
- Crisp pass back across body leading directly to shot.

SKILL 4

TIMING AND PRECISION PASSING

At this level, defenders are quicker, bigger, and stronger and adapt to situations and personnel at a much higher level. Consequently, passing has to be completed with exact timing and precision without much room for error. Below are few examples by position.

PERIMETER

Throughout the passing section, the importance of post entries and back-door passing has been alluded to. Another example that is often neglected is the precision involved in passing in transition or advantage situations. For example, let's take a situation of a ball handler having an offensive teammate out in front and a defender picking up the basketball. Add in another defender running alongside the ball handler but slightly behind the teammate who is ahead and running at full speed. What type of pass would be appropriate in this situation? Many would say a lob pass, but this pass is highly difficult not only to complete, but also to catch and finish without a turnover. A long bounce pass splitting the two defenders would be more effective. This type of pass requires a great deal of timing and precision. The basketball will likely be thrown with one hand, splitting the two defenders, with the bounce occurring close to the defender in order to keep hands out of the way. It should hit the offensive player at the waist in stride, leading directly to a layup.

POINTS OF EMPHASIS

- Take advantage of small windows of opportunity to complete precise passes.
- In transition, bounce passes are easier to complete and handle than lob passes.
- Pass with one hand; bounce at defender's feet.
- Hit teammate in stride at waist level leading directly to a shot.

POST

Making a high-low pass can require a great deal of timing and precision and should be mastered at this level. Part of becoming a successful high-low passer is knowing how teammates play. For example, one teammate may clear the lane allowing more room for error on the pass. Another teammate may give up a seal on the left side, while tending to hold a better seal on the right side. Knowing these elements can assist on where and when to deliver a high-low pass. In general, on the high post catch teammates should always look for the post player sealing. Squaring up and creating an attack presence so the defense cannot anticipate such a pass is necessary. The actual pass should have some touch on it, between a crisp chest pass and a lob with too much air under it. Many times, the pass will need to travel over the defender's outstretched hand and drop into the hands of the teammate without traveling out of bounds or going too far under the basket to complete the layup. It is important to have vision of the entire floor and an understanding of where the help side might be rotating from. The basketball should be delivered to the target hand, possibly leading the player, and be away from the help-side defender. The timing and precise delivery can be challenging to master, but can be a nightmare to defend if completed properly.

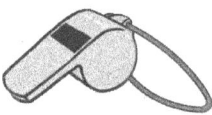

POINTS OF EMPHASIS

- Know teammate's tendencies.
- Square up in attack mode.
- Have vision of the entire floor.
- Put air under the pass, but not too much. Pass over the defender's hand but not out of bounds.
- Hit target hand and lead player into layup.

SKILL 5

DECISION-MAKING AND PASSING USING ON-BALL SCREEN

The golden rule coming off of an on-ball screen as a ball handler is to have a scoring mindset. The momentum and actions coming off the on-ball screen should also make the defender believe this is the first intention, regardless if there is another offensive option preferred at that moment in time. The ball handler should also be aware of how the defense is defending the screen in addition to the rest of the floor to understand how help side is rotating.

Below are different options to attack off the ball screen using the pass, which, as mentioned before, are secondary options for the ball handler who is first looking or indicating an intention to score.

OPTION: HIT ROLLER

As a ball handler, the decision-making process begins when the shoulders clip the waist of the screener. From this point, how the defenders play the screen will determine next steps. If the defenders switch the screen, this allows the screener to roll to the basket, sealing a smaller defender behind. The ball handler must come off of the screen hard and immediately create space and an angle to complete this pass, most times, using a bounce pass. Vision of the entire court is imperative once it's determined how the defenders involved in the screen are playing the screen. The bounce pass will travel between the two defenders, so the angle needs to be opened at the correct time. This falls on the ball handler, moving the basketball from one side of the body to the other, to complete the pass. Delivering the pass on the run leading to an immediate shot is preferred to cut down on the chances of the help side rotating in time.

OPTION: HIT POP

This option opens up when attacking off of the screen; both defenders go with the ball handler, either trapping, hedging, or through miscommunication. In this scenario, the individual who sets the screen will recognize this advantage and pop, creating space and an angle from the ball handler to receive a pass in order to make an immediate jump shot or attack the basket on the catch. The ball handler must attack the two defenders and help with creating this space, also buying time for the screener to pop and get feet set to receive the basketball. Many times, this pass has to be made off of the dribble using a crisp overhead pass to allow the individual popping to get a shot off before the help side rotates. In other instances, mainly if being trapped, a pivot back toward the popper may be necessary to protect the basketball and provide a controlled pass that can be received ready to score or attack.

OPTION: PENETRATE KICK TO TEAMMATE BEHIND ROLLER

A situation such as this requires the ball handler to see the next defender (besides the two involved in the screens) in order to make the correct decision. While using the on-ball screen, the two defenders switch, allowing the individual setting the screen to roll, sealing the switching defender. The individual defending the offensive player in the corner recognizes the disadvantage this creates and slides into help side to take away the roller. In this scenario, the offensive player in the corner should relocate toward the ball handler, making the run for that defender to recover much longer. The ball handler should recognize a situation like this and find the open teammate rotating out of the corner. Again, the actual pass often will be directly off of the dribble, but could be off of a pivot if necessary. As always, delivery of the pass should be received leading to a scoring opportunity without adjustment.

 # POINTS OF EMPHASIS

- Decision-making process begins at point of screen.
- Have awareness of defenders involved in screen and in help side rotating—floor vision.
- Immediately create space and angles to complete successful next pass.

SKILL 6

RECEIVING: TYPES OF SQUARE-UP BASED ON SITUATION

The use of pivots seem to be underutilized, yet at this level can be used effectively to create space for scoring or passing opportunities. Being able to understand situations and read defenders while using both feet in both directions on receipt of a pass should be maximized at this level. Below are a few examples per position.

PERIMETER

While receiving the basketball on the wing, an offensive player frequently will use a front pivot, or inside foot, in order to establish an attack mode to the defender. This allows the offensive player to create momentum to the basket while forcing the defender backward. It also leads the offensive player into a position to make multiple moves through jab steps or off of the dribble, while also allowing for a clear vision of the court. If an offensive player squares up using a reverse pivot, if the defender is not completely overplaying, then the defender would have an opportunity to jam up the offensive player, making the offensive player the reactor with the defender dictating the action. An example where an offensive player would want to use a reverse pivot while receiving the basketball on the perimeter would be if the defensive player is overplaying on the denial, getting out of position, and allowing an opportunity to attack the basket. In this case, the offensive player would receive the basketball with the shoulders facing the passer, catching the basketball most likely on the outside of the body. On the catch, the offensive player would make a reverse pivot a full 180 degrees heading in a straight line to the basket. The pivot allows the offensive player to protect the basketball and take advantage of how the defender is playing the pass.

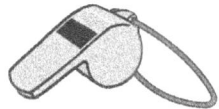

POINTS OF EMPHASIS

- Be in attack mode as often as possible on offense, which typically means using a front pivot.
- Use pivots into jab steps, to attack off the dribble and to create vision of the court.
- If the denial defender overplays, there is an opportunity to use a reverse pivot to attack rim.
- Reverse pivots should be used to create space without falling out of attack mode.

POST

Use of the pivot is critical in post play and is dependent on the three Cs: Catch, Chin, Check, and the overall feel of where the defender is located. In the low block, a reverse pivot can be used to establish space from the defender, in many cases allowing for a quick turnaround jump shot. This type of pivot can be especially effective if a front pivot is used with success several times. At this time, a defender may be anticipating the front pivot. Use of the reverse pivot will give a different look and create space for a scoring or passing opportunity. A reverse pivot in the low block may also be utilized to buy time on a double-team, creating an extra second to make an appropriate pass, or even create a scoring opportunity in the opposite direction prior to the double-team arriving. In addition to low block play, receiving the basketball at the high post, short corner, or anywhere outside of the lane is critical. If a defender is playing in the lane, a front pivot into a short jump shot is highly effective. The front pivot allows the momentum to be going toward the basket, squaring up for a scoring opportunity while allowing vision of the floor to look for a higher percentage shot or advantage opportunity. Whether in the low block or at the high post, reading and feeling where the defender is located is imperative to creating solid, offensive opportunities at this level.

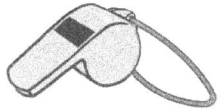

POINTS OF EMPHASIS

- Three Cs: Catch, Chin, Check.
- Feel where the defense is; understand how the defense is playing and what they are trying to take away.
- Use appropriate pivots to create space from defender for shot or passing opportunity.

DEFENSIVE PRINCIPLES

GENERAL OVERVIEW: *The amount of time spent playing defense off the basketball far exceeds the time spent playing on-ball defense, making denial defense imperative. At the Performance Level, teaching game application of denial defense to impact the outcome of the basketball game is required and accomplished by understanding the opposing team's offensive and personnel tendencies and how to use denial concepts within the team defensive philosophies. Application through strategy is key.*

SKILL 1

USING DENIAL TO DISRUPT OFFENSIVE FLOW

The use of denial defense can accomplish far more than just resulting in a steal. It is important, at this level, to understand how the offensive team is comfortable scoring—from where on the floor, from which player, where the passes come from, etc. For example, a team may be highly effective once the basketball is reversed through the high post. Denying the high post, thereby not allowing ball reversal, will take away the offensive team's first option, potentially creating a far more challenging offensive flow. The denial did not necessarily create a turnover, but it could create a bad shot being taken from an offensive player who is not comfortable with the shot. In many scenarios, this is just as impactful as a steal. In another example, an offensive team may be highly effective when they catch the basketball on the wing at the three-point line, allowing for screening action and good angles to make difficult timing passes. If a defender can make the catch two steps off of the three-point line, those timing passes become much more challenging to complete. Another example to consider is against a highly effective dribble penetrating team. In this case, a team may choose to deny farther up the line toward the basketball, making the floor look smaller with fewer gaps to be able to penetrate into to get to the rim. This type of defense forces jump shots or outside shots, which can be advantageous to a defensive team if the offensive team's strength is dribble penetration to the rim.

It is important to remember that many nuances of the game do not show up directly on a stat sheet but can impact and change the outcome of games.

POINTS OF EMPHASIS

- Understand how the opposing team is comfortable scoring and make adjustments to alter this comfort level.
- Use denial to extend the offense beyond normal spacing or to throw off offensive timing.

SKILL 2

DENIAL BASED ON OFFENSIVE PERSONNEL

Similar to using denial defense to disrupt offensive flow, the same concepts hold true for specific player personnel. A player, for example, may be most comfortable catching the basketball at a certain position on the floor, scoring at a high percentage when this occurs. The use of strategic denial defense can deter the catch at this position, making an effective scorer catch out of the comfort zone. This could result in several fewer points in the game, directly impacting the outcome. Below are examples specific to position.

PERIMETER

When playing against a team with a dynamic offensive scorer, one who can penetrate, shoot a three-point shot, and is the center of the entire offense, it might make sense to adjust the defense on this player. Have the defender in an all-out denial position, essentially face-guarding the player, not allowing a catch or making every catch as difficult as possible. This can be highly frustrating to the offensive player and can impact the point production of an individual player and team. Further, a denial position may look different based on if the offensive player is a three-point threat or more of a penetrator. If the player is a three-point shooter, an all-out overplaying denial position would be appropriate. If the player is a penetrator, more of a soft denial might make sense, allowing for a cushion on the catch to defend the penetration.

POST

If there is an offensive player who scores efficiently on the right block turning over the left shoulder, a strategic adjustment may be to deny on the low side to make a catch difficult on the player's preferred side. Further, establishing position on the low side will allow the defender to sit on the left shoulder on the catch should the offensive player receive the basketball. A defensive player can also use the denial position to make the post player catch one step off of the block. This can result in making a post player who is more comfortable with the back to the basket now have to face up, throwing off the rhythm of the player.

The more a defensive player understands personnel, the more strategic denial positions can disrupt offensive possessions and scoring opportunities.

POINTS OF EMPHASIS

- Denial principles are necessary for team defense. Adjusting and altering from the principles based on the opposing team's player personnel can impact a game at this level.
- Have an overall understanding of how individual players score and overall tendencies, adjusting accordingly to disrupt the rhythm.

SKILL 3

DENYING PERIMETER L-CUT

If executed properly, L-cuts can be much more challenging to defend than standard V-cuts, due to the offensive player's ability to get into the body of the defender closer to the spot of the catch, assuming the catch is on the wing. The goal of the offensive player on this type of cut is to establish a foot higher than the top foot of the defender and to physically get into the body of the defender in order to change directions effectively, creating an opening for an entry pass. Because of this, positioning of the defender denying the basketball is critical. The defender must work early, establishing position up the line toward the passer, creating some space from the cutter in order to maintain the positioning at the most critical point, not allowing the offensive player to win the top foot positioning. If this positioning is established and maintained, it makes it difficult for the offensive player to gain an advantage. Proper denial of the L-cut either results in a steal, impacts timing, or pushes the catch farther out than desired.

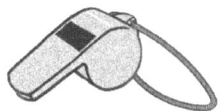

POINTS OF EMPHASIS

- Do work early.
- Establish position and maintain space from cutter.
- Do not allow offensive player to win top foot positioning at pinnacle of cut.

SKILL 4

IN-GAME ADJUSTMENTS

In-game adjustments at this level can be critical to player and team success. Being able to quickly communicate adjustments to an individual and the team is important to the success of any team defense, and players should be trained accordingly to be able to understand and quickly react to such adjustments. It is encouraged to prepare for these types of adjustments through training so the adjustments and terminology are not new during the heat of the game. Further, teams will begin to excel when players can recognize and make in-game adjustments without a coach's word. Coaches are encouraged to empower players to make quick decisions based on personnel and how teams are effectively scoring. This trust is established in practice and through game situations and post-game reflections over time. Empower players to think and understand the game of basketball, understanding situations and reacting accordingly to team defensive philosophies to impact the outcome of the game.

POINTS OF EMPHASIS

- Communicate effectively on all in-game adjustments—this should be practiced and not something new during a game.
- Prepare for such situations in practice and discuss adjustments that could have been made in post-game reflections.
- Establish trust with players—empower players, as coaches cannot always get messages into fast-paced game situations.
- Create an environment for players to think and understand the game of basketball.

PERFORMANCE LEVEL

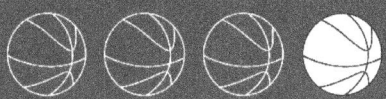

OFFENSIVE PRINCIPLES: REBOUNDING

GENERAL OVERVIEW: *Rebounding—both offensive and defensive—is a fundamental skill to teach as possession of the basketball comes more often from missed shots than any other way. The success of offensive rebounding relies largely on players' desire and courage. In this level, the skills are defined by tactical positioning for offensive rebounding. Tipping the ball, getting the ball out of your area, and designated offensive rebounding spots are examples of tactical rebounding work.*

SKILL 1

TIPPING THE BASKETBALL

Offensive rebounders may tip the basketball away from the board for possession in situations when they are not in position to get either an offensive tip in or a clear possession. Offensive rebounders should learn to use their wrists and fingers for tipping and not to bat at the basketball. They should also keep the palms of the hands toward the basket in order to have better tipping control. The offensive rebounder must always be active to give the second and third effort. Many offensive baskets have been made simply because the rebounder refused to give up and kept giving the extra effort until the basket was made.

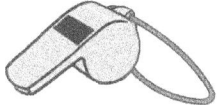

POINTS OF EMPHASIS

- Use wrist and fingers to tip the basketball.
- Use the tip to keep the basketball alive if the basketball cannot be grasped with both hands.
- Be ready to jump several times to tip the basketball in the basket or to a teammate.
- Jump quickly to tip the basketball.

SKILL 2

GETTING THE BASKETBALL OUT OF THE AREA

Movement for offensive rebounding is key to securing the rebound when it is out of your area. This is a great skill but one that few master, as players need much determination, desire to get the basketball, quickness to the basketball, and a keen understanding of the angles for missed shots. Players who constantly move and keep the hands above the shoulders have a better chance to rebound the basketball when it goes outside of their area.

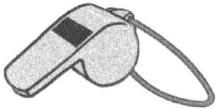

POINTS OF EMPHASIS

- Movement as the shot is taken is a key to rebounding.
- Know the angle of the missed shots—opposite and long for deep shots.
- Be quick to react to the missed shot and jump to get the basketball.
- If you cannot grab the basketball with both hands, tip the basketball to a teammate or to the basket.

SKILL 3

DESIGNATED OFFENSIVE REBOUNDING AREAS

This skill is only done at the Performance Level, as it takes time and mature basketball players to mentally get to offensive rebounding areas. This involves the offensive players to get to a preassigned spot when the shot is taken by a teammate. While the offensive rebounders may not get to that spot, they will be moving toward that area, which makes it much more difficult to block them out. Coaches can assign these rebounding spots to players or by position based on personnel and team strengths.

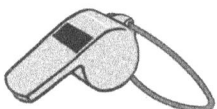

POINTS OF EMPHASIS

- As the shot is released, the offensive players move to the designated spots on the court for rebounds.
- Hands should be above the shoulders.
- Keep eyes on the basketball to watch the angle of the rebound.
- Stay low in the ready basketball position in order to jump for the missed shot.

DEFENSIVE PRINCIPLES

GENERAL OVERVIEW: *Tactical positioning for defensive rebounding may include many of the defensive rebounding skills discussed in the Foundational and Advanced Levels, with more emphasis on these same skills in order for the defensive rebounder to overcome better offensive rebounders.*

SKILL 4

BLOCKING OUT AND GOING AFTER THE REBOUND

Strength is an obvious part of this level of rebounding. Going up between several players to get a rebound is crucial. Strong wrists, hands, and fingers all are necessary when discussing defensive rebounding at the Performance Level.

DRILL 1: WAR

This drill involves three players in the lane area who try to get the missed shot and score.

- The coach will shoot the basketball and the players will fight for the rebound. Even before the coach releases the basketball for the shot, players will begin working for positioning and boxouts.
- The player who gets the rebound will immediately go up and try to score while being fouled by the other two players.
- If the basketball hits the floor or goes outside the lane, the play ends and the coach will shoot the basketball again.
- Play to three baskets off of putbacks and then a new player will come into the drill to replace the winner while the other two players continue in the drill at their current score, trying to get to three. Play a made basket as a missed shot.

 **POINTS OF EMPHASIS**

- Be very aggressive to grab the missed shot.
- Use good basketball positioning to rebound in traffic.
- The players who do not get the rebound will try to stop the shot of the offensive player.
- Catch the basketball cleanly and finish strong.

DRILL 2: RED-WHITE REBOUNDING

This is a very aggressive rebounding drill to develop blockout skills at the highest level.

- Set up two lines at each elbow and two more lines at the baseline corner of the lane. The two lines on the baseline should face the elbow lines.
- The first two players in the baseline lines are defensive teammates and the first two players in the elbow lines are offensive teammates.
- The basketball is tossed by one of the baseline players to either of the players at the elbow who shoots the basketball.
- The shot, made or missed, is rebounded by either the baseline players or the elbow players and put back in by the player who gets the basketball. On the rebound, the team who secures the ball should first try for an immediate putback but can play 2-on-2, if needed, to score.
- Once the basketball is rebounded and scored, the two losers, nonscorers, go to the top elbow lines and the two winners, scorers, go to the bottom baseline lane lines. If the blockout is done correctly, the baseline players should always remain in the bottom lines.

POINTS OF EMPHASIS

- Stay low to absorb the contact from the rebounders.
- Hands need to be above the shoulders.
- Bend knees in order to get the best height on rebounding the basketball.
- Use the rear end to block out the legs of the opponent so the offensive player has a difficult time to jump.

PERFORMANCE LEVEL

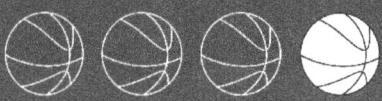

OFFENSIVE PRINCIPLES: SCREENING

GENERAL OVERVIEW: *The screen at the Performance Level now includes much more tactical approaches to maximize offensive efficiency. The purpose of the offensive screen is to create indecision by the defenders, which will allow a shot or a pass for a shot. With every screen set, the defenders must decide how to rotate and play the screen. At this level, misdirection can also be used before the screen is set so the defenders have a hard time communicating and anticipating the screen.*

SKILL 1

TACTICAL USE OF OFF-BALL SCREENS

The advanced use of off-ball screens includes the combination of the screener and the player using the screen working together to create indecision by the defense, which can lead to easy baskets.

- As the screener sets the screen away from the basketball, the screener's eyes are on the defender and the player receiving the screen. The actions of all these players will determine the screener's movement. If the player receiving the screen makes a curl cut around the screen, the screener will then go opposite of the curl cut or step up to receive a pass.
- If the defender being screened is anticipating the screen coming and moves out of defensive help position, the screener slips the screen by planting the top foot and making a hard basket cut looking for the basketball on the cut.
- If the defender on the screener reads the cut of the player receiving the screen and steps up to hedge, the screener will slip to the basket.
- The screener will set up a flare cut if the defender on the player receiving the screen is caught on the ball side of the screener. The screener turns and sets the screen on the outside of the defender so the pass will go over the top of the screener to the offensive player for a shot. Usually the flare cut is set up by the offensive player faking the curl cut.
- The screener may also use a rescreen, which involves a second screen for the offensive player. This could be a down screen first followed by a back screen for the same player.
- Anytime there is a screen across the lane, such as a post-to-post screen, the screener will turn back to the basketball in the opposite direction of the cutter. If the cutter goes low off the screen, the screener will roll back high to the basketball.
- The screener may look for more than one player to screen. For example, the player may set a down screen and then a cross screen across the lane.
- Screening the screener occurs when a player sets the first screen and then receives a second screen by another teammate. This causes a great deal of indecision on the part of the defenders reacting to this action.

POINTS OF EMPHASIS

- The offensive player should not watch the basketball during the screen but should keep eyes on the defender to make the proper decision based on the defender's action.
- The screener will plant the top foot and cut straight to the basket when the defender attempts to cheat the screen by playing over the top of it.
- When using the flare screen, the screener pivots toward the basketball to screen the defender who is caught on the ball side of the screener. The offensive player steps back from an attempted curl cut to use the screen.
- Spacing becomes important after the screen is set. The offensive player using the screen must clear out to allow proper spacing for the screener to pivot back to the basketball.
- Communication by the two offensive players is just as important as the communication for the two defenders. The screener must use hand signals and words to let teammates know a screen is coming.

SKILL 2

TACTICAL USE OF ON-BALL SCREENS

At higher levels and against better defenders, on-ball screens are very useful to create indecision for the defenders and more efficient offense. Setting screens on the basketball creates scramble situations for the defenders, which leads to easy baskets for the offensive team.

- A slip can be used on the basketball as well as off the screens. As the screener runs to set the screen for a teammate who has the basketball, the screener will get within two steps and then plant the front foot to make a quick change of direction to the basket with the hand up calling for the basketball. The key for the screener is to slip if the defender starts to hedge.
- An option for the screener on wing screens is to roll baseline if the dribbler is double-teamed or the defender hedges.
- As the dribbler comes off the screen, the defender on the screener may hedge or flatten out so the dribbler does not turn the corner. Rather than roll to the basket, the screener may find a good passing angle by popping back out. In this instance, the dribbler can also try to split the defenders with the dribble.
- The screener may be able to rescreen the dribbler—set one screen and then turn to set another screen for the dribbler—by reversing directions. This can be called a twist.

POINTS OF EMPHASIS

- The screener needs to run to set the screen to make it more difficult for defenders to hedge or double-team the dribbler.
- On side screens, the screener needs to read the defenders and either pop back out or roll to the baseline.
- When splitting the defenders, the dribble and the dribbler must stay low and attack the basket.
- A rescreen is a good option when the defender on the dribbler gets over the top of the screen. The dribbler can change direction and use the same screener again.

DEFENSIVE PRINCIPLES

GENERAL OVERVIEW: *A team must have one primary method to cover screens, whether it be switching, hedging, double-teaming the screen, or getting over the top of the screen. The offensive matchups will then determine if the defense will change for a particular offensive player. The objective of defending screens is to keep the defense intact and avoid scramble situations.*

SKILL 1

DEFENDING OFFENSIVE PLAYER MOVEMENT AWAY FROM BASKETBALL

- The defender guarding the offensive player moving away from the basketball must immediately be alert for a cutback—slipping the screen.
- The defender must warn teammates in the direction the offensive player is moving to be alert for a screen.
- As the offensive player moves away from the basketball, the defender will stay in a position to help on the basketball and be ready for any screens away from the basketball.

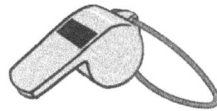

POINTS OF EMPHASIS

- Defender must communicate a possible screen to teammates.
- Stay in good help-side position so the off-ball screen is much more difficult to set on the defenders.
- The defenders must be in a flat stance so the defender can see the basketball and the offensive player.
- This type of screen away from the basketball is a comparatively easy switch.

SKILL 2

DEFENDING A SCREENER ADVANCING FROM SIDE

- The defender being screened should open up toward the possible screener and move one step toward the opposite side of the offensive player.
- By moving over and opening up toward the potential screener, the chances to avoid the screen improve.
- Opening up will also make a switch possible by placing the defense in a better position to prevent the screener from getting open on a roll.
- The step away prevents the offensive player from playing a possible switch and cutting by the defense on the opposite side.

 ## POINTS OF EMPHASIS

- Have an awareness of the possibility of being screened if guarding the offensive player with the basketball.
- As the defender on the basketball anticipates a screen, open up to the side of the screener by dropping the foot closest to the screener back.
- Communication should take place between both defenders as the screener comes closer to the defender.
- Defenders must stay in a stance with the head up and the hands and arms above the waist.

SKILL 3

DEFENDING THE BLIND SCREEN

- The defender must open up by dropping the baseline foot back as soon as the teammate warns the defender of the approaching screen.
- By opening up, the defender can see the basketball and react to the pass.
- It is much more difficult to screen players when their body and shoulders are in perpendicular position to the screener.
- Try to drive the offensive player who wants to use the screen toward the congested area where help-side defenders are in position.
- On specific offensive players, it may be necessary to get on the offensive player's hip so the defender can follow the offensive player.

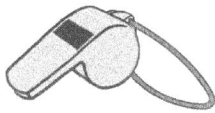

POINTS OF EMPHASIS

- As the blind screen is set, the defender on the screener must loudly call out the screen to the teammate who will be screened.
- A quick pivot by the defender receiving the screen will allow that player to open up and see the basketball and slide with the offensive player.
- The defender should work to go on the ball side of the blind screen, which will prevent a direct pass to the offensive player.
- Keeping the hands high will prevent a pass to the offensive player using the blind screen.

SKILL 4

ROTATIONS WHEN DEFENDING PICK AND ROLL

- Defending screens involves all five defenders. Those defenders not directly guarding the screen or the screener must be in a position to help on the screening action.
- Anytime a screen takes place on the court, the three defenders not involved in the screening action must be ready to rotate to the basketball when the dribbler uses the screen.
- On a hedge by the screener's defender, the weak-side player will drop off to defend the roll by the screener who will be open for a short time because of the hedge.
- The hedger must scramble back to the screener who has rolled or popped to the open area.
- If a side screen takes place and the screener rolls to the baseline on a hedge, the weak-side post player must cover the screener and the screener's defender who hedged will quickly cover the weak-side post.
- On middle screen action, baseline defenders must be open to the basketball and in a position to help stop the penetrating dribble if the basketball is advanced on the dribble to the basket.
- On a guard-to-guard screen or a post-to-post screen, a switch is easy to execute, as the players are the same position.
- On a post-to-post screen, a general rule is to switch if the post using the screen goes under the screen and stay if the offensive post goes over the top. The help-side wing should be in a position to help on a post who rolls to high post.

POINTS OF EMPHASIS

- Defenders not directly involved in the screening action must be in help-side position to stop the dribbler or the screener rolling to the basket.
- Hands and head of the help-side defenders are up and eyes are on the basketball and the offensive player they are guarding.
- If the screening action requires a switch, all five defenders must be in position to be ready to rotate to the basketball in the event the switch does not stop the basketball.
- The main responsibility of the defenders is to not get caught up in a scramble situation but to stop the screening action with as little rotation as possible.

PERFORMANCE LEVEL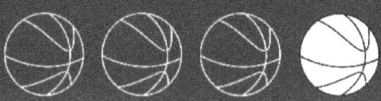

OFFENSIVE PRINCIPLES: SHOOTING

GENERAL OVERVIEW: *Although it is important to always revisit proper shooting mechanics to maintain muscle memory, this level will focus elsewhere. At this stage of player development, the focus should be on the mentality of a shooter, decision-making abilities, making shots with consistency, and developing creativity with the basketball to increase scoring potential.*

SKILL 1

LAYUPS: FLOATER

A floater is often useful when a player is penetrating the lane and a defender slides in to help who is either taller or a talented shot blocker. In this situation, shooting a typical layup will likely result in a blocked shot, making a floater an effective option.

- The footwork for a floater is the same as a normal layup. Players jump off of one foot and rise with the knee on the same side as the shooting hand.
- The upper body movement, however, differs. Players must extend the shooting hand straight up and shoot an overhand layup that arcs high over a defender's hand. The basketball will travel significantly higher than a typical layup, as it must travel over a defender's extended arm at the peak of a jump.
- This shot requires a different type of touch, as the basketball will likely fall directly through the hoop as a result of its high-arching trajectory. This isn't always the case, but it is most common.
- This type of shot should be practiced with the dominant and nondominant hand. Players should also practice attacking the rim from different angles and allow defenders to step in to help at various times from various angles.

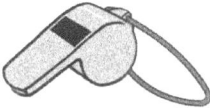 **POINTS OF EMPHASIS**

- Typical layup footwork; elevate and extend straight up.
- Overhand shot.
- High-arching shot over defender.
- Work on timing and shot with both hands.

SKILL 2

LAYUPS: CRAFTY FINISHES

The higher the level of play, the less likely it is for a player to shoot an uncontested layup. Players will be forced to be more creative and craftier around the rim in order to get a layup off. There are countless ways to execute a shot around the rim. Below are a few examples.

STEP-THROUGH

- Many times, a defender will cut off the offensive player attacking the rim and will be anticipating a shot. With these two elements in play, the offensive player can use a step-through to finish the layup.
- Once the defender cuts the offensive player off, the player will pick the basketball up and shot-fake the anticipating defender. If the defender leaves the floor, the offensive player will use a front pivot to step-through the defender, creating a seal with the rear end. Then, once around the out-of-position defender, the player can elevate up for a layup.
- Protect the basketball with the body and keep it high in order to take the layup quickly. This particular move can be used in a congested lane with much success.

 ## POINTS OF EMPHASIS

- Shot fake at the rim; lift eyes and basketball.
- Quick step-through using front pivot.
- Seal defender on rear end.
- Protect basketball with body and keep high.
- Elevate quickly into layup.

SPIN MOVE

- The spin move also counters a defender attempting to cut off an attacking offensive player. If the lane is less congested, a spin move could be a good skill to go to should the defender make a definitive move to cut off the attacking offensive player.
- As the defender cuts the dribble off, the offensive player will quickly jump-stop, making one additional hard dribble, pivot quickly on the inside foot, and keep the basketball tight to the body on the spin.
- The tighter the offensive player can spin, the better. This will prevent the defender from recovering or moving to the help side to adjust.
- Coming out of the spin, players should find the rim with their eyes and elevate quickly into a layup.

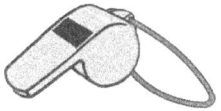
POINTS OF EMPHASIS

- Survey the lane prior to performing the move.
- Jump-stop combined with hard dribble to start the spin.
- Keep basketball tight to the body to protect.
- Spin as tightly as possible.
- Immediately find the rim with the eyes.
- Elevate up for layup; control momentum.

DOUBLE-PUMP/CLUTCH

- A double-pump or clutch can be used to create opportunities while in the air that may not have been there when first elevating. It can be used to completely change directions to dodge a defender. It may also help to absorb contact from a defender in midair.
- To use a double-pump to change directions, the offensive player will first elevate into the air. While this happens, a defender may come from the help side and try to contest the layup.
- The offensive player can pull the basketball back to the shoulder while still in the air, ducking under the defender, and adjust the positioning of the basketball and the body to get a clean layup attempt.
- This takes significant practice in order to understand the skill and body control, how to incorporate the needed strength, and to become comfortable with midair adjustments. Further, this skill requires great court vision and a creative mind to make quick decisions before implementing.
- Using a double-pump to absorb contact and then create a second opportunity to get the shot off also requires a great deal of skill and creative ability. As the defender comes from the help side to contest the layup midair, the offensive player will need to absorb the contact with the inside shoulder in order to reserve enough strength to complete the double-pump.
- The offensive player will show the basketball, making the contest even more encouraging for the defender. Once the contact is absorbed in the air, the player will again bring the basketball back to the shoulder, allowing time for the defender to descend.
- As this occurs, the player will raise the basketball from the shoulder to shoot the layup. Many times, the actual shot will occur while the offensive player is on the way down. The body should protect the basketball if the offensive player absorbs the contact on the inside shoulder, allowing for space to get the shot off successfully, even if it is on the way down.
- Again, this takes a great deal of practice.
- Both of these examples should be practiced attacking the rim from different angles with help side coming from different directions and with varied timing.

POINTS OF EMPHASIS

- Court vision prior to elevating into the layup.
- Attack from various angles.
- Use body to either change directions or absorb contact.
- Protect the basketball.
- Finish the layup even if fouled.
- Be creative.

SKILL 3

MINDSET OF A SHOOTER

So much of being a great shooter is a mindset, a mentality. Shooters truly believe that any shot they take, from anywhere in the gym, will go in, no matter if they have missed or made the last twenty shots.

- This sense of confidence does not waver and is built from watching the basketball go in day after day in practice. Players earn this confidence and begin to trust themselves. Additionally, great shooters have a short memory, which enables them to step up and hit a shot late in the game regardless of their performance up to that point.
- Being able to block out everything up to the point of taking a critical shot is imperative and is a skill that is also developed over time. Confidence and poise under pressure are developed and earned, much like the physical mechanics of a shot.
- As a coach, it is important to understand the mentality the player has, and either build on what is already established or help develop a stronger and more confident mindset. This can be done through conversation, drill work in practice, and even verbal praise to that player directly, if need be. Pushing the right buttons to help a shooter is an important art for a coach.
- This mentality that a shooter will develop may not always be a positive for the team. For example, a player may be struggling with shots in a game and may still be shooting on every touch of the basketball. At this point, it is important to help the player out of this slump while also not jeopardizing the team in that particular game.
- This can be a slippery slope. Many times, a shooter just needs to see the basketball go through the hoop, even if it's a layup or a free throw.
- Encourage players in this position to get to the rim, or give them a defensive assignment so they see some success on the basketball court. This will help get their mind off of the poor shooting and provide them an opportunity to positively impact the team.
- Something as small as this can help a shooter get back on track. Again, it is important to understand the mentality of players in order to help put them in a position to be successful individually, while producing for the team at large.

 ## POINTS OF EMPHASIS

- Help develop a shooter's mentality through work in practice.
- Provide an environment where a player can gain confidence while still pushing to be better.
- Instill trust in players.
- Understand the mentality—reinforce the existing mentality or help develop a stronger one.

SKILL 4

SHOOTING OFF THE DRIBBLE: STEP-BACK

Using a step-back off of the dribble can be an effective way to get a shot off against a defender pressuring the basketball.

- The key, just as with getting a jump shot off in the half court off of the dribble, is to get the defender moving backward. The offensive player will take a hard dribble (or two) at the rim, getting the defender to react with a drop step.
- As this happens, the offensive player puts the inside shoulder into the chest of the defender, plants the inside foot, and pushes hard backward, creating the step-back. The more space that is created at this moment, the easier it will be to get the shot off prior to the defender recovering.
- On the step-back, it is easiest to gather on a hop. Pay attention to controlling the movement that is created going backward. It will be important to gather this momentum and rise up into the shot straight up or slightly in front of where the player took off.

POINTS OF EMPHASIS

- Hard, urgent dribble at the rim to get defender on heels.
- Plant inside foot and urgently push back off of that foot.
- Gather on the hop.
- Control momentum.
- Rise into shot; proper shooting mechanics.

SKILL 5

UNDERSTAND GOOD SHOTS

Part of being a great shooter or scorer is establishing an understanding of the difference between a good shot and a forced shot. There is no way to document or go through every situation that will present itself in a game situation and declare what is a good shot and what is not. This must be assessed and determined in the moment.

- To a certain extent, this is a feel that a player will develop on the floor, through the guidance, conversation, experience, and review of the coach, as well as the player's team.
- At this level, this can be a constant evaluation and review with the player to help generate trust and understanding between the player and the coach to enable the player to make positive decisions in a game environment that fits within the confines of the team offensive goals.
- Below are a few general examples to consider in starting the thought process.

FLOW OF OFFENSE

- The best shooters tend to understand all of the nuances of the entire team offense: understanding the location of the basketball, the timing of teammates' cuts and screens, and consequently understanding where possible shots may arise for themselves. This comprehension also allows a shooter to take shots that will occur within the flow of the offense.
- For example, when attempting to break a zone offense, a shooter may be open on the first pass but likely will be even more open to catch the basketball in the flow on the seventh pass. Shooting with the defense rotating and while in the flow of the offense allows for a better shot. It also helps the entire offense be ready to grab an offensive rebound.
- Additionally, the more patient the offense is, the harder the defense works.

PERSONNEL STRENGTHS

- Players on a team must understand the strengths of each teammate on the floor. For example, imagine there are two players spotting up on offense, one at the top of the key and one on the wing. If both are wide open on ball reversal for a three-point shot, it is critical to understand who is a better three-point shooter.
- If the player at the top of the key is most productive off of the dribble and the player on the wing is a pure three-point shooter, the player at the top of the key should make the extra pass to the player on the wing for the shot.
- It is not to say that both players cannot make a three-point shot but, rather, the team is playing to the strengths of the personnel who are on the basketball floor.
- This is the beauty and puzzle of a team—being able to utilize the strengths of all players and put them to the test of an opposing team's strengths.

WHO IS HOT?

- High-level players keep track in their mind of who is making things happen on both sides of the floor throughout the course of a game. Specifically, they pay attention to who is scoring effectively.
- Many times, certain players will find themselves in what you may call "the zone," where they feel like they can take any type of shot from anywhere on the floor and it will go in.
- As a team, if a teammate gets into this type of zone, it's advantageous to feed that player the basketball in a scoring position as many times as possible. It is amazing how many times an opportunity such as this goes unutilized due to players simply being unaware.
- This really means two things: (1) get the basketball to the player who is hot, and (2) if the player who is hot has an open opportunity to shoot, take it.

DEFENSIVE TENDENCIES

- Great shooters can outline the defensive tendencies of the players and teams who play them better than the actual defenders can.
- For example, if a certain player tends to overhelp on dribble penetration, this should be noted by all players on the floor. If that particular player gets matched up on a shooter in transition, dribble penetration toward that defender could draw the defender over and free up a shooter for a three-point attempt.
- Another example is if there are defenders who tend to turn their heads on the backside of a zone on an inbounds play. Here, a shooter may sneak down to the three-point line on the opposite side for an open look. These types of tendencies can lead to an easy shot attempt that has the potential to change a game, especially since games can come down to one possession.

TIME AND SCORE

- Coaches should be able to stop play at any moment in a game and any player in the gym should be able to state the time on the clock and the score. This knowledge is critical at this level.
- Further, shot selection and decision-making should reflect time and score situations as well, especially late in a game. Aside from obvious situations, such as shooting a three-point shot when a team is down by three points with seconds to go, there are other situations that need to be considered.
- For example, if a team is up by fifteen points late in the game and the opponent scores six unanswered points quickly, it would make sense to work the shot clock rather than shoot the first open shot. Working the clock in this example is far more important than taking an open three-point shot early in the possession.
- Again, every situation cannot be outlined here, but it is important as a shooter, and as a basketball player in general, to understand time and score situations.

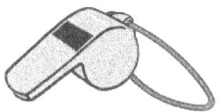 **POINTS OF EMPHASIS**

- Constant conversations to increase knowledge and understanding of in-game situations.
- Empower and build trust with players.
- Drill various situations in practice often.

SKILL 6

SHOOTING OFF THE PASS: DEVELOPING QUICKER RELEASE

As defenders get better, it is important that shooters are able to adjust accordingly.

- One way is to get the shot off more quickly. Some of this can be achieved by understanding angles and spacing, which makes the defenders cover more ground when recovering to a shooter. Even if a player can make the defender take one additional step, this will buy one valuable second that can help get the shot off.
- Another way to help buy another second is to develop a quicker release. Much of this can be accomplished by doing the work prior to actually catching the basketball. This includes quick footwork, catching the basketball low, and being ready to shoot immediately after catching the basketball.
- If all of this is already complete prior to receiving the basketball, all the player has to do is rise up into the shot, which makes for an extremely efficient and quick shot.
- It is important to understand there is a difference between being quick in preparation and footwork, but not quick in the actual shot. The player does not want to rush the actual shot; it's the preparation leading into the shot that can be quick.
- This skill is one that must be practiced at game speed and repeated very often.

POINTS OF EMPHASIS

- Quick preparation.
- Efficient and quick movements leading to actual shot.
- Once into shot, do not rush.
- Practice at game speed.

SKILL 7

BECOME A MARKER RATHER THAN A SHOOTER: DEVELOPING QUICKER RELEASE

The mindset and expectation for a player at this level is to make shots consistently, rather than just attempt shots. This has to be developed in practice and carried over into the game environment.

- From a practice standpoint, every drill and repetition should be competitive. Constantly trying to shoot a perfect shot, beat a previous record, or reach a new goal prior to moving on is important.
- Putting pressure on the player at game speed is necessary in order to increase consistency through the repetition. The goal should be to increase consistency throughout a season at every type of shot. In order to shoot a high percentage in a game, the expectation and desire is to shoot a much higher percentage in practice, due to game slippage.
- Further, on shooting drills that require less movement, the shooting percentages should be even higher. Continually push players to be better and expect more on every drill and shot.
- Lastly, put players in high-pressure situations in practice, such as taking the game-winning shot. This will help players become more comfortable with wanting to take the shot in games and gain confidence from previous experiences.

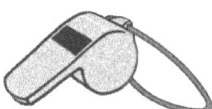

POINTS OF EMPHASIS

- Document makes and misses; everything should be competitive with self or team.
- Game speed.
- High repetitions with consistency.
- Strive for much higher percentages in practice to account for game slippage.

SKILL 8

FREE THROWS: PRESSURE SITUATIONS

An interesting statistic to keep in basketball would be a player's free-throw percentage in the last two minutes of the game with a close score. This type of situation presents a great deal of pressure; many times players rise to the challenge and many times players do not. What is it that makes the difference between these two outcomes?

It is likely a combination of things that culminate together into that one moment, standing at the free-throw line trying to win a game. First, does the player actually want to be the individual taking that key free throw? So much of shooting free throws is a mentality, a calm confidence and trust in the preparation, and flat out wanting to take the shot. This mentality may be more important than the physical act of shooting a free throw. It is critical to put the player into situations like this, a high-pressure situation with a consequence if the shot goes in or not, prior to it happening in the game. This can be simulated through drills in practice, moments standing in front of the team having to make a free throw, while tired, while fresh—countless ways. The player will likely miss some of the free throws in this situation; help them recover and gain confidence to want to take the shot again until they are successful. Through time, the player will gain confidence in the situations, which could culminate to a high-pressure opportunity in a game.

In addition to developing a mentality, it is critical that free throws are drilled and taken every day. Muscle memory and correct shooting form should continue to be a focus at high repetition. Many times, free throws are neglected at this level in order to cover other elements of team play, but the importance of a free throw in a game will always be present. Fit them in!

 **POINTS OF EMPHASIS**

- Drill high-pressure situations in practice.
- Help players develop calm confidence mentality.
- Continue to focus on shooting mechanics from free-throw line.
- Repetitions are always important.

PERFORMANCE LEVEL

TEAM DEFENSIVE CONCEPTS

GENERAL OVERVIEW: *Team defensive concepts in the Performance Level focus on execution in the full court and half court and game strategy. There are not many new concepts offered in this level which were not already explained in the Advanced Level. With more practice and more experience, the concepts discussed in the Advanced Level are now more defined and more easily performed by players.*

SKILL 1

HELP THE HELPER SITUATIONS

- In defensive rotation situations, the first step for proper execution is for all defenders to be in help position when playing off the basketball.
- The second part of the rotation is for the help defense to play off their player and be aware of the ball handler attacking the basket. This will allow the defender to take a charge or be in a position to stop the drive, so that the offensive player must give up the basketball.
- The third part of the rotation is to cover the offensive player who is left open due to the rotation, which is referred to as helping the helper. If all the defenders are in proper position on each pass, helping the helper should be a smooth rotation.
- Half court 3-on-3 will drill this "help the helper" situation. Start with three offensive players—one at each wing and one at the top of the key.
- When the ball is passed to the wing from the top, the defenders will move to the proper position, either in denial or help side in the lane.
- If the wing defender is beat, the opposite wing defender must step up and stop the drive to the basket.
- The defender at the top of the key now must be in position to help the helper and drop down to cover the opposite wing player left open by the defender helping on the driver.
- In a 5-on-5 scenario, the post defender will often times be the defender who helps on the dribble drive. In the case of the post player helping on defense, the "help the helper" situation comes into play from the perimeter defender.
- As the post player steps out to help stop the drive, the opposite wing defender must rotate down to help on the offensive post player, which may cause a size mismatch.

 ### POINTS OF EMPHASIS

- All the defenders must move on the pass. Movement occurs when the ball is in the air, so defenders are in proper position when the pass is completed.
- Defenders should have an awareness of what could happen with each pass and be ready to help stop the ball if needed.
- Communication is extremely important when rotations occur on defense.

SKILL 2

FULL-COURT DEFENSIVE SITUATION

There are several full-court situations that may be helpful as players become more advanced physically and mentally.

- A 1-2-1-1 full-court zone press is a basic press that can be used to create turnovers and trapping situations.
- The normal 1-2-1-1 press traps the basketball in the corner on the first pass with the middle player then taking the first pass down the sideline. The opposite defender guards the ball-side elbow. The back defender comes to the half line to play the middle offensive player.
- Several adjustments to this press can cause problems for the offensive players. Instead of trapping immediately in the corner, the press can rotate to a 2-2-1 press. The defender on the ball will drop to the free-throw line area with the defender at the free-throw line dropping back to the half line. The middle defender goes to the ball-side sideline just as in the regular trapping press. The back defender stays back to cover the long pass.
- The press can also take a different look when the defender on the ball stays with the inbounder and does not allow this player to receive the basketball back. Instead of leaving to trap, the defender stays with the inbounder until the free-throw line and then forms the 2-2-1 press.
- The press may also cover the inbounder with the opposite defender, who will come over and defend the inbounder while the trap is set in the corner.
- The press can be a "one and done" press where the defense attempts one trap in the corner and then retreats to a half-court player-to-player defense or a zone defense.
- The press can stay the same but have different points of attack—drop the players back so the defender on the inbounder now starts at the free-throw line and the two wing defenders drop back to the half-court line with the middle defender dropping back in the half-court circle. Now the trapping area is at the half-court sideline area instead of in the corner of the full court.
- A third type of attack is dropping the press back to the half-court line with the top defender starting at the half-court circle area and the other defenders dropping back to the defensive end with the same 1-2-1-1 set on the half court. The trapping area now is on the offensive end of the half court, so as the offense crosses the half-court line a trap will occur.

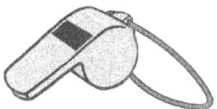 **POINTS OF EMPHASIS**

- Different press defenses all have the same set of 1-2-1-1 with different points of attack.
- The players in a press must all move as the pass is in the air so the proper coverage occurs as the pass is completed.
- The fundamentals of trapping are very important and need to be practiced repeatedly to ensure proper technique.

PERFORMANCE LEVEL
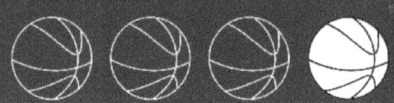

TEAM OFFENSIVE CONCEPTS

GENERAL OVERVIEW: *These concepts at the Performance Level deal more with the understanding of the game. This understanding of the game includes overall awareness of where every player is on the court, thinking two to three passes ahead of the present situation, making an extra pass within the offensive structure, and setting teammates up for success. The Performance Level also emphasizes players making wise choices within the offense to get open or to get a teammate open for a shot.*

SKILL 1

PRIMARY AND SECONDARY TRANSITION

- The secondary transition is more likely to lead to a basket than the primary break at this level due to the defender's ability to stop the layup initially.
- In the secondary transition, the basketball should find the open player when the offense is spaced appropriately.
- If the offense attacks the right-hand side of the court, the players on the left-hand side of the court should be in position to receive the basketball and shoot when the basketball is reversed across the rim line to them.
- Often times, the offense needs to make one more pass to an open teammate as the defense closes out to the basketball for the best shot opportunity.

 ## POINTS OF EMPHASIS

- The basketball must be centered in the middle of the floor between the free-throw lane lines as soon as possible on transition.
- Use the rim line, an imaginary line that goes from basket to basket down the middle of the court, as the point of reference.
- One more pass is usually needed, as the defense can close out to the first pass that crosses the rim line but not the second pass.

SKILL 2

UNDERSTANDING ADVANTAGE/DISADVANTAGE

Advantage/disadvantage in the Performance Level now gets more complicated, as the players are bigger, stronger, and faster. Offensive decisions must come more quickly and be more reactive as well and overall awareness must increase.

DRILL 1: LAKER DRILL

This is one of the best drills for this higher-level offensive awareness. In this drill, decisions must be made quickly while being cognizant of the defenders sprinting back in transition.

- Put players in three lines at each baseline. The drill starts with 4-on-4 play on one half court.
- The offense and defense play 4-on-4 until a basket is made, the defense forces a turnover, or the defense gets a rebound.
- The defensive player who secures the rebound, made basket, or turnover now becomes the new offense and is joined by three new teammates from the line under the basket.
- The offensive team from the initial possession becomes defense and both teams transition 4-on-4 to the other basket.
- The drill continues play up and down and coaches can add time or score limits.

 **POINTS OF EMPHASIS**

- The basketball needs to get to the middle of the court either by the dribble or with a pass as soon as possible.
- Keep score so there is a winner for the drill. Play to a certain number of points or time.
- The defensive team does not need to take the basketball out of bounds after a made basket.
- The rotation is always offense to defense then out to the lines on the baseline, except for one defender who gets the basketball and stays in with the three new players entering the drill from the baseline.
- The offense must have awareness of where the basketball and teammates are on the court and then try to think two passes ahead, which would lead to an easy jump shot.

SKILL 3

OFFENSIVE WEAK-SIDE PLAY

- The offensive players on the weak side are very important when attacking the defense. They must have overall awareness of what may take place two or three passes ahead of the action.

- The weak-side offensive players should keep the defenders busy so they are not as quick to help stop the basketball. This can be done by movement, such as cutting or screening, or by properly spacing out to receive a pass for a shot.
- Weak-side players should try to make their defenders turn their back to the basketball to keep them from helping on the offensive player with the basketball. When defenders have to divide their attention, weak-side players have a better chance to get open.
- When getting open to receive a pass, look to make a cut. If the basketball is not passed, go opposite the basketball to the weak side.

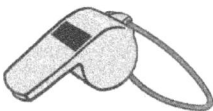

POINTS OF EMPHASIS

- The act of cutting to the basketball or at least making the defender think you are going to make a cut to the basketball when on the weak side occupies the defender's attention and energy.
- If cutters do not get the basketball, find a teammate to screen.

SKILL 4

SCRIMMAGING

- Scrimmaging both half court and full court is a vital part of the practice program at this level.
- Half-court scrimmaging is necessary for the development of regular team offenses and defenses, floor balance and timing, and special offensive and defensive plays.
- Full-court scrimmaging is necessary for the development of physical conditioning, quick transition from offense to defense and defense to offense, adjusting to all changing situations, and simulating game conditions.
- It is through scrimmaging that the best opportunity for developing teamwork can be emphasized, which needs to be done continually during practice.
- During full-court scrimmages, opportunities are presented for the development of self-control, reacting positively to officials' calls, acknowledging a good pass from a teammate, complimenting a teammate's good play, adjusting to rare or unusual game situations, and showing restraint to critique from a teammate or coach.
- Vary up half-court scrimmage games in practice. Keep one team on offense until they have been stopped by the defense five times, then flip the offense and defense. Keep track of scores accumulated during possessions. A defensive foul gives a point to the offense without counting as a stop. An offensive foul will count as a stop.

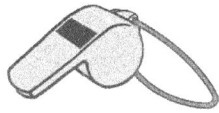

POINTS OF EMPHASIS

- Since both offense and defense are worked on in scrimmage situations, place special emphasis on offense one day and defense the following day.
- Mental and emotional adjustments are as necessary for a player to approach maximum potential as are the physical adjustments.
- Full-court scrimmaging should be done almost every day for the first couple of weeks of a season, then twice a week until your first several games are completed. Continue with scrimmages primarily for the players who did not play much in the previous game.

SKILL 5

COMPETITIVE WARM-UP

- Adding competition to warm-ups each day in practice will add some pressure to execute the warm-up correctly and quickly.
- Competition can be done in the form of keeping score, setting time goals, or both.

FULL-COURT LAYUPS

- Put players in two lines with a line starting under the basket at each end. The first three players in each line have a basketball.
- The players speed dribble full court and make a layup at the other end. Players stay at the end they shoot the layup at and the next player in line without a basketball grabs the made layup out of the net and dribbles to the other end for a layup.
- Goal = 50 made layups in one minute.

FULL-COURT JUMP SHOTS

- Put players in four lines with a line starting at each of the four corners of the full court. The first two players in two of the lines, on opposite corners, have a basketball.
- The basketball is passed straight down the court to the first player in the line that does not have a basketball. The passer sprints the length of the court and receives a pass back for a jump shot.
- The shooter fills the end of the passing line and the passer rebounds the shoot and rotates to the opposite corner line after passing the basketball to the next player in that line.
- Goal = 22 made field goals in one minute.

FIVE-BALL SHOOTING

- Lines are again in the four corners of the court with one basketball at the front of each line.

- Three players start the drill under one basket; the player in the middle has the fifth basketball and the outside players are wide.
- The three players weave to the opposite end, making only two passes: the first from the middle player to the outside and the second from the outside player to the opposite-side player who will score the layup.
- The players will follow their pass and weave behind the receiving player as they move down the court.
- The two players who did not shoot the layup will continue to sprint to the elbow areas and each catch a pass from the corner line for a jump shot. The shooters will rebound their shot, give it to the next player in the corner lines, and fill the end of the corner lines.
- The player who shot the layup stays in the drill and rebounds the layup, now becoming the middle player to weave back down the court with the two corner passers joining the three-player weave.
- This is a continuation drill where all layups and jump shots are counted out loud on scores.
- Goal = 25 baskets in one minute.

PERFECT LAYUP DRILL

- Players will be in three lines on one baseline with the first two players on one of the outside lines with a basketball.
- The first three players in line advance up the court by passing the basketball and running in their lanes, no weaving. The basketball is passed from the side to the middle, back to the same side, back to the middle, then from the middle to the opposite side for a layup.
- The second basketball is started when the first basketball gets to half court so that the drill becomes a continuous drill.
- The middle player runs to the sideline to be the outlet for the player who shot the layup.
- The opposite player from the layup rebounds the layup and makes a two-handed overhead outlet pass.
- The outlet makes a baseball pass to the next player in line at the other end in the corner, who now starts the drill from the other side while the three players who finished the drill run back to the starting baseline.
- The layup earns two points for a make where the basketball does not touch the rim and one point for a make where the basketball touches the rim. Zero points are earned for missed layups.
- Goal = 25 points in one minute.

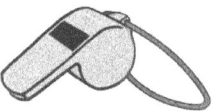# POINTS OF EMPHASIS

- Do the warm-up drills for several days before making them competitive so players know the skills involved and the rotation for the drills.
- On the full-court layups, use right-handed dribbling and layups one day and use left-handed dribbling and layups the next day.
- On full-court jump shots and five-ball shooting, two points may be counted for made three-point shots.
- Emphasize running hard in the five-ball drill with the player laying up the basketball turning around immediately to get the basketball out of the net to be the middle player going the opposite direction.
- In the perfect layup drill, make the players touch the baseline before they get back in line for the drill.

- These drills build a sense of accomplishment for players and are best performed when teammates encourage one another throughout the drill.

SKILL 6

STRATEGY

- A strategy starts with tactics that the coach thinks are necessary to have the team be competitive and have a chance to win. Fast break or half-court offense, player-to-player or zone defense, and press or half-court defense are examples of strategies to use.
- However, no matter how experienced the coach, coaches cannot only rely on strategy to outsmart and beat opponents.
- There is no substitute for three essentials: proper execution of the fundamentals, good conditioning, and great team spirit.
- Pressing defense strategies can be designated for a bigger, slower team, a mechanical team that wants to use a ball-control type of offense and go through specific patterns, a team not well conditioned, a zone press against teams that like to advance the basketball by dribbling, or a team with inexperienced or poor ball-handling guards.
- Use a specific set play following a timeout and after every intermission from play.
- Use more screening attack against a close guarding or tight player-to-player defense.
- Zone a player in the key area against a strong post attack.
- Float deep against teams that want to drive and tight on those teams that prefer to shoot from the outside.
- Face-guard a star scorer all over the floor.
- Play the strong points of the individual players as well as the team.
- Change defense occasionally for a few minutes to some other type and occasionally use a different set offensively.
- Play a style of game to which the players are best adapted, providing everyone is comfortable with this style.

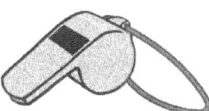 **POINTS OF EMPHASIS**

- May need to play a slow, deliberate, and controlled game in an effort to slow the tempo and control over the fast break.
- Double-team the defensive rebounder to slow the outlet pass and the fast break of a team.
- Play at least two players back on defense to stop transition.
- Many of the strategies will deal with the scouting of the team and players and may change as the season progresses.

PRACTICE PLANNING & GUIDELINES

PRACTICE CULTURE

Players will spend far more time in practice settings than competing in games. Therefore, it is the practice culture that you create that can make or break a player's love for the sport. As a coach, strive to create an atmosphere in practice where players enjoy coming to improve.

Practices must be positive. To combat this setting where players are constantly being taught new things and critiqued, make sure you have established genuine relationships with players off the court so they trust and hear you in practices. Find time to connect with your players to understand what things they are going through outside of basketball, share what you believe are their strengths, and set individual goals for the season that are challenging but attainable.

Let players know it is okay to make mistakes in practice and encourage them to try new things. It should not be the mistake you are concerned with, but a player's attitude and reaction after the mistake. Reward hustle plays and recognize all players throughout a season. It is easy for the most talented player or your best shooter to feel valued in games, but practices provide opportunities for every player to embrace their role and contribute to the team.

Practices are a great time to work on team building. Spend a few minutes at practice start or conclusion, or at different times in the season, to do something creative with your team to develop team bonding. Set up a fun obstacle course and pair up teammates so one is blindfolded and navigates through the course with the help of a partner giving directions. Surprise your team with a pizza party after practice. Invite a motivational speaker, community leader, or school figurehead to speak to your team about a topic of value. Let your players write up one of the practices in a season and pick all of the drills to work on. Team-building actions can be big or small, and all contribute to your team's culture and affinity to work hard together.

SETTING THE PRACTICE PACE

Organizing a good practice is composed of two parts: what you are going to teach and how you are going to teach. The best coaches prioritize both elements to devise effective practices that flow.

Practice flow is a byproduct of the pace you set. Pace is the intensity of movement between practice drills and the adherence to a standard of how athletes are expected to perform at any given moment. A coach must dictate the pace based on what is being taught and how it's being taught. If left to chance, athletes likely will pick a cadence that is short of the coach's expectations.

Let's examine how the "what" and "how" of teaching impact pace.

EXAMPLE

I'm putting together a practice plan for advanced-level players. We are about midway through our season, so my practices strongly emphasize individual skill development, but also dedicate time to offensive and defensive concepts and strategy. In today's practice, I have selected drills to work on footwork, ball handling and dribbling, passing and receiving, and shooting. I also have built in time to run through our offensive sets for competition and defensive tactics to stop the opponent.

I want my practice to have high intensity. Therefore, the instructional drills I've selected must be modified to encourage an active pace. Every drill will have a competitive aspect to it and a consequence for nonwinners. I'll add a time to complete drill goals within or set achievable numbers for scores that my team should be able to hit. I'll be able to recognize a winner for each drill, and nonwinners will have to carry out a reasonable consequence, such as a timed stationary ball-handling drill or a full-court dribbling sprint.

As we transition to the offensive and defensive team concepts, we will run through our sets with all five players going at game speed. I'll only stop action to break down a key emphasis tied to our strategy for the upcoming opponent.

By identifying what I will teach in my practice and how I will teach it, I can set the pace for practice and flow between drills, concepts, and teaching points to be efficient and effective.

THE IMPORTANCE OF HOW YOU TEACH

There are two key reasons to focus on how you teach just as much, if not more, than what you teach:

- Focusing on the how improves communication between the coach and players by emphasizing what is important to the coach.
- By adapting drills to match the how and the desired pace, athletes will develop skills relative to their role on the team.

STRATEGIES TO FOCUS ON HOW YOU TEACH

- Examine the training methods you currently are using. Do your current techniques develop player skills and growth that advance the team?
- Follow the teaching methods for learning: explain what should be done in a drill, show and demonstrate the drill, put players through repetitions, correct the repetitions, and perform correct repetitions to create habits.
- Organize activities for maximum efficiency by planning a pace that matches your purpose.
- Devote a certain amount of time each day for planning out practice time. Make a list of the skills and drills to emphasize at that particular practice session. Then determine how you will communicate and teach the skills to move your team closer to your objective.
- Step back from time to time and reflect on the methods you are using. Are the methods communicating what is important to you as a coach? Seek opinions of others, whether assistant coaches or parents, that you trust for honest, unbiased feedback. Do they agree that you are communicating clearly?

SKILL DEVELOPMENT DURING PRACTICES

Players never graduate from a skill. From the first practice of a season to the very last practice, time should always be set aside to work on skill development. This concept applies to players in any of the four levels of the USA Basketball Curriculum. As a coach, your emphasis on skill development trickles down to your players. If you don't value skill development, players won't believe it is important.

One common pitfall to avoid is thinking your players are performing skills well enough "in relation to their level or the competition" and abandon continued development. Remember that skill development is not a comparison to others but a personal and ongoing progression in a player's basketball journey. A player with some natural ability and an early advantage on skills who doesn't commit to continued skill development will be passed up down the road by those who have a stronger fundamental foundation.

USA Basketball identifies eight skills as part of the player development curriculum:

1. Ball handling and dribbling
2. Footwork and body control
3. Passing and receiving
4. Rebounding
5. Screening

6. Shooting
7. Whole defensive concepts
8. Whole offensive concepts

The curriculum also outlines four levels of skill development—Introductory, Foundational, Advanced, and Performance—with corresponding drills per level to establish and progress the eight skills. These drills guide coaches and players through skill development and mastery.

Depending on the level of player you are coaching, the amount of practice time spent on skill development will vary. In general, practices can be structured into thirds. One third of practice time should be spent exclusively on skill development, another third for whole offense, and a final third on whole defense.

When you are working on skill development in practice, it is important to incorporate as many repetitions as possible. Keeping players in shorter lines, spreading out to maximize available basketballs and baskets, and ensuring players stay active while waiting their turn all help players stay focused and repetitions be efficient.

Players learn by doing. As repetitions increase, habits for a skill can form. Correct repetitions as you go so players form correct habits and continue to improve.

While the eight basketball skills are the basis for player development, coaches should also emphasize two other key attributes of a complete player: the skill of competing and the skill of communicating. Reference the section on the four Cs of culture for practical actions to teach these skills (page 25).

HOW TO PICK THE RIGHT DRILLS FOR PRACTICES

Understanding the importance of skill development and the starting point of your players leads to the selection of the right drills for a practice. For players in the Introductory and Foundational Levels, repetition of drills is a good way to build familiarity and confidence in skill work and eventually form habits. Don't try to impress your players with your library of drills; instead identify the handful of drills that are realistic, practical, effective, and challenging, and revisit these drills in consecutive practices so players can see personal growth. Start with drills that are easy enough for the players to perform and then gradually add some complexity.

As players plateau in a drill, and before transitioning to a new drill, find ways to advance the current drill. Change the shooting finish, add defense, make players use their offhand only, deduct points for poor passes, or add contact to the drill. These all are ways to reduce explanation time while increasing performance.

For more experienced players, the best drills are the ones that directly improve players' skills related to the actual game. After a new drill is taught and repetition takes place, quickly advance the drill to be competitive and game-like.

Starting practice off with a competitive drill is a good way to get your team focused and in the proper frame of mind for practice. Competitive drills can be any that include a time and/or score element. Putting your players in positions where they struggle in drills helps them fight through adversity in game situations as well. Competitive drills also encourage leadership and communication from players as they strive to achieve the goal.

As a coach of Advanced and Performance Level players, balance your desire to teach with the value in allowing players to lead. There is such a thing as overcoaching your team. Sometimes, a coach's desire to explain every detail of a drill, even with the best of intentions in mind, can make players tune out and lose interest. Be concise in your instruction and let your players communicate as a team to figure out the best way to set the drill up and execute.

MIND CANDY

WHAT IS MIND CANDY?

"Mind Candy" is a short phrase that serves as the thought of the day prior to practice start. Just like we warm our bodies up before physical activity, it is important to warm our minds up to be focused on the upcoming practice. Recognize that players may come to the gym preoccupied with other things and use Mind Candy as an opportunity to get them focused mentally before beginning training. Mind Candy is a phrase that relates to the team's needs and motivates players.

WHAT IS THE PURPOSE OF USING MIND CANDY?

There are a number of catch phrases or quotes coaches use to provide inspiration to teams in a season. The concept of Mind Candy is to purposefully select the phrases that best establish and elaborate on the culture you are building to constantly keep your team on the same page. Effective Mind Candy drives home key concepts and sets or reinforces a standard of expectations.

HOW DO YOU IMPLEMENT MIND CANDY IN A PRACTICE?

Every practice plan should be unique to the focuses of the day. Similarly, select Mind Candy phrases that apply to the stage your team is in or the topic you want them to reflect on. Write the Mind Candy on the practice plan so you as a coach are reminded of the greater purpose throughout the practice session.

Prior to practice start, hold a brief team meeting to share the Mind Candy verbally and encourage players to discuss how it relates to them and the team. Make sure you are encouraging all players to contribute to the discussion and be open to the many different ways these phrases may be interpreted.

As Mind Candy is discussed, the tone for practice is set and players are able to focus on the task ahead. Continue to reinforce the Mind Candy throughout the practice if you hit challenges within drills or with players' attention to allow them to reset in a positive manner.

MIND CANDY EXAMPLES FROM USA BASKETBALL NATIONAL TEAMS

- There are four Cs that separate talented players: Communication, Competition, Comfort Zone, and Choices.
- These things require zero talent: being on time, work ethic, effort, body language, energy, attitude, passion, and being coachable.
- It is just as important to be respectful as it is to be good. Being respectful will help get you through times when you aren't so good.
- Three things that lead to success: work hard, stay humble, and surround yourself with good people.
- There is power in the now! Don't drain today with worrying about yesterdays and tomorrows.
- You have to be a family first to be a team. Being a family begins and ends with communication.
- The thing that drives all success is passion and enthusiasm for what you do.
- Three things about success: it does not happen in a vacuum, it takes time, and it is hard.
- How you practice, good or bad, is how you play in a game.
- The best players are the ones who play the best.

DEVELOPING WEEKLY, MONTHLY & SEASON PRACTICE PLANS

Each practice, and correspondingly each practice plan, fits into the overall vision of what you want your team to accomplish and improve on within a season. While practice plans can be modified to highlight specific areas of focus needed, you should first sit down and determine what you want your team to accomplish by the last day together. Once you've charted out the skills and team concepts you want to teach in the season, you can then formulate practice plans with an eye on achieving the goals.

Coaches who work with young players should be most focused on each player's individual fundamental development. End-of-year goals may be for all players to be able to dribble with confidence with the basketball in both the dominant and nondominant hand. Another goal may be for players to understand spacing and sharing the ball, so practices may focus on passing and court awareness.

For coaches working with Advanced and Performance Level players, end-of-the-year goals may be more outcome focused. At these higher levels, team goals may revolve around tournament success and records. While not the sole emphasis, competition is a big factor at these levels. Therefore, more practice time may revolve around strategy development and execution of offense and defense for in-game success.

With the end goal in mind, break your season down month by month and structure practice plans based on what you'd like to accomplish each month. A Foundational Level team may focus on dribbling on the move with their dominant hand in month one and then dribbling on the move with their nondominant hand in the second month. A Performance Level team may focus on player-to-player offenses, defenses, and out-of-bounds plays in the first month and then in the second month spend practice time on zone defenses and press defense.

Another helpful strategy in building practice plans with your whole season in mind is to document the day or practice number when new concepts were introduced and how often certain elements were revisited. You can reference these notes in the future to assess if the time spent on concepts was enough based on the success you're having.

If your team is not progressing at the pace you believe they should be for a certain skill and your notes show you only spent two practices developing the skill, you can reasonably assume that you need to add more drills in future plans to teach the concept. Make your practice plan decisions based on an honest assessment of player abilities, not on instinct or guesses of what to teach.

Remember, as you decide on drills and concepts to include in your practice plans, make sure you include things that are out of your players' comfort zone. Challenge players with new drills, by modifying current drills with advanced execution elements and by adding competition to drills. Push your players to be uncomfortable while performing drills, and they will increase their learning and skill levels.

YOUTH GUIDELINES

USA Basketball and the National Basketball Association (NBA) came together in 2016 to establish three expert working groups charged with developing guidelines designed to promote a positive and healthy youth basketball experience. The three working groups focused on player health and wellness, playing rules and standards, and curriculum and instruction.

The overall objective was to develop guidelines for youth basketball that promote health and wellness, on-court skill development, and help to create a lifelong love for the game of basketball.

The full recommendations from the working groups can be found at www.usab.com/youthguidelines.com but below are some fundamental guidelines to incorporate into youth practices and games.

PARTICIPATION GUIDELINES

Players ages 7–8

- Participate in a maximum of 3 hours per week of organized basketball.
- Participate in one practice per week that lasts 30–60 minutes.

Players ages 9–11

- Participate in a maximum of 5 hours per week of organized basketball.
- Participate in two practices per week that last 45–75 minutes.

Players ages 12–14

- Participate in a maximum of 10 hours per week of organized basketball.
- Participate in two to four practices per week that last 60–90 minutes.

Players grades 9–12

- Participate in a maximum of 14 hours per week of organized basketball.
- Participate in three to four practices per week that last 90–120 minutes.

EQUIPMENT AND COURT SPECIFICATIONS

Players ages 7–8

- Size of ball: boys and girls—size 5 (27.5").
- Height of basket: 8 feet.
- Size of court: 50 feet by 42 feet.
- A 3x3 half court also is recommended.
- Distance of 3-point arc: Not applicable.
- Distance of free-throw line: 14 feet.

Players ages 9–11

- Size of ball: boys and girls—size 6 (28.5").
- Height of basket: 9 feet.
- Size of court: 74 feet by 50 feet.
- Distance of 3-point arc: Not applicable.
- Distance of free-throw line: 14 feet.

Players ages 12–14

- Size of ball: girls—size 6 (28.5"); boys—size 7 (29.5").
- Height of basket: 10 feet.
- Size of court: 84 feet by 50 feet or 94 feet by 50 feet.
- Distance of 3-point arc: 19 feet, 9 inches.
- Distance of free-throw line: 15 feet.

Players grades 9–12

- Size of ball: girls—size 6 (28.5"); boys—size 7 (29.5").
- Height of basket: 10 feet.
- Size of court: 94 feet by 50 feet.
- Distance of 3-point arc: 22 feet, 2 inches, or the next available line under 22 feet, 2 inches.
- Distance of free-throw line: 15 feet.

EQUIPMENT AND COURT SPECIFICATIONS RATIONALE

Distance of 3-Point Arc: For 7–8 and 9–11-year-olds, although the 3-point arc may exist on the floor, all baskets made beyond this arc only count as two points. Therefore, the distance of the line is not applicable for these age segments. Eliminating the 3-point basket at these age segments will encourage players to shoot within a developmentally appropriate range. For ninth through twelfth graders, a twenty-two-foot-two-inch arc is preferred, but if this line is not on a court, the next available line under twenty-two feet two inches is recommended.

Distance of Free-Throw Line: 7–8 and 9–11-year-olds should take free throws fourteen feet from the basket to develop proper form and increase success.

Height of Basket: Utilizing a lower basket height for 7–8 and 9–11-year-olds allows children to develop proper shooting form and increases the opportunity for shooting success.

Scoring: All field goals for 7–8 and 9–11-year-olds are worth two points to encourage children to shoot within a developmentally appropriate range. This allows for proper mechanics and form. While these age segments may attempt a shot behind the 3-point arc, any field goal made behind the arc will only count as two points.

Size of Ball: A smaller basketball for the younger age segments is advised due to the size of a child's hand as well as their developing skill level. A smaller ball allows for better control and success.

Size of Court: For 7–8-year-olds, a fifty-by-forty-two-foot court is contemplated to be a cross-court game on a full-sized basketball court. This dimension is more appropriate for younger children based on their relative size in space.

GAME STRUCTURE

Player ages 7–8

- Game length: four 8-minute periods.
- Time between periods: 1 minute.
- Extra period: 2 minutes.

- Scoring:
    - Free throw: 1 point.
    - All field goals: 2 points.
    - No 3-point field goals.
- Timeouts:
    - Two sixty-second timeouts permitted in the first half of play. Two sixty-second timeouts permitted in the second half of play.
    - One sixty-second timeout granted for each extra period.
    - Unused timeouts may not carry over to the next half or into extra periods.
- Start of game possession: coin flip. Team awarded possession starts with throw-in at half court.

Players ages 9–11

- Game length: four 8-minute periods.
- Time between periods: 1 minute.
- Extra period: 2 minutes.
- Scoring:
    - Free throw: 1 point.
    - All field goals: 2 points.
    - No 3-point field goals.
- Timeouts:
    - Two sixty-second timeouts permitted in the first half of play. Two sixty-second timeouts permitted in the second half of play.
    - One sixty-second timeout granted for each extra period.
    - Unused timeouts may not carry over to the next half or into extra periods.
- Start-of-game possession: coin flip. Team awarded possession starts with throw-in at half court.

Players ages 12–14

- Game length: four 8-minute periods.
- Time between periods: 1 minute.
- Extra period: 4 minutes.
- Scoring:
    - Free throw: 1 point.
    - Field goals inside the 3-point arc: 2 points.
    - Field goals outside the 3-point arc: 3 points.
- Timeouts:
    - Two sixty-second timeouts permitted in the first half of play. Three sixty-second timeouts permitted in the second half of play.
    - Maximum of two timeouts permitted in the final two minutes of the fourth period.
    - One sixty-second timeout granted for each extra period.
    - Unused timeouts may not carry over to the next half or into extra periods.
- Start-of-game possession: jump ball.

Players grades 9–12

- Game length: four 10-minute periods.
- Time between periods: 2 minutes.
- Extra period: 5 minutes.
- Scoring:
    - Free throw: 1 point.
    - Field goals inside the 3-point arc: 2 points.
    - Field goals outside the 3-point arc: 3 points.
- Timeouts:
    - Two sixty-second timeouts permitted in the first half of play. Three sixty-second timeouts permitted in the second half of play.
    - Maximum of two timeouts permitted in the final two minutes of the fourth period.
    - One sixty-second timeout granted for each extra period.
    - Unused timeouts may not carry over to the next half or into extra periods.
- Start-of-game possession: jump ball.

GAME STRUCTURE RATIONALE

Start-of-game possession: For 7–8 and 9–11-year-olds, a coin flip will determine the team that starts with the ball to mitigate significant differences in height and coordination among children. Alternating possession rules will then ensue throughout the game.

Timeouts: Managing the way timeouts are called allows for better game flow and decision-making by the player(s).

INTRODUCTORY LEVEL PRACTICE PLANS

BUILDING A PRACTICE PLAN AT THE INTRODUCTORY LEVEL

Practices in this level need to always have a starting point. Find a way to signal to your players that practice is ready to begin so they can shift their attention away from other distractions. Sitting your players down in lines is a good method to signal this start.

Establish a way to regain attention throughout practice to help players refocus during the time block. Recognize that young players have a shorter attention span, and implement ways to get them back on track proactively to avoid frustration in the moment. A whistle can be implemented to signal freezing in place and listening to the coach for the next instruction. Have your players clap twice anytime they hear the coach shout out "eyes" to indicate that eyes should be back on the coach. Do this as often as needed throughout practice to help players slow down and regroup.

Drills should be short in this level, with a maximum of five minutes spent per drill. Keep lines short so players get to participate frequently, which will help them stay engaged and interested. Incorporate games in addition to drills for skill development. Games like red light–green light or tag (without the ball to start) teach a player to start and stop in balance, work on movement and spacing, and establish the fundamental building blocks for basketball skills in later levels.

In this level, most of the time with your team should be spent on developing individual skills and making sure practices are fun. Do not focus on 5-on-5 concepts or positions. Recognize the small successes of players so they are encouraged to continue playing the game.

EARLY-SEASON PRACTICE PLAN
INTRODUCTORY LEVEL

Date	Duration: 60 Minutes	Practice #

PRE-PRACTICE

5 MIN	Team Meeting	*Mind Candy:* Working hard is a choice that you control.

Warm-Up

Duration	Exercise	Description
3 MIN	Running Jump Stops with Skills	Players run the floor, stopping at three to five designated places on the court to complete a jump stop, then perform a skill (pivot, shot, rebound, tip).
2 MIN	Running with V-Cuts	Players start on the baseline and make diagonal V-cuts while running.
5 MIN	Defensive Slides	Players spread out and slide up and down the court in a defensive slide position on the coach's command.

SKILL DEVELOPMENT

Skill: Ball Handling and Dribbling

Duration	Drill Name	Drill Description/Focus
5 MIN	Rolling Figure 8	Players roll the ball on the ground in a figure-8 motion around and through the legs.
5 MIN	Circles around Waist	Players move the ball around their waist in a clockwise motion switching hands as the ball goes around the waist. Switch directions.

Skill: Passing and Receiving

Duration	Drill Name	Drill Description/Focus
5 MIN	Stationary Partner Pass	Hold ball with one hand on each side and step to pass to a stationary partner. Start with bounce passes and move to air passes once confident. Count the number of completed passes.

Skill: Shooting

Duration	Drill Name	Drill Description/Focus
2 MIN	Form Shooting, No Ball	Players spread out and face the coach. Follow coach's command to shoot without a basketball. Explain form—BEEF.
3 MIN	Form Shooting at a Basket	Form line directly in front of basket. Use an eight-foot basket if possible. Player shoots the ball, rebounds, and goes to the end of the line.
5 MIN	Step and Shoot	Players start six to eight feet from basket in two to three lines. Player stands with non-shooting foot in front of shooting foot. Player steps with the shooting foot as the shot is taken.

WHOLE OFFENSIVE CONCEPTS

Duration	Drill Name	Drill Description/Focus
10 MIN	Pass and Cut	Player passes to a coach and then cuts to the basket. Touch the spot under the basket before getting back in line.

COMPETITION

Duration	Drill Name	Drill Description/Focus
5 MIN	Half-Court Tag	One player is the tagger. All players must stay within the half-court lines. When tagger touches a player, that player must go stand on the baseline until all players have been tagged.

MIDSEASON PRACTICE PLAN
INTRODUCTORY LEVEL

Date	Duration: 60 Minutes	Practice #

PRE-PRACTICE

5 MIN	Team Meeting	*Mind Candy:* Choices are who you are.

Warm-Up

Duration	Exercise	Description
5 MIN	Line Drills	Player takes two dribbles, performs a jump stop, pivots, and passes to next player in line.

SKILL DEVELOPMENT

Skill: Ball Handling and Dribbling

Duration	Drill Name	Drill Description/Focus
5 MIN	Review Triple Threat	On command, players stop dribble and get into triple-threat position. May dribble stationary or on the move.

Skill: Passing and Receiving

Duration	Drill Name	Drill Description/Focus
5 MIN	Passing for a Layup	Form two lines. One line passes to other as player runs to basket and catches for a layup.

Skill: Shooting

Duration	Drill Name	Drill Description/Focus
5 MIN	Form Shooting, No Ball	Players spread out and face the coach. Follow coach's command to shoot without a basketball. Explain form—BEEF.
5 MIN	1–2 Shots	Form two to three lines facing the basket six to eight feet from the rim. Players drop the ball in front of themselves and step with nonshooting foot then shooting foot into the dropped ball for shot.

WHOLE DEFENSIVE CONCEPTS

Duration	Drill Name	Drill Description/Focus
5 MIN	Help Side/Ball Side	Explain ball side and help side. Two players are on wings facing basket with defenders. Ball is dribbled to baseline and back to wing—defenders adjust their alignment when the ball is dribbled.
5 MIN	4x4 Shell Drill	Set four offensive players around the top of the arc with four defenders. Ball is passed from around the perimeter with defenders adjusting.

WHOLE OFFENSIVE CONCEPTS

Duration	Drill Name	Drill Description/Focus:
10 MIN	5 Out Offensive Movement	Six cones on the court: two at wing, two at corners, one at top of key, and one under basket. Players pass the ball to player closest to them and touch the cone under the basket. Players rotate to fill open spot and cutter runs to open cone. Cut hard and look for pass back.

COMPETITION

Duration	Drill Name	Drill Description/Focus:
10 MIN	1x1	Start with one line at top of key or at wing. First player plays defense and second player plays offense. Play until score or defensive rebound.

LATE-SEASON PRACTICE PLAN
INTRODUCTORY LEVEL

Date	Duration: 60 Minutes	Practice #

PRE-PRACTICE

5 MIN	Team Meeting	*Mind Candy:* Hard work beats talent when talent doesn't work hard.

Warm-Up

Duration	Exercise	Description
5 MIN	Line Drills	Player takes two dribbles, performs a jump stop, pivots, and passes to next player in line.

SKILL DEVELOPMENT

Skill: Ball Handling and Dribbling

Duration	Drill Name	Drill Description/Focus
5 MIN	2-Ball Dribbling	Two lines facing each other. First player in line has two basketballs. Player dribbles to the other line pounding both basketballs at the same time with both hands.

Skill: Passing and Receiving

Duration	Drill Name	Drill Description/Focus
5 MIN	2-Line Passing Full Court	Players make two lines facing each other. Players slide in a defensive position while chest-passing the ball up and down the court.

Skill: Shooting

Duration	Drill Name	Drill Description/Focus
10 MIN	Oiler Drills	One line at top of key to start. Second and third player in line have a ball. First player runs and touches the baseline, turns, and receives a pass from the second player in line. Player pivots and shoots in front of rim. Passer becomes the next shooter. Shooter gets own rebound and passes to the next player in line without a ball.

WHOLE DEFENSIVE CONCEPTS

Duration	Drill Name	Drill Description/Focus
5 MIN	Close Out	Players form three lines under the basket with three players opposite them at the free-throw line holding basketballs. When coach says "shot," the three baseline players run then pitter-patter and shuffle the last two steps with their hands high and yell "shot."

WHOLE OFFENSIVE CONCEPTS

Duration	Drill Name	Drill Description/Focus
10 MIN	Keep Away	Played either 4x4 or 5x5. The first team with the ball makes as many passes as they can before a turnover occurs. No dribbling allowed and use the entire half or full court to cut, run, and move to make passes. After a turnover, switch sides. The team with the most passes completed wins.

COMPETITION

Duration	Drill Name	Drill Description/Focus
10 MIN	4x4x4 Exchange	Split the group into three equal teams and start on the baseline. A coach will referee to call fouls. Scoring team stays on. If defense fouls, possession counts as an offensive score. If defense gets a stop, they become the offense and the third team rotates in. Drill will progress in difficulty as player ability develops.

FOUNDATIONAL LEVEL PRACTICE PLANS

BUILDING A PRACTICE PLAN AT THE FOUNDATIONAL LEVEL

The Foundational Level player is ready to expand on basic movement skills and learn more basketball-specific fundamentals. In this level, three skills are of key importance to develop in every practice: shooting, footwork and body control, and passing and receiving. Players are more likely to progress in the other skills if they have a solid grasp of these three core skills, as they are an underlying aspect of every part of the game.

Skill development still is the primary focus in this level, and practices should be well organized to pick drills that allow for the most repetitions of skills. With increased repetition, proper habits can develop.

Later in the level, as skill mastery advances, competition can be introduced. Many think of competition as 5-on-5 half- or full-court play, but USA Basketball strongly encourages small-sided games like 2-on-2 or 3-on-3 to start.

Small-sided games help to develop a young player's ability to "play the game" and make decisions. With fewer players on the court at a time, spacing improves and there are more opportunities to teach movement and cutting principles. Players also are forced to perform all skills in this setting as positions aren't defined, which is critical in this level.

Allow players to figure things out on their own and try to resist the urge to coach every movement. As players grow in their abilities, they will feel excited and encouraged as they problem solve in this level and begin to develop their own relationship with the game.

EARLY-SEASON PRACTICE PLAN
FOUNDATIONAL LEVEL

Date	Duration: 65 Minutes	Practice #

PRE-PRACTICE

5 MIN	Team Meeting	*Mind Candy:* Listening occurs with your eyes as much as your ears.

Warm-Up

Duration	Exercise	Description
5 MIN	Dynamic Stretches	Jog forward, jog backward, karaoke, knee raisers, and Frankensteins.

SKILL DEVELOPMENT

Skill: Passing and Receiving

Duration	Drill Name	Drill Description/Focus
5 MIN	Stationary Bounce Pass	Break players into pairs. Spread five to ten feet apart and make two-handed bounce passes. Step into the pass with thumbs down and elbows in.
5 MIN	Passing with a Coach	Pass to coach and receive it back. Make a W with thumbs and fingers for the target

Skill: Shooting

Duration	Drill Name	Drill Description/Focus
5 MIN	Form Shooting, No Ball	Players spread out and face the coach. Follow coach's command to shoot without a basketball. Explain form—BEEF.
10 MIN	Form Shooting at a Basket	Form three lines facing the basket. First player in line shoots the ball with two hands using BEEF form, rebounds, and goes to the end of the next line. Gradually move the lines back but continue to emphasize the focus on proper form. Adjust height of basket if possible, depending on player need.

Skill: Ball Handling and Dribbling

Duration	Drill Name	Drill Description/Focus
10 MIN	Dribbling on the Move	Four lines across the baseline with each player having a ball. Dribble length of court while walking and keeping ball close to body with elbow close to hip. Gradually increase speed from walking to jogging. Switch dribbling hands.

WHOLE OFFENSIVE CONCEPTS

Duration	Drill Name	Drill Description/Focus
10 MIN	Pass and Cut	Player passes to a coach and then cuts to the basket. Touch the spot under the basket before getting back in line.

COMPETITION

Duration	Drill Name	Drill Description/Focus
10 MIN	Sharks and Minnows	Line all players on baseline; they are the minnows. Start with one shark, who starts at half court. Players use stop-and-go techniques to avoid being tagged as they try to get from one baseline to the other baseline. Players who are tagged now also become sharks as everyone resets positions before the next run from baseline to baseline.

MIDSEASON PRACTICE PLAN
FOUNDATIONAL LEVEL

Date	Duration: 80 Minutes	Practice #

PRE-PRACTICE

5 MIN	Team Meeting	*Mind Candy:* Don't be afraid to try something new and fail.

Warm-Up

Duration	Exercise	Description
5 MIN	Static Stretches	Circle up at half court and stretch in place.
5 MIN	Line Drills	Player takes two dribbles, performs a jump stop, pivots, and passes to next player in line.

SKILL DEVELOPMENT

Skill: Passing and Receiving

Duration	Drill Name	Drill Description/Focus
5 MIN	Indiana Passing	Lines in each corner of the lane. Going clockwise, one player passes to the line to the right, follows the pass, receives it back, then performs a handoff to the same player at the front of the line. First player goes to end of new line and player who receives the handoff continues pattern of pass, pass back, handoff, to the line on their right. Once team is comfortable, you may add a second ball.
5 MIN	Decision-Making Passes	Half court two versus one. Start with three lines on baseline. On signal, first three players sprint to half court, where coach passes the ball to either outside line. Middle player sprints back to basket to play defense against other two, who become the offense.

Skill: Shooting

Duration	Drill Name	Drill Description/Focus
5 MIN	Form Shooting, No Ball	Players spread out and face the coach. Follow coach's command to shoot without a basketball. Explain form—BEEF.
5 MIN	Layups	Two lines facing the basket outside the lane. Each player has a ball. Coach stands in the middle of the lane five feet from basket. Player passes ball to coach, cuts to the basket, and gets the ball back for a layup.
10 MIN	Shooting from a Pass	One line at each elbow and baseline. Baseline players bounce pass to partner at the elbow. As ball is passed, the shooter at the elbow steps into pass with nonshooting foot then shooting foot to catch in rhythm.
10 MIN	Shooting off the Dribble	Player starts at the elbow, takes one hard dribble toward the basket for the shot.

WHOLE OFFENSIVE CONCEPTS

Duration	Drill Name	Drill Description/Focus
10 MIN	Attack and Move 3x0	Half-court spacing. Once a player passes the ball, they make a scoring cut to the basket and go out opposite the pass. Opposite wing fills the vacated spot at the top of the key.

COMPETITION

Duration	Drill Name	Drill Description/Focus
5 MIN	Baseline Out-of-Bounds Plays	Implement a new baseline out-of-bounds play.
10 MIN	4x4x4 Exchange	Split the group into three equal teams and start on the baseline. The offensive team must follow one rule to maintain possession: on every catch, the player must square up to the basket. A coach will referee to enforce the rule. Scoring team stays on. If defense gets a stop or offense breaks the rule, the defense becomes offense and the third team rotates in.

LATE-SEASON PRACTICE PLAN
FOUNDATIONAL LEVEL

Date	Duration: 95 Minutes	Practice #

PRE-PRACTICE

5 MIN	Team Meeting	*Mind Candy:* You can't let praise or criticism get to you—it's a weakness to get caught up in either one.

Warm-Up

Duration	Exercise	Description
10 MIN	Texas Drills	A series of four team drills: Full-court layups—players dribble full length of court and finish with a layup. Full-court shots—players dribble full length of court and finish with a jump shot. Three-line layups—players run a three-player weave and finish with a layup. Three-line full-court shots—players run a three-player weave and finish with a jump shot.
5 MIN	Line Drills	Player takes two dribbles, performs a jump stop, pivots, and passes to next player in line.

SKILL DEVELOPMENT

Skill: Footwork and Body Control

Duration	Drill Name	Drill Description/Focus
5 MIN	Close Out	Form three lines on the baseline. One player stands in front of each line at the free-throw line. Baseline player passes to player at the free-throw line and performs a close out. Player at the free-throw line goes to the back of the line.

Skill: Shooting

Duration	Drill Name	Drill Description/Focus
10 MIN	Keyhole Shooting	Form a line on each wing. Players one and two in line on the right wing have basketballs. Players two and three in line on the left wing have basketballs. Player one on the left wing, without a basketball, will be the first shooter and starts the drill by running to the midpoint of the free-throw line and receiving a pass from player one on the right wing. Upon the catch, pivot to the basket and shoot. The passer now cuts to the free-throw line to receive a pass from opposite line, then pivots and shoots. Rebound own shot and fill opposite line.

Skill: Ball Handling & Dribbling

Duration	Drill Name	Drill Description/Focus
10 MIN	1x1	Start with one line at top of key or at wing. First player plays defense and second player plays offense. Play until score or defensive rebound.

WHOLE DEFENSIVE CONCEPTS

Duration	Drill Name	Drill Description/Focus
5 MIN	3 Player Run and Slide	Three players in a group. One starts with ball on the baseline, one defender, one pass receiver. Player with the ball dribbles to sideline while being defended, pivots, and passes back to the third player. New player with ball dribbles to opposite sideline while defender sprints to defend.
5 MIN	4 Player Run and Trap	Same concept as above. Use four players, two players trap on one sideline, then the other sideline.

WHOLE OFFENSIVE CONCEPTS

Duration	Drill Name	Drill Description/Focus
10 MIN	UCLA Drill	Divide team into teams A and B and line each team up on opposite sidelines. Team A starts with three offensive players a few feet behind half court. Team B sends two players to play defense. Offense attacks three versus two, but as soon as they cross half court the defensive team adds a third player, who runs in from sideline, touches the half-court middle circle, then joins action. Team A sends two defenders to wait under opposite basket. Play 3x3 until a score or stop. Team B's three players then take the ball and attack opposite basket three versus two until Team A's third player runs in. Continuous play.
10 MIN	5x5x5	Form three equal teams. One team starts as the offense at half court. Other two teams are defense, one defending each basket on each side. Offense plays 5x5 half court until there's a score or stop. If offense scores, they transition to the other half court to play 5x5 against the third team and defense stays. If defense gets a stop, they become new offense and transition to other end of court to play against third team.

COMPETITION

Duration	Drill Name	Drill Description/Focus
10 MIN	4x4x4 Exchange	Split the group into three equal teams and start on the baseline. The offensive team must follow two rules to maintain possession: on every catch, the player must square up to the basket and on a made basket, the scorer must thank the passer. A coach will referee to enforce the rules. Scoring team stays on. If defense gets a stop or offense breaks the rules, the defense becomes offense and the third team rotates in.
5 MIN	Free Throws	Each player shoots a free throw—whole team runs on a miss. Same player shoots again (no penalty if misses again). Continue until all players have shot a free throw.
5 MIN	Communication Circle	Players circle up and hold hands. One at a time, look at the player to the left or right and answer the question of the day to the teammate while making good eye contact and speaking loud enough for all to hear. (Question examples: What basketball skill do you want to keep improving on? What is something the teammate you are looking at did well today at practice? What is something no one knows about you?)

ADVANCED LEVEL PRACTICE PLANS

BUILDING A PRACTICE PLAN AT THE ADVANCED LEVEL

Individual skill development plays a role in practice planning for all four levels. Coaches working with Advanced Level teams, however, must also take into consideration the importance of implementing team concepts and game strategy into practice plans as well as adding competition to drills.

Effective practices begin by first determining what your practice involves, how to emphasize your practice goals, and when to implement each aspect of your practice plan to achieve your overall team goals.

Teaching techniques should focus on the Whole-Part-Whole Method. Coaches should show the end result and the overall drill concept, then break down each drill element to teach to players. A good way to do this is by using 3-on-3 and 4-on-4 to teach parts of your offense and defense. After explaining the full offense or defense, set up on the half court with limited players on the floor to go through each segment of the offense or defense. This allows players to learn step by step without being overwhelmed. After confidence is established, build up to five players on the court and a live opponent.

The Advanced Level player is ready to test the skills they've developed from prior levels. Use competition to challenge players and increase their skill levels. Once players have learned a drill, add competition with either time or score. This also allows players and teams to set measurable goals and track progress throughout a season.

EARLY-SEASON PRACTICE PLAN
ADVANCED LEVEL

Date	Duration: 120 Minutes	Practice #

PRE-PRACTICE

10 MIN	Team Meeting	*Mind Candy:* Three things about success: it doesn't happen in a vacuum, it takes time, and it is hard.

Warm-Up

Duration	Exercise	Description
5 MIN	Running Jump Stops	Players run the floor, stopping at three to five designated places on the court to complete a jump stop.
5 MIN	Jump-Stop Pivots	Players run the floor, stopping at three to five designated places on the court to complete a jump stop, accompanied by a reverse or front pivot.

SKILL DEVELOPMENT

Skill: Footwork and Body Control

Duration	Drill Name	Drill Description/Focus
5 MIN	Dribble-Pivot-Pass Work	Four lines on sideline, first player in each line has a basketball. Players take two dribbles in straight line, jump-stop, perform a reverse pivot, then pass to the next player in line and run to the end of the line. Coach calls out different types of pivots for variation.
10 MIN	Texas Drills	A series of four team drills: Full-court layups—players dribble full length of court and finish with a layup. Full-court shots—players dribble full length of court and finish with a jump shot. Three-line layups—players run a three-player weave and finish with a layup. Three-line full-court shots—players run a three-player weave and finish with a jump shot. Set a goal for made baskets for each drill.

Skill: Passing and Receiving

Duration	Drill Name	Drill Description/Focus
5 MIN	Indiana Passing	Lines in each corner of the lane. Going clockwise, one player passes to the line to the right, follows the pass, receives it back, then performs a handoff to the same player at the front of the line. First player goes to end of new line and player who receives the handoff continues pattern of pass, pass back, handoff, to the line on their right. Once team is comfortable, you may add a second ball.
5 MIN	Passing out of Double Team	Two players on offense try to go full length of court against three players on defense. The trap is occurring on sidelines with the player forcing the trap coming from middle of the floor.
5 MIN	Passing Using On-Ball Screen	Coming off of the ball screen, drill several options: hit roller, hit pop, penetrate kick to teammate behind roller.

Skill: Shooting

Duration	Drill Name	Drill Description/Focus
5 MIN	Form Shooting, No Ball	Players spread out and face the coach. Follow coach's command to shoot without a basketball. Explain form—BEEF.
10 MIN	Form Shooting at a Basket	Player shoots the ball with one hand only using BEEF form, rebounds, and goes to end of the line. Add a second hand and gradually move the line back, but continue to emphasize the focus on proper form.
10 MIN	Keyhole Shooting	Form a line on each wing. Players one and two in line on the right wing have basketballs. Players two and three in line on the left wing have basketballs. Player one on the left wing, without a basketball, will be the first shooter and starts the drill by running to the midpoint of the free-throw line and receiving a pass from player one on the right wing. Upon the catch, pivot to the basket and shoot. The passer now cuts to the free-throw line to receive a pass from opposite line, then pivots and shoots. Rebound own shot and fill opposite line. Players count made baskets out loud and work toward a set goal.

WHOLE DEFENSIVE CONCEPTS

Duration	Drill Name	Drill Description/Focus
5 MIN	Stance and Movement	Mass work on defensive stance. Big step out with lead foot in direction of movement. Shuffle other foot to follow while maintaining a low position. Coach can point to direction of movement.
5 MIN	Zigzag Defense 1x1	Start one offensive player and one defender on baseline. Offense dribbles side to side using one-third of the court from sideline to free-throw lane while defender slides to stay in front of dribbler. Work on turning the offense. May go live when offense hits half court and attempt to score 1x1.
10 MIN	Ball Side/Help Side	2x2 passing the ball from wing to wing with ball-side to help-side positioning.

WHOLE OFFENSIVE CONCEPTS

Duration	Drill Name	Drill Description/Focus
10 MIN	Offense Intro	Introduce the offense and work 5x0 with offensive patterns.

COMPETITION

Duration	Drill Name	Drill Description/Focus
15 MIN	4x4x4 Exchange	Split the group into three equal teams and start on the baseline. A coach will referee to enforce the rules. The three main rules for the offensive team: on every catch the player must square up to the basket, after a pass the player must move, and on a made basket the scorer must thank the passer. Scoring team stays on. If defense gets a stop, they become the offense and third team rotates in.
5 MIN	Communication Circle	Players circle up and hold hands. One at a time, look at the player to the left or right and answer the question of the day to the teammate while making good eye contact and speaking loud enough for all to hear. (Question examples: What basketball skill do you want to keep improving on? What is something the teammate you are looking at did well today at practice? What is something no one knows about you?)

MIDSEASON PRACTICE PLAN
ADVANCED LEVEL

Date	Duration: 130 Minutes	Practice #

PRE-PRACTICE

10 MIN	Team Meeting	*Mind Candy:* These things require zero talent: being on time, work ethic, effort, body language, energy, attitude, passion, and being coachable.

Warm-Up

Duration	Exercise	Description
10 MIN	Running Jump Stops	Players run the floor, stopping at three to five designated places on the court to complete a jump stop.
5 MIN	Jump-Stop Pivots	Players run the floor, stopping at three to five designated places on the court to complete a jump stop, accompanied by a reverse or front pivot.

SKILL DEVELOPMENT

Skill: Footwork and Body Control

Duration	Drill Name	Drill Description/Focus
5 MIN	Dribble-Pivot-Pass Work	Four lines on sideline, first player in each line has a basketball. Players take two dribbles in straight line, jump-stop, perform a reverse pivot, then pass to the next player in line and run to the end of the line. Coach calls out different types of pivots for variation.
10 MIN	Texas Drills	A series of four team drills: Full-court layups—players dribble full length of court and finish with a layup. Full-court shots—players dribble full length of court and finish with a jump shot. Three-line layups—players run a three-player weave and finish with a layup. Three-line full-court shots—players run a three-player weave and finish with a jump shot. Set a goal for made baskets for each drill.

Skill: Rebounding

Duration	Drill Name	Drill Description/Focus
10 MIN	Offensive Rebounding	Shot is taken by coach—three offensive rebounders called crashers must get to paint for rebound. "Junk" player goes to top of key for long rebound and "back" player goes to opposite key.

WHOLE DEFENSIVE CONCEPTS

Duration	Drill Name	Drill Description/Focus
10 MIN	Ball Side/Help Side	2x2 passing the ball from wing to wing with ball-side to help-side positioning.
15 MIN	3x3 Defensive Emphasis	Divide team up into even 3x3 teams. Set up 3x3 in the half court. Team on defense must stay on defense until they get three stops in a row. Offensive teams can keep rotating in each possession

WHOLE OFFENSIVE CONCEPTS

Duration	Drill Name	Drill Description/Focus
10 MIN	Pick and Roll Shooting	One line at baseline and one line on opposite-side wing. Baseline will go to elbow, set a ball-side screen, and roll to basket. Wing player comes off screen and shoots at elbow area. Screener rolls to basket and receives pass from next baseline player for shot on the roll.
15 MIN	5x5x5	Form three equal teams. One team starts as the offense at half court. Other two teams are defense, one defending each basket on each side. Offense plays 5x5 half court until there's a score or stop. If offense scores, they transition to the other half court to play 5x5 against the third team and defense stays. If defense gets a stop, they become new offense and transition to other end of court to play against third team.

COMPETITION

Duration	Drill Name	Drill Description/Focus
10 MIN	Defensive 4x4x4 Exchange	Split the group into three equal teams and start on the baseline. A coach will referee to enforce the rules. Same drill as offensive 4x4x4 exchange, but with three defensive rules to stay on the court—no paint touches by ball, rotate over and down on baseline drives, and close out on all catches. If defense breaks any of these rules or if offense scores, the defense rotates out. First defense to have three successful stops while following the rules wins.

| 5 MIN | Communication Circle | Players circle up and hold hands. One at a time, look at the player to the left or right and answer the question of the day to the teammate while making good eye contact and speaking loud enough for all to hear. (Question examples: What basketball skill do you want to keep improving on? What is something the teammate you are looking at did well today at practice? What is something no one knows about you?) |

LATE-SEASON PRACTICE PLAN
ADVANCED LEVEL

Date	Duration: 105 Minutes	Practice #

PRE-PRACTICE

| 10 MIN | Team Meeting | *Mind Candy:* Three things that lead to success: work hard, stay humble, and surround yourself with good people. |

Warm-Up

Duration	Exercise	Description
5 MIN	Dribble-Pivot-Pass Work	Four lines on sideline, first player in each line has a basketball. Players take two dribbles in straight line, jump-stop, perform a reverse pivot, then pass to the next player in line and run to the end of the line. Coach calls out different types of pivots for variation.
10 MIN	Texas Drills	A series of four team drills: Full-court layups—players dribble full length of court and finish with a layup. Full-court shots—players dribble full length of court and finish with a jump shot. Three-line layups—players run a three-player weave and finish with a layup. Three-line full-court shots—players run a three-player weave and finish with a jump shot. Set a goal for made baskets for each drill.

SKILL DEVELOPMENT

Skill: Passing and Receiving

Duration	Drill Name	Drill Description/Focus
10 MIN	Half Court 2x1	Three lines on baseline with coach at half court with one ball. First player from each line sprints to half court and touches half-court line, then turns back to basket. Coach throws ball to either player on the outside to attack basket as offense. Player from middle line becomes defense for 2x1. Progress to five lines on baseline all sprinting to half-court line; outside players and middle-line player are offense after touch and coach throws ball to any of the three. Other two lines become defense for 3x2.

Skill: Shooting

Duration	Drill Name	Drill Description/Focus
10 MIN	Keyhole Shooting	Form a line on each wing. Players one and two in line on the right wing have basketballs. Players two and three in line on the left wing have basketballs. Player one on the left wing, without a basketball, will be the first shooter and starts the drill by running to the midpoint of the free-throw line and receiving a pass from player one on the right wing. Upon the catch, pivot to the basket and shoot. The passer now cuts to the free-throw line to receive a pass from opposite line, then pivots and shoots. Rebound own shot and fill opposite line. Players count made baskets out loud to work toward a set goal.

Skill: Rebounding

Duration	Drill Name	Drill Description/Focus
10 MIN	War Rebounding	Three players are in the lane area. Coach shoots; players will fight for the rebound. The rebounder will try to score while being fouled by the other players. If the ball hits the floor or goes outside the lane, the play stops and the coach will shoot again. Play to three baskets and then a new player will come into the drill. Play a made basket as a missed shot.

WHOLE DEFENSIVE CONCEPTS

Duration	Drill Name	Drill Description/Focus
5 MIN	Zigzag Defense 1x1	Start one offensive player and one defender on baseline. Offense dribbles side to side using one-third of the court from sideline to free-throw lane while defender slides to stay in front of dribbler. Work on turning the offense. May go live when offense hits half court and attempt to score 1x1.
10 MIN	Shell Drill	4x4 defensive drill. Offense moves ball around arc and attacks the basket by dribbling and passing. Defense works to get stops. Off-ball defenders stay open to help on dribbler. Add defending basket cuts and defending down screens to drill.
10 MIN	Perfect Defense	4x4 defensive drill. Defensive team must prevent the offense from scoring for a full thirty-second count. If offense scores, thirty seconds starts over. New offensive team comes on court against the same defensive team until defense gets a stop.

WHOLE OFFENSIVE CONCEPTS

Duration	Drill Name	Drill Description/Focus
10 MIN	5x5 Turnover Scrimmages	Play two-minute games keeping score. On a turnover, the other team wins.

COMPETITION

Duration	Drill Name	Drill Description/Focus
10 MIN	4x4x4 Exchange	Split the group into three equal teams and start on the baseline. A coach will referee to enforce the rules. The three main rules for the offensive team: on every catch the player must square up to the basket, after a pass the player must move, and on a made basket the scorer must thank the passer. Scoring team stays on. If defense gets a stop, they become the offense and third team rotates in. Add competition—play for five minutes and the team with the most scores wins. Repeat.
5 MIN	Communication Circle	Players circle up and hold hands. One at a time, look at the player to the left or right and answer the question of the day to the teammate while making good eye contact and speaking loud enough for all to hear. (Question examples: What basketball skill do you want to keep improving on? What is something the teammate you are looking at did well today at practice? What is something no one knows about you?)

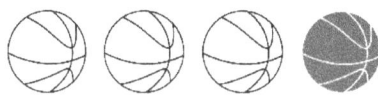

PERFORMANCE LEVEL
PRACTICE PLANS

BUILDING A PRACTICE PLAN AT THE PERFORMANCE LEVEL

Coaches working with Performance Level athletes must be demanding of players, understanding how to push them to achieve their highest potential of success, without being demeaning. Players all have different needs and different responses to coaching methods. A good coach reads cues well and understands how to manage behaviors. Pushing an athlete to their peak ability does not look the same for everyone. It is important to adapt to each player while still staying true to your coaching principles and upholding team expectations.

Performance Level practice plans must be structured to work on your team's nonnegotiables. Nonnegotiables are the core offensive and defensive philosophies you want to execute in games. Decide on these nonnegotiables, communicate them to your team, and then enforce them through practice drills while making sure to address times when they were or were not executed.

Examples of nonnegotiables include not allowing dribble penetration into the lane by the offense, prohibiting baseline drives to the basket, limiting teams to one shot attempt, or always taking two dribbles off the ball screen.

Limit your team to only one or two offensive and defensive nonnegotiables to allow players to fully concentrate on those elements while playing at game speed.

EARLY-SEASON PRACTICE PLAN
PERFORMANCE LEVEL

Date	Duration: 130 Minutes	Practice #

PRE-PRACTICE

10 MIN	Team Meeting	*Mind Candy:* The 4 Cs of culture: Communication, Competition, Comfort Zone, and Choices.

Warm-Up

Duration	Exercise	Description
15 MIN	Dribble-Pivot-Pass Work	Four lines on sideline, first player in each line has a basketball. Players take two dribbles in straight line, jump-stop, perform a reverse pivot, then pass to the next player in line and run to the end of the line. Coach calls out different types of pivots for variation. Add step-out passes, step-through passes, push passes, and same-side passes.

SKILL DEVELOPMENT

Skill: Passing and Receiving

Duration	Drill Name	Drill Description/Focus
10 MIN	Texas Drills	A series of four team drills: Full-court layups—players dribble full length of court and finish with a layup. Full-court shots—players dribble full length of court and finish with a jump shot. Three-line layups—players run a three-player weave and finish with a layup. Three-line full-court shots—players run a three-player weave and finish with a jump shot. Set a goal for made baskets for each drill.
5 MIN	Indiana Passing	Lines in each corner of the lane. Going clockwise, one player passes to the line to the right, follows the pass, receives it back, then performs a handoff to the same player at the front of the line. First player goes to end of new line and player who receives the handoff continues pattern of pass, pass back, handoff, to the line on their right. Once team is comfortable, you may add a second ball. Coach may call out "switch" and players must switch directions. Start with two balls and keep adding balls throughout.

Skill: Shooting

Duration	Drill Name	Drill Description/Focus
10 MIN	Full-Court Shooting Drill	Three lines under each basket with one ball per line. First person from each line on one end sprints the full length of court to catch a pass from the opposite line for a shot. After making the pass, three passers sprint the length of court to opposite end for their shot. Every basket counts as one. Goal is to make 110 baskets in five minutes.

WHOLE DEFENSIVE CONCEPTS

Skill: Passing and Receiving

Duration	Drill Name	Drill Description/Focus
5 MIN	Stance and Movement	Mass work on defensive stance. Big step out with lead foot in direction of movement. Shuffle other foot to follow while maintaining a low position. Coach can point to direction of movement.
5 MIN	Zigzag Defense 1x1	Start one offensive player and one defender on baseline. Offense dribbles side to side using one-third of the court from sideline to free-throw lane while defender slides to stay in front of dribbler. Work on turning the offense. May go live when offense hits half court and attempt to score 1x1.
10 MIN	Shell Drill with Transition	4x4 defensive movement on the pass. Offense doesn't move while the defensive players adjust to each pass. On the coach's whistle, offense drops the ball and runs to opposite end to play defense. Defense picks up ball and offensive transitions to other end to score.
10 MIN	UNLV Defensive Transition	Line team up under the basket as defense. On the opposite basket, coach has one ball and two offensive players take position each on a wing. First two defenders step out and both jump to touch the backboard three times, then sprint to opposite end of the court. Coach throws ball to either offensive wing player as defense arrives and play 2x2. Can increase to 3x3 and 4x4.

WHOLE OFFENSIVE CONCEPTS

Skill: Passing and Receiving

Duration	Drill Name	Drill Description/Focus
5 MIN	Review Offense	Review offense 5x0—go at both ends. Change ends on the whistle to simulate transition offense.

Duration	Drill Name	Drill Description/Focus
10 MIN	Fast Break Work	Five players run in a circle inside the lane. Coach acts as offense and shoots the ball. After securing the rebound, all five players run the lanes on the initial break. Post players fill the rim run spot and trail spot while wings run wide.
10 MIN	5x5x5	Three teams of five, with two teams playing 5x5 at one end and third team waiting as defense under opposite basket. On shot or turnover, transition to 5x5 at the other end against waiting team.
10 MIN	5x5 Mini Games	In your three teams, two teams to play a 5x5 full-court game while the third team is off and waiting. Game is first team to score three baskets and then waiting team rotates in to play winner in a new 5x5 game to three.

COMPETITION

Duration	Drill Name	Drill Description/Focus
10 MIN	4x4x4 Exchange	Split the group into three equal teams and start on the baseline. A coach will referee to enforce the rules. The three main rules for the offensive team: on every catch the player must square up to the basket, after a pass the player must move, and on a made basket the scorer must thank the passer. Scoring team stays on. If defense gets a stop, they become the offense and third team rotates in. Add competition—play for 5 minutes and the team with the most scores wins. Repeat. Coach can add personal rules (all scores must be in paint, etc.).
5 MIN	Communication Circle	Players circle up and hold hands. One at a time, look at the player to the left or right and answer the question of the day to the teammate while making good eye contact and speaking loud enough for all to hear. (Question examples: What basketball skill do you want to keep improving on? What is something the teammate you are looking at did well today at practice? What is something no one knows about you?)

THE USA BASKETBALL COACHING GUIDE FOR ALL LEVELS

MIDSEASON PRACTICE PLAN
PERFORMANCE LEVEL

Date	Duration: 130 Minutes	Practice #

PRE-PRACTICE

10 MIN	Team Meeting	*Mind Candy:* Under pressure you don't rise to the occasion, you sink to the level of your training.

Warm-Up

Duration	Exercise	Description
10 MIN	Texas Drills	A series of four team drills: Full-court layups—players dribble full length of court and finish with a layup. Full-court shots—players dribble full length of court and finish with a jump shot. Three-line layups—players run a three-player weave and finish with a layup. Three-line full-court shots—players run a three-player weave and finish with a jump shot. Set a goal for made baskets for each drill.
10 MIN	Partner 2 Ball Handling	First player in line on one side only has two basketballs. Two-ball dribble to partner in the line across, pounding balls at same time to opposite line. Jump-stop and pass each ball with one hand at a time. Switch types of two-ball dribbles—alternate dribbles, both balls low, one low and one high; and windshield wipers side-to-side dribble.

SKILL DEVELOPMENT

Skill: Rebounding

Duration	Drill Name	Drill Description/Focus
10 MIN	War Rebounding	Three players are in the lane area. Coach shoots; players will fight for the rebound. The rebounder will try to score while being fouled by the other players. If the ball hits the floor or goes outside the lane, the play stops and the coach will shoot again. Play to three baskets and then a new player will come into the drill. Play a made basket as a missed shot.

Skill: Shooting

Duration	Drill Name	Drill Description/Focus
10 MIN	Keyhole Shooting	Form a line on each wing. Players one and two in line on the right wing have basketballs. Players two and three in line on the left wing have basketballs. Player one on the left wing, without a basketball, will be the first shooter and starts the drill by running to the midpoint of the free-throw line and receiving a pass from player one on the right wing. Upon the catch, pivot to the basket and shoot. The passer now cuts to the free-throw line to receive a pass from opposite line, pivot, and shoot. Rebound own shot and fill opposite line. Add competition to the drill with a team goal of thirty baskets made in two minutes. Once two minutes expire, team sprints to other end and sets up the drill at the other basket with a new goal of making five in a row to finish drill.

WHOLE DEFENSIVE CONCEPTS

Duration	Drill Name	Drill Description/Focus
5 MIN	Zigzag Defense 1x1	Start one offensive player and one defender on baseline. Offense dribbles side to side using one-third of the court from sideline to free-throw lane while defender slides to stay in front of dribbler. Work on turning the offense. May go live when offense hits half court and attempt to score 1x1.

Duration	Drill Name	Drill Description/Focus
10 MIN	6-Point Defense	This is a defensive positioning drill where the defensive player must adjust as the offense moves to different spots on the court. One offensive player at top of key with basketball and one defender guarding the ball. Coach is on wing. Offense passes to coach and begins sequence: (1) Offense cuts to basket; defender adjusts positioning to defend cut. (2) Offense posts up on block; defender adjusts positioning for post defense. (3) Offense breaks to ball-side baseline on three-point line; defender adjusts positioning to deny pass from wing. (4) Offense cuts backdoor to basket; defender adjusts positioning to guard backdoor. (5) Offense relocates to weak-side wing; defense adjusts positioning to play help-side defense. (6) Coach throws ball to offense on wing; defense closes out on ball and play 1x1 until a score or stop.
10 MIN	Full-Court Defensive Trapping	Set up 5x5 full-court defense with the offense inbounding from the baseline. Defense works on trapping the ball and rotating to fill spots.

WHOLE OFFENSIVE CONCEPTS

Duration	Drill Name	Drill Description/Focus
10 MIN	Specials	Review sideline and baseline out-of-bounds plays. Run plays into 5x5 scrimmage.
15 MIN	Catch-Up Drill	Five players line up on baseline as the offensive team, and five players line up opposite these players at free-throw line as the defensive team. Coach throws ball to one of the baseline players. Defensive player opposite the ball touches the baseline as offensive team starts a 5x4 transition break to the opposite end. Defensive player who touched the baseline catches up to the play.
15 MIN	Scrimmage 5x5 Build-Up	Start with two players on offense at half court and one on defense at the basket. Play 2x1; on a score or stop the defense adds two more players to team and transitions to other end as offense now playing 3x2. Continue with the defensive team always adding two new players for 4x3, then 5x4. Finish playing 5x5 full court until time runs out.

COMPETITION

Duration	Drill Name	Drill Description/Focus
10 MIN	4x4x4 Exchange	Split the group into three equal teams and start on the baseline. A coach will referee to enforce the rules. The three main rules for the offensive team: on every catch the player must square up to the basket, after a pass the player must move, and on a made basket the scorer must thank the passer. Scoring team stays on. If defense gets a stop, they become the offense and third team rotates in. Add competition—play for five minutes and the team with the most scores wins. Repeat. Coach can add personal rules (all scores must be in paint, etc.).
5 MIN	Communication Circle	Players circle up and hold hands. One at a time, look at the player to the left or right and answer the question of the day to the teammate while making good eye contact and speaking loud enough for all to hear. (Question examples: What basketball skill do you want to keep improving on? What is something the teammate you are looking at did well today at practice? What is something no one knows about you?)

LATE-SEASON PRACTICE PLAN
PERFORMANCE LEVEL

Date	Duration: 105 Minutes	Practice #

PRE-PRACTICE

10 MIN	Team Meeting	*Mind Candy:* Success begins with the attention to and the perfection of the details.

Warm-Up

Duration	Exercise	Description
10 MIN	Fast-Break Cycle Work	Coach shoots the ball with five players in the lane. On the rebound, all players run the floor in transition. There will be five trips up and down the floor in total, each time using a different sequence of passes and players who score. The four players will always in-bound and the outlet always goes to the one player. The progression up and down the floor goes 1-2-3, 1-2-5, 1-2-1-4, 1-2-1-4-5, and 1-2-4-3.
10 MIN	Indiana Passing	Lines in each corner of the lane. Going clockwise, one player passes to the line to the right, follows the pass, receives it back, then performs a handoff to the same player at the front of the line to the right. First player goes to end of new line and player who receives the handoff continues pattern of pass, pass back, handoff to the line on their right. Coach may call out "switch" and players must switch directions. Start with two balls and keep adding balls throughout. Set a goal and count passes.

SKILL DEVELOPMENT

Skill: Team Offense

Duration	Drill Name	Drill Description/Focus
10 MIN	Position Work	Divide players into frontcourt and backcourt, one coach with each group. Work on offensive skills relative to that particular group.

Skill: Shooting

Duration	Drill Name	Drill Description/Focus
10 MIN	Hawkeye Shooting	Divide your team up by positions one through five with multiple players for each role. Once the drill starts, three total players will be in action together. All ones are at half court, all twos and threes are split into a line at each baseline, all fours and fives are split under each basket. First one player dribbles to free-throw line for a shot; a four and a five step into the paint and battle for the one's rebound, make or miss. Whichever player rebounds the shot then outlets back to the one. A two/three player sprints from the baseline to opposite end and the one passes the ball to the two/three for a shot. The four/five sprints the floor after the outlet pass to catch a pass from the coach under the opposite basket for a post score. The two/three rebounds their shot and outlets back to the one, who gets back in line at half court. Try to operate the drill with both sides going at same time, so a one would start in each direction.

WHOLE DEFENSIVE CONCEPTS

Duration	Drill Name	Drill Description/Focus
5 MIN	Sideline Slide Drill	Players start on sideline facing baseline with outside foot on sideline. Players say "big step" as they slide to opposite sideline. Mix in turn to sprint.
15 MIN	Perfect Defense	4x4 defensive drill. Defensive team must prevent the offense from scoring for a full thirty-second count. If offense scores, thirty seconds starts over. New offensive team comes on court against the same defensive team until defense gets a stop.

WHOLE OFFENSIVE CONCEPTS

Duration	Drill Name	Drill Description/Focus
10 MIN	Laker Drill	Three lines at each baseline. Offense and defense sets up at half court on one side only to play 4x4. Play until a made basket, defensive rebound, or turnover. Defensive player who secures the rebound or turnover turns into offense and is joined by three new teammates from the line under the basket. Offensive team becomes defense and all transition 4x4 to other end of basket. Continuous play for a set time.
10 MIN	5 Player Weave into 5x5	One team starts with a five-player weave. Other team waits on baseline where weave ends, gets ball out of the net, and plays transition offense against the team that completed the weave.

COMPETITION

Duration	Drill Name	Drill Description/Focus
10 MIN	Free Throws	Each player shoots a free throw—whole team runs on a miss. Same player shoots after running with a consequence if missed again. Continue until all players have made a free throw.
5 MIN	Communication Circle	Players circle up and hold hands. One at a time, look at the player to the left or right and answer the question of the day to the teammate while making good eye contact and speaking loud enough for all to hear. (Question examples: What basketball skill do you want to keep improving on? What is something the teammate you are looking at did well today at practice? What is something no one knows about you?)

ABOUT USA BASKETBALL

USA Basketball, which celebrated its 50th anniversary in 2024, is the national governing body for the sport of basketball in the United States. As the recognized governing body by the International Basketball Federation (FIBA) and the United States Olympic and Paralympic Committee (USOPC), USA Basketball is responsible for the selection and training of USA teams that compete in FIBA-sponsored basketball competitions and select national events and for the development of youth basketball initiatives that address player development, coach education, and safety.

The USA Basketball Youth & Sport Development Division is tasked with the development of youth basketball initiatives that address player development, coach education, and safety, while promoting, growing, and elevating the game. USA Basketball is committed to providing youth throughout the country safe, fun, and developmentally appropriate environments in which they can enjoy the game.

USAB.COM